Methods in Experimental Psychology

Methods in Experimental Psychology

Charles L. Sheridan
University of Missouri
and Veterans Administration Hospital
Kansas City, Missouri

Holt, Rinehart and Winston
New York Chicago San Francisco
Dallas Montreal Toronto London Sydney

Library of Congress Cataloging in Publication Data

Sheridan, Charles L. 1937–
Methods in experimental psychology.

Bibliography: p. 269
Includes index.
1. Psychology, Experimental. 2. Psychological research. 3. Psychology—Methodology.
I. Title. [DNLM: 1. Psychology, Experimental—Methods. BF181 S552m]
BF181.S433 150′.7′24 78-21925

ISBN 0-03-045231-7

Printed in the United States of America
9 0 1 2 090 9 8 7 6 5 4 3 2 1

Preface

This book should be useful for a wide range of students in undergraduate courses in experimental methodology or in general research methodology. While it is comprehensive enough to serve as a central text in many such courses, its modest length and paperback format make it feasible for the instructor to select supplemental materials such as books that cover specific content areas or that discuss nonexperimental methods more fully. I believe that instructors who structure their courses as purely methodological will find this text provides adequate coverage, but they will also have the option of providing in-depth material from other sources in topic areas they want to treat in more than average depth. The book is particularly well adapted to the instructor who wishes to cover both methodology and content, but who is not entirely satisfied with the particular examples of research content provided in available texts. They will probably find full coverage of their methodological materials here, and can provide content-oriented materials from other sources.

The organization of the book developed from my experiences in teaching courses in experimental psychology and research methodology that require research projects during the semester. It was necessary to provide information to the students as they needed it, so I began teaching the materials in the order in which one actually does research. This is the pattern underlying the present work, with an occasional deviation based on the need to delay certain topics until prior information has been given. For example, single-subject experimental designs and the experimental analysis of behavior are discussed late in the book because issues involved in evaluating this approach are most easily explained after a number of other matters have been clarified (for example, the concept of power, the role of signal/noise ratios in judging reliability of findings).

This pattern of organization leads to some interesting modifications of the usual ways of treating topics. For example, the concept of interaction is explained prior to the introduction of detailed statistical procedures. At first I considered making a concession to pedagogy and presenting the concept out of the originally intended order. But I realized that a difficult concept like that of interaction is probably best presented in its barest and simplest form, with statistical details added later.

Another implication of this method of organization corollary to the one just mentioned, is that is invites redundancy. Teachers may think "They have already had statistics, so I don't need to explain statistics!", but students usually think otherwise. With respect to statistics and many other topics, it helps to have repetition and to see the subject from several different angles.

Statistics is dealt with at three distinct levels. First, the logical framework underlying statistical as well as nonstatistical procedures is treated in various contexts (for example, under sampling and generality, and under reliability). Second, the particulars of major statistical methods are explained in several places (in Chapters 7 and 9). Third, student-tested computational procedures are provided in the appendixes. These computational procedures include those for fairly complex multifactor designs. My reason for going so far is that I have found that students cannot read the contemporary literature without some knowledge of multifactor designs. Most articles involve use of multifactor designs, and it does not require an exceptional student to understand them at the early undergraduate level. Assignment of the appendixes is, of course, optional.

Is this book intended for students who have had or for those who have not had statistics? My students fall into both categories. I find that the students who have had statistics usually need a review and a second opportunity to grasp the essential logic of statistics. Those who have not had statistics get a good introduction to the essential logic, and to the most important particulars. Both groups usually welcome the routinized, student-tested computational procedures. So the book is really designed to be used by both classes of student.

The preceding paragraphs might give the impression that there is a great emphasis on statistics in this book. Actually, the book is best characterized as an account of the *research process* as it takes place for the experimental psychologist. In one place (Chapter 5) I have dealt with preexperimental methodology, but this is to place experimental method in context. As the early Gestalt psychologists showed, clear perception of figures requires contrast. Students are more likely to understand the nature of experimental work if they have a basis for comparison.

I have tried in this book to emphasize the pragmatics of the research process. One of the ways in which this book may differ from others in the same area lies in the coverage of informal as well as the formal aspects of research. I have attempted to provide a printed approximation to a research apprenticeship. In this way I intend that those who do research will have the needed information at hand, and that those who will only read about research will have a realistic understanding of it.

A number of people have made substantial contributions to the development of this book. Roger Williams and Johnna Barto helped create the concept, and Johnna fostered the development of the book through most of its phases. The editorial work of Arlene Katz was of great value in clearing up errors and clarifying imprecisions. An especially important contribution was made by the substantial number of psychologists, who remain anonymous, but who acted as editorial consultants and were often very helpful in improving the organization, clarity, and correctness of the book.

Kansas City, Missouri
September 1978

C.L.S.

Contents

CHAPTER 1

Experimental Psychology: Definition and Scope

The Need For Evidence in Psychology

If our society's present interest in psychology got any more intense, we could rightly call it an obsession. Bookstores, magazines, and bestseller lists are laden with advice on how to get other people to do what you want, how to quit worrying and relax, how to make love, how to stop overeating, raise children, face death, be creative, or go out of your body.

It would be hard to imagine a whole week's passing without the publication of at least one "new discovery" about how our minds work, how we ought to deal with each other, or how this or that technique can give our lives new meaning and wholeness. Books and articles advocate open marriage, intimate fighting, assertiveness, intimidation, relaxation responses, meditation, biofeedback, developing psychic powers, recording biorhythms, and so on. People pay substantial amounts of money for training in techniques such as Transcendental Meditation, est, and Primal Therapy.

This is not necessarily a bad thing. But, then again, it is also not necessarily good. We need to ask, "How convincing is the evidence for these various proposals?" We do not put drugs on the market without giving them a good screening, yet psychological systems sometimes are promulgated on the basis of nothing more than their author's opinion. Assuming that psychology *really does* have the power our society attributes to it, should we not exercise caution in adopting new methods?

I am certainly not proposing a system of censorship of new (or even old) ideas. The answer must lie in defending ourselves by becoming sophisticated about evaluating claims. We have to realize that just because someone has a prestigious degree or writes a book that gets a big, nationwide promotion, it does not follow that the proposed theories are correct or that the method works. To believe this would be to slip into the fallacy called the *argument from authority.* It is fallacious to believe that something is necessarily true simply because it comes from an authoritative source. Both logic and science discourage us from accepting arguments based on the authority of their source.

This is not to say that all of the psychological approaches coming to our attention today are merely based on the argument from authority. In truth, they vary greatly in the degree and kind of evidence supporting them. Some *are* merely based on unfounded claims, but others have considerable scientific evidence supporting them.

Unfortunately, it is not enough to determine whether a system has scientific evidence supporting it. Nonscientific evidence is useful for some purposes (for example, to stimulate new ideas). Nor is all evidence obtained within a scientific framework entirely convincing. There are many, many facets to the application of science. A given investigation may be strong in some ways but still contain deficiencies. Not all "scientific" investigations are adequate. It is a complicated business to learn how to create and evaluate scientific work. This is why entire books, like this one, are written in an attempt to lay down certain principles of methodology.

You might be inclined to feel that this is all unnecessarily exacting, and perhaps not of much practical importance. But an understanding of scientific methodology must be exact, and is often of great practical importance. Let me illustrate with a personal example. A colleague of mine is interested in the treatment of obesity. She has spent a great deal of time researching the literature on the causes of overweight. Much of this literature is based on evidence that would be considered quite weak from the point of view of an experimental psychologist. On the basis of not very compelling evidence, students of obesity have often "explained" overeating by appeal to various early childhood fixations and other psychodynamic concepts. These interpretations may be correct, but we cannot be sure until more extensive research has been done.

My colleague was alert to the deficiencies of such speculative explanations. However, she was quite impressed by a body of research literature indicating that obese people are more "dependent" than others (see, for example, Bruch, 1973). Since her main interest lies in developing treatment programs, you can easily imagine that dealing with the problem of overdependence would, on the basis of such research, become a staple of her program. It struck me as worth probing a little further into the strength of the evidence for the relationship between obesity and dependence. Assuming that there was a statistically significant relationship between measures of obesity and dependence, how *strong* was the relationship. We will have much more to say about statistical significance (see Chapters 9 and 10), but for now let us just say that a statistically significant relationship is one that is unlikely to happen by chance; it is therefore presumed to be a real relationship. However, a real relationship is not necessarily a very strong one. I may really have five dollars in a savings account, but it may be a negligible portion of my wealth. Similarly, obese people might have a tendency to be dependent, but it might be a minor aspect of their character. The therapist might be making a poor investment of effort if she concentrated on changing the dependency.

To make a long story short, closer scrutiny of the investigations on which the obesity-dependency relationship was based indicated that, though in some sense "scientific," the evidence was weak, nor did it indicate a particularly strong relationship between the two characteristics. It would have been unfortunate if a treatment program had been constructed with emphasis on decreasing dependency. (Further discussion of the strength of relationships will be presented in Chapters 8 and 10.)

There are many more or less subtle aspects of evaluating research similar to the issues of statistical significance and strength of relationships. The major purpose of this book is to stress the most important of these issues, especially those that affect the use of experimental method in psychology.

The Nature of Experimental Psychology

Experimental psychology is a specialized way of gaining information about psychological phenomena. It is not the only way—not even the only *effective* way. But it is a way with certain special advantages. In particular it has the advantage of letting us know which factors actually *control* psychological reactions.

Experimental psychology is simply that branch of psychology in which experimental methods are used.

It is a comprehensive discipline. The users of methods of experimental psychology can raise and answer questions about hatred, memory, meditation, vision, mutual attraction, decision making, or any other psychological matter.

Experimental psychologists have helped to create the impression that their field is a narrow one. For instance, journals of experimental psychology do not often have articles on experimental clinical psychology, experimental social psychology, or even physiological psychology. But such traditions are just accidents of history. Like most scientific disciplines, experimental psychology started out with emphasis on the simplest of its potential topics. These came to be identified with the field as a whole. Only later was the full range of experimental psychology made apparent.

Whenever experimental method is applied to psychological events, it is an instance of experimental psychology. It's just that simple.

Implications of the Definition of Experimental Psychology as Method

Basic experimental science often produces information of great practical value. An understanding of the laws underlying a phenomenon is worthwhile in its own right. But there is great advantage in recognizing the direct applicability of experimental method to complex, socially meaningful subject matter. Psychologists should recognize that their questions, socially applicable or otherwise, can generally be handled within the framework of experimental method.

Furthermore, it is only logical to define experimental psychology to include the widest possible range of topic areas. There is no rational basis for excluding those instances in which experimental method is applied to complex clinical and social subject matter. Experimental psychology is not realistically represented today by the old narrow definition. The fact is that experimentalists *do* carry out research on complex psychological phenomena, such as conformity, attraction between persons, and mental illness.

The Objectives of Experimental Psychology

Experimental psychology has three main objectives (see Figure 1.1). The first objective is to *measure* psychological events. The second is to *specify* and *predict* the conditions under which given psychological events will occur. The third is to become able to *produce* a desired psychological event at will, given adequate physical and technological support.

These are merely the general objectives of experimental science, adapted to psychology. Scientists *measure* phenomena, they *analyze* them, and they *synthesize* them. Measurement helps greatly in the process of analysis. Analysis helps us discover basic principles or laws. These laws eventually allow us to predict events not yet observed. Synthesis means reproducing something after the laws underlying its occurrence are known. Synthesis benefits us in two ways: by assuring us of the accuracy and completeness of our understanding of the phenomenon under study and by working out how to put our knowledge to practical use.

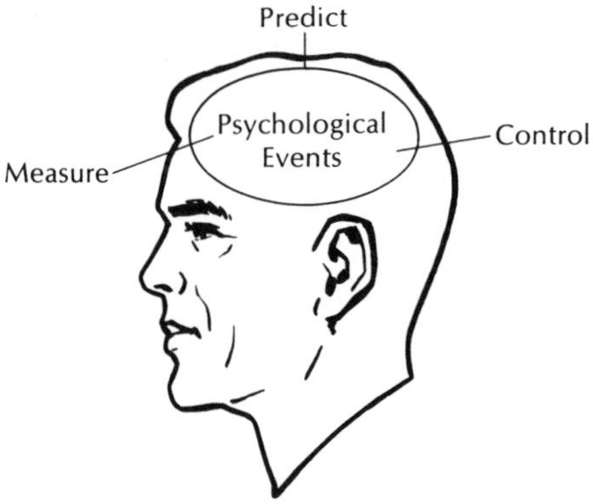

FIGURE 1.1 Objectives of experimental psychology.

Science, Measurement, and Risky Prediction

What is it that experimental psychologists are trying to accomplish? Their enterprise began when physicists and physiologists were starting to apply their familiar techniques to the study of psychology. Science had been eminently successful in its other areas of application. So why not try it in the mental sphere? This is not so easy as it sounds. It requires that we identify the hard core of scientific method—what is essential to it. We need to distinguish that core from the nonessential attributes that stem from the application of science to a particular subject matter. The mind cannot be weighed in an analytical balance. Nor can it be burned to find how many calories it yields. But does this mean that it cannot be dealt with scientifically?

Some people insist that psychology, if it claims scientific status, must slavishly imitate the methods of physics. Such an approach is called *physicism.* But some of the characteristic methods of physics are probably unique to its subject matter and not essential to a science as such. To restrict the designation "science" to such a close imitation of physics would be a mistake. On the other hand, we should not use the term "science" too loosely. Some people have characterized science by its *empiricism.* Empiricists say that experience, especially that of the senses, is the only source of knowledge. But empiricism is not a sufficient criterion of science, since even something as nonscientific as a poem or a novel is usually based on the experience of the writer. Even mysticism, the very opposite of physicism, uses a kind of experience.

If empiricism fails to identify "science," what does? Actually, scientific method can be characterized in many different ways. For our purposes, its most important characteristic is the demand for measurement. The lowest kind of measurement is simple agreement between observers about the presence or absence of something (interobserver agreement or reliability) and, of course, consistency from one time to another in the same observer (intraobserver reliability). In science there are often disagreements about how to *interpret* observations, but rarely do we have disagreement about the observed facts themselves. In science, observers agree on the facts unless someone is in error. It may be necessary to instruct observers in order to get high levels of agreement.

Some have identified science by the tendency of scientific theories to generate *risky predictions.* It might seem that the best theory would be one that explains every possible event that might occur. But such a theory would be useless in helping us to predict. Imagine a theory that could only let us predict that coin-tossing would result in either heads, tails, or balancing on edge. Assuming that these are all the possible outcomes, it would be no better than one that said "We cannot predict which of the possible outcomes will actually occur." To predict everything is no better than to predict nothing. A scientific theory must enable us to make predictions that can prove wrong, depending on the outcomes of observations in the real world.

Risky prediction (which places emphasis on theory) and inter- and intraobserver reliability (which emphasizes fact) have much in common. A prediction is risky if observers can reliably agree on an observation or fact that will refute the theory. Agreement among observers is the backbone of science. This is what is meant when we hear it said paradoxically that scientific knowledge, the most objective form of human knowledge, is social in nature. It is objective precisely because observers can agree on the facts—indeed, this is the very meaning of "objective."

Philosopher of science, Karl Popper, illustrated the role of risky prediction by contrasting the theories of Einstein and Freud. Einstein's theory made risky predictions. There have been a number of occasions, including during some of the moon landings, when Einstein's theory made very explicit predictions about measurable events (for example, that time would be distorted a little). These predictions were verified.

In contrast, Popper argues that the Freudian theory fails to make specific predictions. Personality is determined by strong attachment to a particular stage of childhood development ("fixation"). But we generally have no real measures of the childhood events leading to such fixations. Fixations can occur, according to the theory, as a result of too much trouble or too much pleasure during a developmental stage. But, since "too much" is not clearly defined, the theory cannot be refuted no matter what kind of example is described. Furthermore, the person can react to the fixation in many different ways. People with fixations can persist in the early behavior ("continuation"), can do the opposite ("reaction formation"), or can do something only symbolically related to the fixation ("sublimation"). The theory has so much leeway that any outcome can be regarded as consistent with it. Therefore it is of little value in predicting adult behavior.

Acceptable Degrees of Reliability

Granting that the criterion of inter- and intraobserver reliability constitutes the heart of science, we may ask just how great the reliability must be before a discipline can be legitimately considered scientific. Must agreement be perfect, or is some high but less than perfect level of agreement acceptable? Who must agree? Must every human being who has sight and speech agree? Does this include psychotics? The problems raised here are formidable.

It is often stated that two or more observers must agree as to whether a thing is present or absent, but this is not entirely clear, nor does it reflect the actual practice of scientists. It is doubtful whether the scientific community would be convinced by agreement on a hallucination by two inmates of a mental institution, though they constitute the minimal two observers. Since a rift between conception and practice tends ultimately to result in confusion, it is important that we realize that *no formal criterion of observational agreement is used by scientific investigators,* nor does it seem likely that such a criterion is feasible.

Most students learn in their introductory philosophy course that it is almost impossible to generate a completely acceptable definition of such commonly used terms as "justice," "good," or even "table" or "chair." Yet we seldom encounter any practical misunderstandings because of our lack of a formally explicit definition. The same sort of procedure is followed among scientific investigators. Observational reliability is sufficient if it does not lead, in practice, to dispute. Occasionally we encounter borderline cases, but most of the time we deal with observations that are unambiguous enough so that no practical problem presents itself. In fact, dispute about the facts does occur sometimes in science, though rarely.

Explicit Methods of Establishing Reliability of Observers

Commonly we have sufficient experience with the class of observations dealt with in an experiment so that no explicit demonstration of inter-observer agreement is necessary. If a rat is pressing a bar, and each pressing action causes a counter to increase its reading by one digit, there is little question that observers will agree on the counter-reading. In other instances, however, it is necessary to give evidence of the reliability of observations. For example, Atkinson and McClelland (1948) placed groups of naval submarine-school trainees under varying degrees of food deprivation, and then recorded from the groups the frequency with which Thematic Apperception Test pictures elicited responses reflecting hunger. What is to be counted as a "response reflecting hunger"? Milking a cow? Bees lighting on flowers in a meadow? In order to be sure that a "response reflecting hunger" constituted an *observable event* in the scientific sense, it was necessary to arrange for more than one judge to observe the same phenomenon *independently.* Then the degree to which these judges agreed on the presence or absence of the event of interest was measured. Frequently the degree of agreement between observers is established by a statistical procedure. We might calculate a correlation coefficient between judgments. But it is probably more common to state simply the percentage of judgments on which independent observers agree.

Operational Definition, Radical Operationism, and Multiple Converging Operations

A major method of producing reliable observations is the use of *operational definitions.* When we define something operationally, we define it by specifying the way in which it will be measured. The *method of measurement* thereby constitutes the definition of the thing. Operational definitions came into vogue with the development of modern physics. Physicists found that certain concepts, such as "time" had no clear meaning until they were operationally defined. Subsequently psychologists, with an eye to the great successes of physics, adopted the use of operational definition.

With an operational definition such psychological concepts as "hunger" become "hours of food deprivation" or "rate of eating" or "number of bar presses emitted for a given quantity of food." We know how to measure the latter phenomena, so they constitute operational definitions.

Operational definitions have the advantage of converting intangible inner psychological processes into scientific measurements. They enable us to make very clear what we are talking about. They are so highly valued that many thinkers have put forth the notion that concepts are *nothing but* their measurement operations. This view is called *radical operationism.* It is a point of view long favored by strict behaviorists in psychology. However, it is not without its difficulties.

Consider the operational definition of a dream. Prior to the introduction of electrophysiological methods of identifying dreams, we supposed that dreams existed because people woke up and told us about them. A reasonable operational definition of a dream, then, was the *verbal report* given in the morning. This sort of definition leads to the odd state of affairs in which, if asked *when* dreams occur, we would have, strictly speaking, to say that they occur in the morning when we are awake! If the verbal report *is* the definition of the dream, we are forced to this odd conclusion.

A further problem is created by the realization that some people dream but can't remember the dreams in the morning. Thus the verbal report seems to give an inadequate account of the dream. Surely verbal reports are *part* of what constitutes a dream, but not all of it.

In recent times, many psychologists have taken the view that *multiple converging operations* provide a desirable way to measure psychological events. With multiple converging operations we select several distinct operational definitions of the event of interest. No particular measurement operation gives a complete reflection of the thing being measured, but each provides a partial indicator of it. Going back to the example of dreams, we can use both verbal reports and a variety of physiological indicators from brain and muscles to indicate the presence of the dream. Today, if a person shows certain brain wave patterns and certain characteristic patterns of muscular activity, we say that he or she had a dream even if the person cannot remember it.

Science and Experimental Science

Some approaches to the study of nature deserve to be called "scientific" even though they do not entail the use of experimental procedures. Thus our subject matter is scientific psychology, but more precisely it is *experimental* psychology. How do the two differ? The answer is that experimental scientists manipulate and control the variables of interest, whereas nonexperimental scientific psychologists content themselves with observing and recording events as they occur naturally.

Naturalistic Observation

An example of a scientific discipline that is not usually experimental is astronomy. Astronomers rarely manipulate the factors involved in their study. Sometimes behavioral scientists also rely on observation and recording without experimental intervention. There may be considerable advantage in passive observation prior to experimental manipulation. Ethologists[1] commonly take great pains to describe the behavior of various species as it naturally occurs and regard this as essential to the development of a behavioral science. Sizable books have been written on the life and habits of such species as the herring gull or the mountain gorilla. On the basis of these descriptions a great deal of intelligent inference can be made about why organisms behave as they do.

Experimental Manipulation

When scientists want to know which factors actually control a given behavior, they must introduce active experimental manipulation. They can decide that a given factor influences variations in behavior *only if they discount the influence of all other factors.* They discount the influence of these other factors by showing that variations in behavior still occur when the factors in question are *absent* or are *held constant.*

For example, ethologists have often asked which of the many features of an organism actually control the release of patterns of behavior such as courtship rituals or fighting. They have moved then from naturalistic observation to experimentation. To illustrate, an experimenter might find that for certain fishes the presence of a red belly and of a certain orientation of the body is responsible for the initiation of fighting. How can this be determined? One way would be to construct artificial models that resemble an opponent in some respects but not in others, and then watch for the fighting pattern. If the pattern of the scales, movements of the gills, or shape of the eyes can be eliminated or changed without preventing this aggressive behavior, the experimenter concludes that these variables cannot be responsible for it. If, on the other hand, a feature such as the red belly precipitates fighting, even when other features differ markedly from those of the natural opponent, then it seems that "red belly" is an important controlling factor.

In general, it is by means of experimental manipulation that we are able to *specify exactly the conditions under which an event occurs.* The development of this method is summarized in Figure 1.2. When we restrict ourselves to natural observation, we cannot tell which of the many naturally occurring changes that take place at the same time actually controls the event of interest.

[1]Ethology is a branch of biology in which animal behavior is studied, often in its natural setting. A delightfully entertaining introduction to it may be found in a book by the man who did most to create it—Konrad Lorenz (1952).

FIGURE 1.2 Experimental science combines reliable observation with manipulation of variables. It yields knowledge of controlling variables.

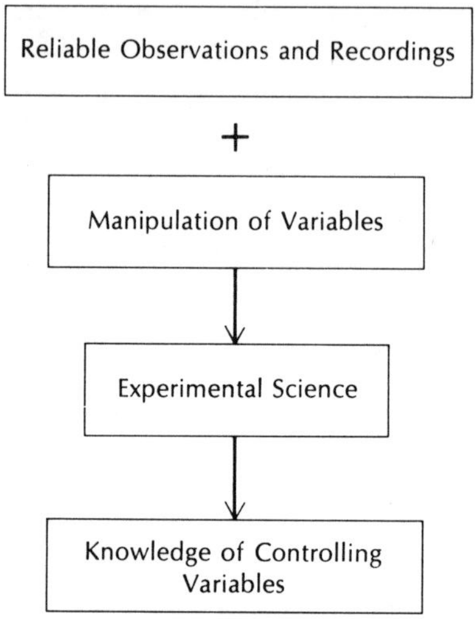

Should One Choose the Experimental Method?

A primary issue is whether to select the experimental approach to psychology. If one feels the objectives of experimental psychology are worth pursuing, the selection of experimental method is thereby determined, since it seems most unlikely that any other method could lead to these goals.

But some people fear the application of rigorous experimental methods to psychology. They feel that attainment of the objectives would lead to a sterile, controlled world shorn of the delights of spontaneity. Such fears are groundless, since even physics does not take away the unpredictability of a leaf falling to the ground. Prediction and control *in principle* imply only that a phenomenon can be reproduced when all the conditions of its occurrence have been specified and controlled. This is hardly applicable to specific situations in everyday life.

But should we try to control people at all? Why not let them be free? An option of this kind does not exist for us. There will be control. The only option is to decide whether it will be systematic or chaotic. Society controls behavior now. It does so in ways that are often clumsy and that have undesirable side effects. For example, the methods of behavioral control most societies have evolved are largely punitive. Experimental science may let us know more constructive methods of control.

Further, the expansion of our understanding of how to control behavior might have unprecedented desirable consequences. There are many situations in which human suffering could be alleviated if we had a greater understanding of psychological control.

Finally, there are no methods of comparable power. People often think that commonsense approaches to psychological helping are superior to the more rigorous approaches, but this is illusory.

Intuitive versus Scientific Procedures

The Main Advantage of the Scientific Approach

What are the advantages of a scientific approach? Put simply, the main advantage of a scientific attack on phenomena is that it makes *progress,* in particular *practical progress,* possible. Practical progress is unlikely without agreement on the facts because disagreement prevents integrated action. In science the rules according to which we can convince each other are relatively clear. Hence, to a great degree, we can reliably compel concerted action in controlling phenomena. For example, there are few people remaining who would propose a quack cure for polio. Science provided Dr. Salk not only with the means of discovering a preventive vaccine, but also with a method for convincing others that his technique would work.

Risks Entailed in Nonscientific Methods

Nature readily seduces us into believing that we understand her laws without the discipline of experimental science. The history of human inquiry is replete with instances of erroneous belief that yielded only to experimental attack.

Presumably, no one likes to believe what is false, but it is worth keeping in mind that *erroneous belief can also destroy human resources, human happiness, and even human life.* Did you know that it was long believed that a wound had to be cut in order to assure that vile "humours" would gather at the surface to be removed? This meant that a lucky individual who had a clean, uninfected wound would be treated with slices from an unclean knife until pus formed! The hapless patient would be *given* an infection.

It was not until modern times that a surgeon, John Hunter (1728–1793), noticed that survival rates seemed to be better in wounded soldiers deprived of treatment. And the surgeon did not content himself with what *seemed* to be. He ran a controlled experiment in which some people received the "treatment" and others did not, then compared their recoveries. It is doubtful that a mere impression could have served to break down such a longstanding belief, but an experimental demonstration could—and did.

Contemporaries tend to dismiss historical accounts of erroneous belief on the grounds that people used to be foolish, gullible, and prone to superstition. But truth comes to us no more easily today than it did in the past.

Nonscientific psychology may be fascinating, but it is on ground no more firm than that of nonscientific disciplines in the past.

Dangers of Intuition in Psychology

Today, the treatment of mental disorder rests heavily on the individual talent of the one doing the treating—on "clinical intuition." But clinical intuition is so called precisely *because* it is unreliable, because one observer cannot agree with another. The intuitive approach is much more direct than a scientific approach and seems often more in tune with "common sense." But remember, common sense told our ancestors, who were no more stupid than we are, that it was silly to suppose that there were people underneath us on the earth, as the absurd notion that the earth was round would imply. Obviously they would fall off! The chief danger entailed by the intuitive approach is that it makes permanent self-deception possible. The situation of one who relies on intuition instead of science is similar to that of the fellow who thinks he is the greatest baritone in the world, even if no one appreciates his voice. There is no method of correcting such errors, since opportunities for external checking are missing.

If clinical intuition were enough without scientific controls, bloodletting would be a well-founded procedure, for centuries of clinical judgment support it. Many an astute barber-surgeon went through life convinced that bloodletting was an effective means of treating various diseases (even though at the time of the bubonic plague, estimates of the amount of blood in the human body were so far exaggerated that people were literally bled to death). Of course the patients sometimes died, but they sometimes got better. No treatment is foolproof, after all! The trouble with the method of the bloodletting physicians was that they had no *objective criterion* of the effectiveness of their treatment—or at least they failed to put it to an objective test. They failed to make risky predictions and test them. Eysenck (1952) has pointed out that psychotherapists are doing exactly the same sort of thing today. They are convinced, on the basis of their clinical experience, that their therapy works, but they have not done the necessary experimental tests that would establish that they are correct.

A Perspective on Nonexperimental Knowledge

My purpose in the previous sections has been to emphasize the value and importance of experimental method. Therefore, I stressed the advantages of experimental method and the disadvantages of other methods. Yet I, like everyone else, must often live and act on the basis of much less reliable information than experiments provide. The ancient Greek notion that wisdom dictates using the best available knowledge in a given area continues to be a good rule of thumb.

Experimental method is, at bottom, an elaborate extension of reality-testing—checking out our ideas and fantasies to see whether they hold up in the real world. It seems to be a superb elaboration of reality testing, though other methods might do very well under appropriate circumstances. For example, the methods of nonexperimental, observational science have been of very great service. And in everyday life we may have to settle for much less than that. But experimental methods can be extended much further than most of us realize. It is difficult, within our cultural traditions, to learn to examine every question for its experimental potential. Whenever possible, we should try to do that. And experiment is possible far more often than we realize. When it is not possible, let us accept the best knowledge available.

What about occult or esoteric knowledge? This would appear to be the polar opposite of knowledge based on experiments, yet reliance on such knowledge today is widespread. Even such forms of gaining truth can often be put to the test of science. Hypnotism is a good example of a phenomenon that made its way from the occult to the scientific. For some people, occult systems are merely sources of entertainment. But for those who take them seriously, reality testing is important. Why not experiment with these systems? If we can predict the degree of advancement of Zen disciples by measured brain waves (Kasamatsu & Hirai, 1966), where are our limits? Attempts have been made to put astrology to scientific test, with most interesting results (Gauquelin, 1973; West & Toonder, 1973).

In some cases, no public test of occult knowledge would appear to be possible. There is an occult tradition that "Knowledge is power and knowledge shared is power lost." The penalty for revelation of secrets among the ancient Pythagoreans was death. But even within these systems some methods of risky prediction can be identified. To what extent they are used we, as outsiders, cannot say. If they are not used effectively, the dangers of intuition are great.

The main disadvantage of experimental method is that it is slow and difficult. But the quality of the results will often make the effort worthwhile. Experimental checking will often show that even our best-founded ideas are mistaken. And we have not *begun* to extend the experimental method over its potential domain.

Experimental Psychology and Traditional Notions of Mind and Body

The attitudes of experimental psychologists might appear to run against traditional notions of mind and body. Actually, this may or may not be the case. Some psychologists take strong philosophical positions in favor of psychic determinism (that there is no free will) and materialistic monism (that all things, including mind, are material). But these are *philosophical,* not scientific, issues. Such questions cannot be answered within the framework of scientific method.

In fact, it is not hard to find experimental psychologists who are not determinists in the philosophical sense or who are dualists (mind and body are distinct substances) or even mentalistic monists (the universe is composed of only one substance, which is mind). Science has a way of conforming itself to changes of philosophy. In fact, one source of the success of scientific method has been its separation from such philosophical questions.

I suspect that most experimental psychologists spend little time thinking about determinism or the mind-body problem. They do their experiments and leave such questions up to the philosophers. Scientific psychologists *do* adopt the working hypothesis that psychological events are lawful. This is the only working hypothesis that justifies doing scientific observations and experiments. But the possibility that there is ultimately a residuum of indeterminacy is of little concern within the framework of science. Physicists now accept indeterminacy with grace; so may psychologists.

The point is that, although any psychologist may have very strong opinions about philosophical matters, one does not speak as a scientist when one shifts to such questions. One may speak as a philosopher, or simply as a human being. But all of the familiar philosophical points of view can be reconciled with experimental psychology.

Controls, Variables, and Relationships

Essential to establishing the effectiveness of a maneuver is properly *controlled* experimentation. If we are to establish the efficacy of a given procedure such as psychoanalytic therapy, bloodletting, or adding a catalyst to chemical reagents, it is necessary that we introduce *controls,* which enable us to determine whether the observed events following it are actually due to our procedure, or whether some other factors are responsible for the events. We must make observations under two conditions: an experimental condition and a control condition. In the *experimental condition* the procedure whose effect is to be measured is introduced (for example, we arrange psychoanalytic therapy for a group of patients). Under the *control condition,* all factors are made identical to those under the experimental condition, but the experimental treatment is omitted (for example, control subjects submit to all factors, such as coming to an office, except psychoanalysis).

As a second example of the use of controls, suppose an experimenter wanted to know whether the caffeine present in coffee improves reading comprehension. An uncontrolled procedure for answering this question would be to have people drink coffee and then take a reading comprehension test. But this would be a woefully inadequate method. The experimental treatment of introducing caffeine-containing coffee needs to be supplemented by a control condition. For example, some subjects (the experimental subjects) could be given regular coffee and other subjects (the control subjects) could be given a coffee with the caffeine removed. The reading comprehension scores of these two groups of subjects could then be compared. If enough subjects were used and they were assigned to the experimental and control groups without bias, a solid conclusion about the effects of caffeine in coffee on a particular test behavior of a particular population could be derived from comparison of their scores.

Any difference between the experimental and the control condition must be due to the introduction of the experimental treatment, if this is the only point on which the two conditions differ. Since the experimental and control subjects are often two different groups of individuals, we often speak of the *experimental group* and the *control group.* It is probably better to think in terms of experimental and control *conditions* or *treatments,* however, because we often use the same subjects "as their own controls." That is, we submit the same individuals to both the experimental and the control condition at different times and compare their reaction under the one condition to their reaction under the other. Under these conditions, there are experimental and control treatments, but there are no separate experimental and control groups. When we design an experiment this way, special precautions must be taken to evaluate the effects of the *order* in which we present the two conditions. It may make a considerable difference which treatment comes first. Methods of dealing with order effects will be discussed later.

Confounded Variables

Although it is not always readily apparent, the reason that control conditions must be introduced in an experiment is to avoid what are termed *confounded variables.* A confounded variable is an uncontrolled factor—one that is allowed to vary along with the experimental treatment, making it impossible to tell whether any observed changes are due to the experimental treatment alone, or whether the confounding factor has made an important contribution (see Figure 1.3).

Independent Variable, Dependent Variable, and Functional Relationship

Thus far, I have used the term "experimental treatment" for the main object of experimental study. Problems of control and confounding are problems of being certain that the effects of the experimental treatment may be measured in an uncontaminated way. At this point, it will be useful to introduce technical terminology to replace the term "experimental treatment" and to designate certain other components of the experiment.

The experimental treatment is usually called the *independent variable.* In science, as in mathematics, a *variable* is something that can have more than one value. A variable is in contrast to a *constant* which has only one value. For example, the relationship between two different types of measure, such as

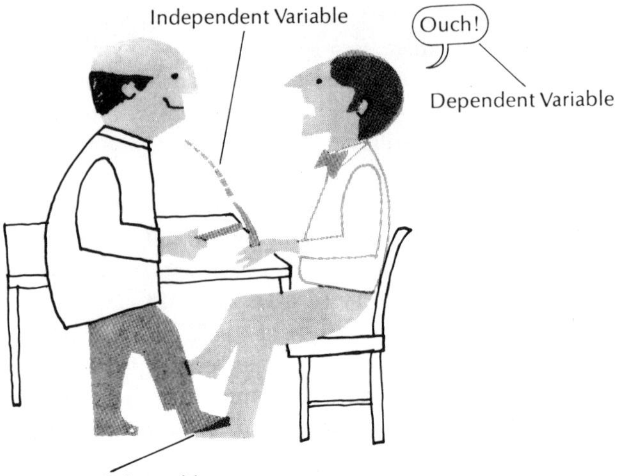

FIGURE 1.3 Relationship of independent, dependent, and confounded variables. The experimenter deliberately manipulates the independent variable and indirectly produces a change in the subject's behavior. If a confounded variable is inadvertently introduced, there is no way to tell whether the independent variable or the confounded variable produced the behavioral change.

inches and feet, can be expressed as a constant multiplier or divisor. Yards times a constant (equal to three) equals feet. To use a related example of a variable, the height of a human being can take a variety of values, such as 3 feet, 4 feet, 7 feet, and so on. Other examples of variables might be the IQs of people, the degree of muscular tension in one's forehead, or the frequency with which one makes direct eye contact during conversation. Each of these can take a range of possible values.

But what is meant by an *independent* variable? This is best explained by looking at an imaginary experiment. Suppose an experimenter wanted to determine the relationship between the height of a male speaker and his ability to persuade an audience. Assume that the experimenter has arranged for males of various heights to deliver a standard persuasive speech to audiences and that there is an accepted way of measuring the degree to which they have been persuaded (for example, a vote). Suppose, further, that the taller the male speaker, the larger the number of votes in the direction of the persuasive argument. Then the experimenter has identified a *functional relationship,* which is a relationship between two variables. In this case, the functional relationship is the relationship between height of the speaker and number of votes in the desired direction. The independent variable in a functional relationship is the variable whose values determine the values of the other variable. In this example, the height of the speaker determines the values of the "vote-gathering" variable, so height is the independent variable. The second variable is called the *dependent variable.* It is the variable whose values are determined by the values of the independent variable.

Another way to describe the functional relationship and its variables is to consider that there is a predictive relationship between the two variables. One of the variables (the independent variable) is *predictive.* The second variable, the dependent variable, is *predicted.* Some experimenters like to restrict the use of the term independent variable to those cases in which the variable not only is predictive of, but also *controls* the values of the predicted or outcome variable. The value of the Dow-Jones Stock Market Average can be predicted from the current length of women's skirts. But skirt lengths surely do not *control* the Dow-Jones average! Many experimenters are reluctant to apply the term independent variable in such cases. The term *predictor* or *predictive variable* can be used in such cases.

Another term that is often used instead of independent variable is the term *factor.* The terms independent variable and factor are synonymous. When we use the word "factor" it is customary to speak of *levels* of the factor rather than of *values.* Further delineation of the subtleties of usage of these terms will be provided later.

Explanation and Pseudoexplanation

Once you have established a functional relationship of the "causal" type, you can use it as an explanatory tool. If you want to explain changes in the pressure of a gas, you can say that they occur because of prior changes in temperature (assuming that such changes and no others actually took place). Thus you establish a functional relationship between the temperature and the pressure of gas. If you want to explain an increase in the tendency for an experimental subject to drink water, you can appeal to an observation of, let us say, a prolonged period of water deprivation. Again you know that a functional relationship exists, and you use it to account for an observed fact or "phenomenon."

There is a highly prevalent counterfeit of such scientific explanation, called a *nominal explanation,* a *tautology,* a *circular explanation,* or (by Skinner, 1953) an *inner cause* explanation. A nominal explanation is a kind of verbal muddle in which the purported independent variable is a mere alias for the dependent variable. In reality, there have not been two distinct observations (corresponding to the independent and dependent variables) at all. Only the dependent variable has been observed and then renamed, the second name being treated as an independent variable.

To cite a comparative example from physics, examine the following question: Why do apples fall toward the earth? The usual answer is, "Because of gravity." But this simplistic answer is a misinterpretation of the concept of gravity. Gravity is merely a *name* for *the fact* that bodies fall toward earth. What observation leads us to conclude that gravity exists? The observation that bodies fall. Hence, if we say that bodies fall because of gravity, we are really saying that bodies fall because bodies fall. Our independent variable is really an alias for the dependent variable we are trying to explain.

This does not contradict the laws of physics. Isaac Newton, the author of the universal law of gravitation, was well aware of the distinction between this misuse of the concept of gravity and the proper use of functional explanation. This awareness was in fact one grave obstacle to his being understood by his contemporaries (see Andrade, 1958). Newton said: *Hypotheses non fingo* (I make no hypotheses). He used the word "hypothesis" in its earlier meaning. Today we use the term to refer to an explanation that we accept provisionally in order to put it to experimental test. Newton had in mind hypothetical entities such as "powers" and "forces," which were used as all too easy pseudoexplanations of events—the very type of explanation we are objecting to here. Newton used the terms "power" and "force," but he defined them in terms of *observable events.* For him, they were mere shorthand forms for functional relationships. In the words of a contemporary physicist:

> What is gravity?
>
> But is this such a simple law? What about the machinery of it? All we have done is to describe *how* the earth moves around the sun, but we have not said what *makes it go.* Newton made no hypotheses about this; he was satisfied to find *what* it did without getting into the machinery of it. *No one has since given any machinery.* It is characteristic of the physical laws that they have this abstract character. The law of conservation of energy is a theorem concerning quantities that have to be calculated and added together, with no mention of the machinery, and likewise the great laws of mechanics are quantitative mathematical laws for which no machinery is available Why can we use mathematics to describe nature without a mechanism behind it? No one knows. We have to keep going because we find out more that way. (Feynman, Leighton, & Sands, 1963)

In the behavioral sciences we are especially prone to slip into nominal explanations. Explanation in terms of what Ryle (1949) has colorfully called "the ghost in the machine" has been particularly common in psychology. If the ghost-in-the-machine account were adequate, there would be little need for the laborious development of psychology as a science, since the development of a complete account of human action is quite simple within such a framework. For every observed action, we would merely propose an inner "power" of the mind as its explanation. We would always have at hand a ready explanation for any human action. But if we were to use this kind of "explanation," it would only make the phenomena to be explained less accessible, and the task of developing a functional explanation would still remain before us.

Two examples of the nominal explanation of human actions are discussed below.

The Primitive Artistic Impulse. Begin with the striking observation that even the most "primitive" humans spent a great deal of time on art forms, even though the time could be alternatively spent in the realistic struggle for food and other basic necessities. Observations made on primates in their natural habitats, up to and including the anthropoid apes, give little indication of any noteworthy artistic strivings, but even in the most hostile of physical environments humans spend long hours on the design of intricate patterns for their shields, their huts, and the like. How do we explain this tendency? If we happen to be addicted to pseudoexplanation, we might say, "It is due to a primitive artistic impulse." But how do we know that the proposed primitive artistic impulse exists? We "know" that it exists because "primitive" men expend their energies on artistry—because of the very observation that we want to explain. Again, the observation corresponding to the independent variable is identical to the observation corresponding to the dependent variable. Put symbolically, this account is of the form "Humans do A because they do A."

The Paranoid Personality. George is suspicious, stubborn, and has delusions of persecution. Why? Because he is paranoid. Once again, "paranoid" is a mere name for his symptoms.

Avoiding Pseudoexplanation

How can we avoid slipping into nominal explanation? It is not easy. We have to keep in mind that the minimum requirement for an adequate functional explanation is that at least two *independent* observations be made. There must be one observation for the dependent variable and another, *distinct* observation for the independent variable.

It is often hard to tell in a brief encounter whether a nominal explanation is being foisted on you. Sometimes an individual who uses rather suspect language will, if pressed, be able to provide the listener with the necessary definition in terms of observable events. Psychologists who have suffered through unpleasant encounters with commonly used nominal explanations are apt to be frightened away by certain linguistic hobgoblins without bothering to determine whether the seemingly loose language is being used in a rigorous fashion. It may be necessary to go to such extremes if you have trouble getting to the core of an explanation in order to see it for what it really is. On the other hand, if you judge explanations merely on the basis of the language in which they are framed you might be taken in by an even more deadly form of nominal explanation—the kind that has been carefully cloaked in scientific jargon.

Nominal explanations are more widely encountered in psychology than we would like to admit. Even respectable explanatory devices such as "reinforcement," or "generalization," or "the central nervous system" can be used in unacceptable ways. The selection of words is not of great importance. The important thing is our ability to put observational backbone into our language. The speaker who uses everyday or phenomenological terminology may be more rigorous than many verbally less colorful colleagues. If the minimal requirement of at least two distinct sets of observations has been met, the explanation is legitimate no matter how it is phrased. If that requirement has not been met, there is no real explanation. No matter how it is phrased, it will be a pseudoexplanation, as Figure 1.4 shows.

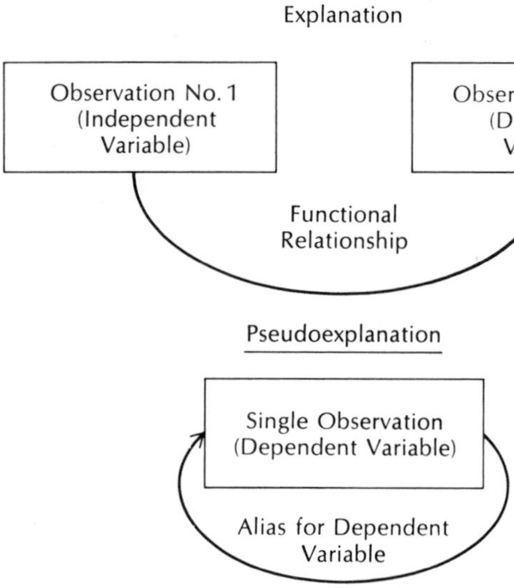

FIGURE 1.4 Contrast between explanation and pseudoexplanation. With explanation, there are at least two independent observations—one for the independent variable and one for the dependent variable. With pseudoexplanation, only the dependent variable is observed, and another name for the dependent variable is treated as though it were an independent variable.

SUMMARY

1. There is a widespread belief in the power and importance of psychology in solving contemporary human problems. Books, magazines and other media barrage us with psychological solutions to our problems. It is not enough to rely on the authority of the source in deciding whether to accept such methods. We need *good* evidence, and a major source of good evidence is the scientific method. Learning to evaluate scientific evi-

dence is a complex task. A major goal of instruction in research methodology is to teach you to make adequate evaluations of evidence, scientific and unscientific.

2. Experimental psychology is distinguished from the rest of psychology by its method, not by its content. Whenever experimental method is applied to any aspect of psychology, we have an instance of experimental psychology.

3. The main objectives of experimental psychology are to measure, predict, and produce desired psychological events. These are merely the general objectives of experimental science as adapted to psychology.

4. Science is characterized by the reliability of its observations, as attained through the use of measurements. It is also characterized by the ability of its theories to make predictions that are specific enough to permit refutation of the theory *("risky predictions").*

5. Though there is no formalized criterion of how reliable scientific observations must be, we usually accept them if they do not generate dispute. Sometimes we have to check specifically to see whether independent observers can agree as to an observation. At times it may be useful to quantify the degree of agreement of observers.

6. A major method of getting scientifically acceptable levels of reliability of observations is to use *operational definitions.* With operational definition, a thing is defined by the way it is measured. Operational definitions are so highly valued that some people have proposed that concepts are nothing but their *measurement operations.* That view is called *radical operationism.* An alternative view is that each operation provides a partial index of the concept under study but that no single operation is identical to that concept. The latter idea leads to the use of more than one measure for a given thing. This is the method of *multiple converging operations.*

7. Not all science is experimental. *Naturalistic science* involves measuring the relationships between things without manipulating and controlling variables in order to ascertain which things control the observed outcomes. With *experimental manipulation* we get knowledge of the controlling influences. Thus we are able to specify exactly the conditions under which an event occurs.

8. No other method will attain the objective of experimental psychology. Thus we must use experimental method if we want to attain those objectives. Many people fear that such use will result in excessive control, but people are controlled in any case. The expansion of our knowledge of controlling factors will permit systematic rather than chaotic control, and may have highly desirable consequences.

9. Methods that lack the reliability and self-corrective measures of science make us highly subject to error. Worse, they may allow us to re-

main in error permanently. Nor do they necessarily permit us, even if we are right, to convince others and get them to act.

10. In an experiment we are looking for a relationship between a *controlling* and a *controlled variable.* The controlling variable is called an *"independent variable"* or *"factor."* The controlled variable is called the *"dependent variable."* If there is a relationship between them it is called a *functional relationship.* A variable that is allowed to vary along with the independent variable is called a confounded variable. A *confounded variable* makes it impossible to attribute variations in outcome to the influence of the independent variable.

11. Once a functional relationship has been established, it can be used to explain instances of that relationship. At a minimum, a true functional relationship requires measurement of an independent variable, and a dependent variable, and establishment of a relationship between them. *Pseudoexplanations* (also called *nominal* or *tautological explanations)* involve measurement or observation of only the dependent variable. The dependent variable is merely renamed and treated as though it were an independent variable. This provides no explanation at all.

CHAPTER 2

Getting Ideas for Research

The main goal of the previous chapter was to explain what experimental psychology is and to identify its primary objectives. In this chapter we deal with the more concrete problem of how one gets started in actually carrying out experimental work in psychology. This will be of value for those who intend to do such work, either as a career or for the more short-range purpose of satisfying various academic requirements. It might also be of some value to the general reader in giving some feeling for how research ideas are generated.

In reality, the sources of ideas are extremely varied. They may range from dreams and visions to carefully calculated implications of formal theories. Here we will deal only with some major sources of research ideas.

Ideas Come from Reading Scientific Literature

If you read scientific books and articles with an active interest, many prospective research problems will be likely to come to mind. This happens even to students reading their first psychology text. However, it is very important to keep a *log of research ideas.* This will serve to fix the ideas in your memory, and it will pull your ideas together in one place. Often pieces will fall together in this way, and sometimes you will notice the same idea recurring in various forms. Furthermore, even if we once had many ideas for research, we may later find ourselves at a loss when the opportunity or obligation to do some research arises. The log will remind you of the ideas you once had.

It is hard sometimes to read research literature until you have done some research yourself. A typical pattern for my students has been to begin a required research project reluctantly, then to be sparked by an exciting new idea from related literature they might otherwise have found tedious.

Searching the Literature

The following information will help you to familiarize yourself with the literature in a given area of interest.

The first and most general sources will be *textbooks.* These will give you a general notion of the kinds of questions that have interested research psychologists, and may stimulate you to extrapolate from previous research.

Once you have a basic notion of the area in which you would like to read, take advantage of one of the most valuable resources in literature searching—*well-informed people in the field.* Students often neglect to make use of such expert sources as their teachers or other faculty members at their college or university. These experts probably have deep knowledge of the area of interest and are likely to be very well aware of available literature sources.

You and the experts may be able to become more specific about the topic of interest. You can make explicit the various forms in which it might be referenced. The more explicit you can get, the easier it will be to identify sources pertaining to your topic.

Look in *library card catalogues* under the topic areas of your interest. Books are exceptionally good starting sources, since they will provide large numbers of references to relevant articles you can look up.

Psychological Abstracts is a journal available at most college and university libraries, that indexes and briefly summarizes most articles in psychological journals. Look in the index of *Psychological Abstracts* under the various names you think might be used for research in your topic area. This will refer you to pages containing summaries of the articles. Having read these abstracts, you can determine whether to search out an article itself. Other reference works such as *Biology Abstracts* or *Index Medicus* may be useful for certain topic areas in psychology.

Review articles are published in several sources, notably *Annual Review of Psychology, Psychological Review,* and *Psychological Bulletin.* Review articles are valuable in giving you a general perspective on a topic area and in providing many further references. However, do not rely entirely on them, since an article may not be well represented by the author, who often will have a strong theoretical point of view to support.

It is extremely important that you seek out articles that are referenced in the articles you first read. You look up the references in a given article, then look up the references in those articles, then look up the references in those articles, and so on until you seem to have covered all the major articles. I have found this to be an extremely effective way of reviewing the literature, and would rely on it far more than the fallible abstracts or computer retrieval services.

You may have access to various computer retrieval services, such as Datrix (University Microfilms, Inc., Ann Arbor), which provides references to most Ph.D. thesis abstracts in North America, or to Medlar, which searches *Index Medicus* for the last two years. These systems rely on coding of articles with key words. The mindless computers, though capable of reviewing enormous quantities of information, may give you a lot of chaff with the wheat, and also may miss some wheat, so don't overvalue this impressive resource.

Several periodicals regularly publish lists of articles by topic area and/or author. Two important ones are *Current Contents—Life Sciences* (Institute for Scientific Information, 325 Chestnut Street, Philadelphia, Pa. 19106) and *Science Citation Index.* These will probably be in your school library. Others may also be available. Check with your librarian.

It is a regular practice for authors to provide without charge copies of their articles (reprints) and even copies of articles they have done that are not yet printed (preprints). You can request these either by postcard or by letter. It is deferential to send a letter, so you should do that if you are making a rather large request. Some authors will not have reprints and preprints, especially in certain countries. But it doesn't hurt to ask.

If you have specific needs for information, you should not hesitate to get on the phone and call an author. In science, even a humble, beginning student can request information from a Nobel prizewinner with good results.

How to Read Articles in Experimental Psychology

Most articles in experimental psychology are not easy to read unless you have a good deal of background. Costs of publication force editors to keep articles down to the bare bones. Keeping certain key questions in mind will help you.

The Problem and Its Significance

First, ask, "What is the problem to be solved, and why is it significant?"[1] The article may not give you much help in answering this question, because authors are expected to write for an audience somewhat familiar with the topic of research. You may have to ask teachers or look for background reference materials before really grasping the significance of the paper. Try not to fall into the fallacy of judging that the article is "trivial" because you do not immediately see why it is significant. It sometimes boggles the mind to see how important a superficially trivial article can be once the background of the problem is understood. One of the advantages of your having had the kind of education you have had is that you can look beyond the superficialities.

Controls and Measures

Next ask, "How were treatments and control conditions assigned to subjects?" and "Were the controls adequate?" Then, "How were the variables measured, and did the measures actually provide a good index of the thing of interest?" Even with little training in research methodology, good common sense can often allow you to recognize missing controls. For example, a study described in *Time* magazine many years ago involved testing the effectiveness of routinely giving antibiotics to surgical patients. The results indicated that patients given the antibiotics were more likely to get infections than those not given them. Many students, even without technical

[1]Your ability to answer all of the listed questions will grow as you work your way through this book.

training, recognize the possibility that surgeons might be more likely to give antibiotics to those patients who were exposed to greater risk of infection. Initial risk of infection is, therefore, uncontrolled.

Similarly, common sense can permit recognition of measures that reflect the wrong thing or that are simply not quantitative enough. For example, studies of obesity commonly use a definition of obesity that stipulates a body weight at least 15 percent above "normal." But it is obvious that there are many finer, and possibly important, gradations of overweight. Are people with 15 percent excess weight just like those with 100 percent excess? Are muscular, athletic types who weigh 15 percent over the norms just like flabby people who are also 15 percent above them?

In the next chapter, I will go into technical considerations about measurement that will make it easier to identify inadequate measures, but common sense can take you a long way toward detecting many of the problems.

By pausing to ask questions about adequacy of controls and of measures, you may see that some controls are not quite right or some measures not good enough.

The Results and Their Reliability

Now ask "What were the results?" and "How likely is it that I can rely on them to hold up in the future?" If the stated statistical probability values are very small, the results are more likely to be reliable than if the results are near the customary cut-off of 5 percent (probability = .05). When statistical analyses indicate that the results were better than chance at the ".05 level," this means that only once in 20 such tests would they in fact be expected to occur by *chance alone.* Such results cannot be relied upon as much as those at, say, probability = .001. The latter case means that only once in a thousand tests can the results be expected to occur by chance alone.

Also ask, "Was the effect obvious or was it a weaker one only clearly revealed by statistical analyses?" Very powerful variables may exhibit their influence without statistical tests, and such variables are more likely to produce similar effects in future studies. If you are familiar with statistics, you can ask, "Were the correct statistics used?" By the time you get to the end of this book, you should be able to answer that question with fair competence.

Further, ask, "Was the study, or some variant of it, done more than once?" Sometimes a paper will contain a series of experiments that, to some degree, are repetitions of each other. Studies that have been repeated are much more reliable than those that have not.

Sensitivity of the Experiment

At this point ask, "Was the experimental arrangement likely to be sensitive to the influences of the independent variables?" In some experimental situations, many random factors are allowed to fluctuate during the study. These are not confounded variables, because, in the long run they influence treatment and control conditions equally. They do not vary systematically with the independent variable. However, their influence may obscure the effects of the independent variable.

You may be inclined to think that any study in which such random variations are permitted is simply badly done. But sometimes the experimenter wants to show that a variable is powerful enough to display its influence in spite of such background fluctuations. I once supervised a thesis (Fawl, 1975) which was designed to detect the effects of a treatment called "electrosleep." This treatment, widely used in the Soviet Union, and used to some extent in this country, purportedly works positive changes on a variety of psychological and psychosomatic disorders. It involves pulsing low-level electric currents through the head.

The claims being made for electrosleep were that it caused beneficial changes above and beyond those produced by routine treatments, and on patients in a variety of diagnostic categories. Fawl therefore studied the impact of the treatment on patients also being treated by whatever other means their therapists thought useful. This made it difficult to detect any effects of the special treatment, since the effects had to reveal themselves over and above those produced by any treatments developed through the ingenuity of the therapists. But what if the effects of electrosleep *did* show up under such circumstances? Wouldn't this be highly convincing? It would mean that this was a very powerful treatment. Unfortunately, Fawl's study produced very little in the way of positive results.

Reading such a study, you could easily devise a further experiment in which the effects of the treatment were submitted to a more sensitive test, one that would be somewhat more generous with the experimental treatment in giving it a chance to show its effectiveness. For example, you could deal with patients with the same diagnosis and arrange for therapists to hold their other treatments constant during your use of electrosleep.

Other considerations that bear on the sensitivity of the experiment are such things as, "How many observations were made?" For example, a study done on only a few subjects, each being measured only a few times, is less likely to detect effects than one done with large numbers of measures.

You should also ask, "What magnitude of effect was the experimenter trying to detect?" In the study on electrosleep just described, Fawl was primarily interested in detecting very large effects. Those using the electrosleep technique had indicated that the effects were large, and she was testing their claim. If she had been interested in detecting effects of small magnitude, she would have been unwise to design her study as she did. You may find studies in which the experimenter fails to see an effect of the independent variable, but the conditions could not reasonably be expected to detect effects of the expected magnitude.

Generality of Findings

You need also consider, "What procedures were carried out to ensure that the findings will occur in other, somewhat different, situations?" "How likely is it that these findings would hold up in other contexts, or with other measures?" If the measures were verbal, they may or may not reflect nonverbal behaviors. If they were taken in a laboratory or under other potentially unrealistic situations, they may not hold up in the wider environment.

"Were the subjects in the study representative of those to whom the experimenter wishes to generalize?" For example, a recent newspaper article reviewed attitudes of current college students, contrasting the current attitudes to those of students in the 1960s. However, the interviewed students were all winners of a high scholastic honor. Are their attitudes really representative of the attitudes of all students? A follow-up study could be done on a more adequate sample of subjects.

Sometimes an investigation will include a direct test of the generalizability of the findings. Then, a useful question is, "Was a direct test of generalizability done?" If it was not, such a test might be a reasonable subsequent study.

You must also consider, "What procedures were used to assure generality of the finding?" Was sampling adequate? Was any empirical test of generality done? Were the measures generalizable (for example, are the authors trying to generalize from verbal reports to nonverbal behavior?).

Significance

Finally, ask, "What was the significance of the findings?" Relate the findings to the question raised in the first place. Does the experiment answer that question? If not, why not? How could it be improved so that it would answer that question? Is the finding relevant to some question the experimenters did not have in mind?

Reading with such questions actively in mind will enhance your understanding of most articles. Sometimes you will not be able to answer some of the questions. For example, you may not know enough about statistics to tell whether the ones used were appropriate. But at other times you might know enough. In any case, it is good practice to keep an eye out for such things. That is one good way to learn eventually how to do it correctly.

Ways of Extrapolating from Previous Experiments

An old saying goes, "The beginning is more than half of the whole." The first experiment in a series is usually harder than those that follow. One experiment tends to lead to others and sets the stage procedurally and technologically for them. Thus, it is a useful strategy to get into a research area the easiest way possible; do not insist on a really fantastic first experiment. That will, hopefully, come later.

There are many ways of following up an initial experiment.

Verification and Replication

The simplest extrapolation from previous research is to attempt to *verify* it. An experimenter who *replicates* (attempts to repeat) a previous finding is trying to verify that finding. Replications make an important contribution to the advancement of scientific knowledge. Psychologists, especially journal editors, should encourage more of them. Many disciplines do not regard a finding as established until it has been "repeated in other laboratories." Unfortunately it is not easy to get simple replications published in psychology.

Variations on simple replication are possible, and of benefit. For example, it may be possible to repeat a finding and also to measure it in a slightly different way. Such studies are more likely to be published.

Recombination

Going beyond simple replication, an experimenter may make a transition into a second mode of extrapolating from previous research, that of *recombining* aspects of previous research. With recombination you take parts of two or more previous experiments and combine them. For example, Donald Blough (1956) was interested in studying the sensory capacities of animals. But how do you ask animals what they see or what they hear? He was aware of the methods used by B. F. Skinner to study operant conditioning. Blough was also aware of certain methods devised by George von Bekesy to study sensory capacities of humans. Essentially, Bekesy had people indicate whether they could or could not detect a stimulus by holding down and letting up on a key. But the operant chamber typically requires animals to press or peck on a key. Why not apply the Bekesy method to animals in operant chambers? This is what Blough did, and he was able to get very refined measures of perception in animals.

Generalization

You can create hypotheses for research by generalizing from previous findings. Generalization can be across various aspects of an experiment. Will the same functional relationship hold with other species? Will it hold in other situations? Will it hold with other kinds of measures (such as a change from verbal to nonverbal measures or a change in type of apparatus)?

Specialization

Specialization is the opposite of generalization. How does a general phenomenon apply in special cases? For example, it is widely known that psychiatrists and psychologists have a higher rate of suicide than the average population. What happens if you look at men versus women in this group? It turns out that the higher rates of suicide are entirely due to more suicides by women.

Unconfounding

A careful reading of the literature will expose many confounded variables, many of them deliberately so. More spectacular findings often have a greater-than-average tendency to have confounded variables, since they tend to be initial efforts toward working in a given area. Many good research projects can be created by putting in the needed controls.

Improving Measurement of the Variables

We briefly discussed improving measurement of the variables in the section on reading the literature. In the next chapter a more detailed account of the nature of measurement will be given, and at that point you will learn a great deal about the various levels of measurement and how to tell which methods of measurement are better and which worse. There are few experiments that could not be improved by taking better measures. This can be as simple as substituting a direct behavioral measure for a verbal report, or for using any other type of measure that is more representative of the target events than the customary measures. It can also be done by using increasingly quantitative measures, such as the higher level scales described in Chapter 3. A valuable way to improve measurement is to use several different measures where a single measure was used before. This is the method of multiple, converging operations, which was explained in Chapter 1.

Identifying Underlying Causes

Research to identify the underlying causes of a phenomenon is probably the most advanced and most satisfying of all research. It commonly comes relatively late in a research attack. To illustrate, I did an experiment that showed that there is a marked difference between albino and pigmented rats in the ability to do visual discriminations with the part of the visual pathway that goes directly from eye to cerebral hemisphere without crossing to the opposite side (Sheridan, 1965a). The first stage of follow-up research had to do with *verification* by replication. The study was repeated with slightly different rats, in a slightly different situation (Sheridan & Shrout, 1965). Next, the phenomenon was verified by establishing it with various measures of neuropsychological (Creel & Sheridan, 1966), anatomical (Lund, 1965), and electrophysiological (Creel, 1971) kinds. Next, but to a degree overlapping the verification stage, was a stage of *generalization.* Tests were done to see whether the phenomenon applied to a range of other species. It is now known to apply to rats, guinea pigs, cats, minks, ferrets, and humans.

But the thrust of contemporary research on this topic is toward identifying underlying *causes.* The first move in this direction came from Sanderson et al. (1972), who began detailed genetic manipulations. A variety of genetic experiments and biochemical experiments are now being done to find the underlying causes of the nervous-system peculiarities associated with albinism.

Ideas from Techniques and Apparatus

Many experimenters center their research on a special technique or apparatus. There is an important distinction between *problem-oriented research* and *technique-oriented research.* In problem-oriented research the experimenter will use a variety of techniques, and even learn or devise new ones, in order to get at the answer to a given question. Problem-oriented research might seem preferable, but it may not be easy in these complicated times to learn all the techniques required to solve a given problem. This leads to the notion that *research teams* of specialists would be ideal for solving research problems, but such teams rarely work out. I think this is because a really good researcher who is master of a given technique will not like to subordinate personal interests to goals imposed by others. First-rate scientists tend to be rugged individualists.

When research is technique oriented, the nature of the problem is dictated by some method or item of equipment. For example, a person might be restricted to working with biofeedback (a type of equipment), or operant conditioning (a method). Though it might be reasonable to expect the inferiority of technique-oriented research, experience does not necessarily support that expectation. Some of the most important research done in recent times has come from technique-oriented researchers.

Ideas from Other People

People naturally want to do research on their own ideas, but there is nothing wrong with picking up a research problem suggested by someone else. Charles Martin Hall was a student in a chemistry class where the teacher suggested the importance of devising an economical way to process aluminum ore. Hall went right to work on the problem and licked it, making a great personal fortune. People often have good researchable ideas while lacking the will or capacity to implement them. Why not put these ideas to use?

Often you do not get people to hand you a research idea, but you get ideas from them in less direct ways. Discussing issues, brainstorming together, and especially *arguing* about ideas are fertile sources.

Apprenticeship

With all due respect for your ideas, it is often good to postpone independent work and to do research under an expert for a while. Most accomplished scientists have done so. Most people have to take a period of time learning a basic framework and developing skills and knowledge of techniques. If you try to go out too far on your own, you may get discouraged and lose interest in science. A lot of students feel guilty or thwarted or put down if they are denied an opportunity to conduct completely independent research. Actually, apprenticing with an expert is just being smart and taking full advantage of the resources available.

Rigorous Evaluation of an Unverified Belief

A fertile source of ideas for research can be found in common beliefs that have not been experimentally established. A good example of this is the belief that clitoral and vaginal orgasms are different. This belief dominated the sex manuals until Masters and Johnson (1966) put it to scientific test.

Particularly at the present time there are many beliefs about psychological matters that have incomplete, or even virtually no scientific backing. Many of the topics alluded to in the opening of Chapter 1 provide excellent examples of such beliefs.

Ideas from Theories

One of the great benefits of having a theory is its usefulness in providing many research ideas. Theories have implications, and experimenters can work these out and test them. Theories also have assumptions or postulates. In psychology, the assumptions or postulates have often been the focus of experimental testing. In the so-called "classical age" of learning theory, a great deal of attention was given to testing the postulates of psychological theories. This is an odd way to use a theory, and probably an improper one.

Many historically great theories have had false assumptions. For example, a look at Bernoulli's earliest formulation of the kinetic theory of gases reveals that every assumption ran counter to the facts. He assumed that all particles are perfectly elastic, that each particle has the same velocity as every other, that the particles never collide, and so on. Yet his was one of science's most successful theories, and an extremely useful one for predicting the behavior of gases. The implications held within a wide range of conditions (though, for instance, when pressure grows very great, the role of collisions of particles becomes too important to ignore).

So the heuristic use of theory (that is, its use as an aid to discovery) comes from the opportunities offered for testing implications. Controversy rages from time to time among psychologists on whether theories should be used to guide research, so let us go into the issue in some detail.

The Role of Theory in Guiding Research

Conventional Description

There is a conventional description of science that says that experiments are done to test hypotheses and that hypotheses are derived by looking at the implications of a theory. This is illustrated in Figure 2.1. Hypotheses are simply "if–then" statements, such as "if I apply heat to a gas, then its pressure will increase"; "if the light rays pass near the sun, they will be deflected"; and "if people must overcome great obstacles in order to join a

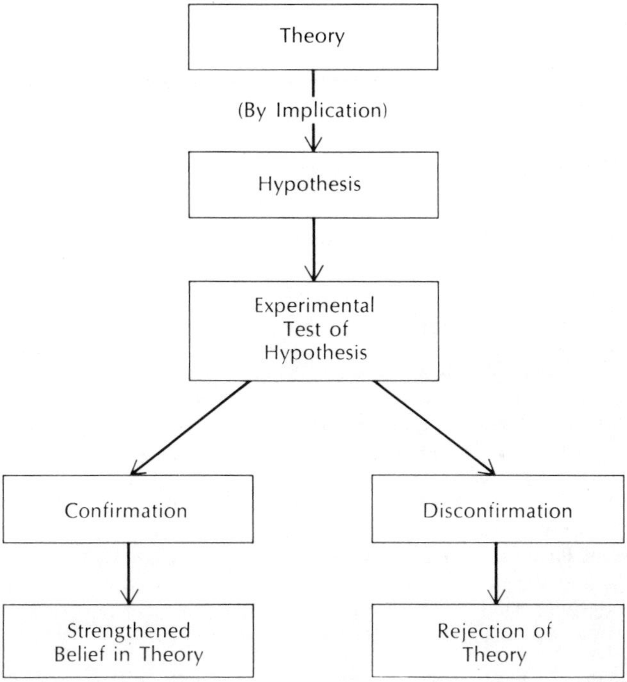

FIGURE 2.1 The "conventional description" of the scientific enterprise. See text for explanation and modern modifications of this view.

group, it will enhance the value of membership to them." If a hypothesis is verified, if observations correspond to it, the theory is *supported.*

The classic form of the conventional theory says that failure of experimental findings to fit the theory means that the theory is *refuted.* A confirmation only strengthens belief in the theory, without proving it correct. This is because many alternative theories might predict the same result. But a disconfirmation means that something necessarily implied by the theory runs counter to the facts. And it indicates that the theory cannot be correct. At a minimum, modification of the theory is required.

More recently, philosophers of science have come to recognize that in fact scientists cling to a disconfirmed theory as long as there is no viable alternative theory. Theories are not rejected so much because of data inconsistent with them; they are rejected because a better alternative theory replaces them.

In psychology, theories have declined in still another way. The learning theory of Hull seems not to have been clearly disconfirmed by data, nor to have been replaced by a better theory. Many findings seemed "kind of" inconsistent with it. Yet it could be stretched to fit most of them. The problem seems to have been that it did not provide a very useful model for predicting measurements not yet observed. The advantages of it were eventually dwarfed by the disadvantages inherent in being fettered by it. Most psychologists lost interest in it, and it went out "not with a bang, but a whimper."

Serendipity

Increasingly, scientists recognize how many discoveries have been made *serendipitously* rather than through theory. Serendipity is the art of finding something while you are looking for something else. Many, if not most, discoveries occur "accidentally," not by testing hypotheses born of theory. It was through serendipity that Pasteur discovered immunization.

> Pasteur's researchers on fowl cholera were interrupted by the vacation, and when he resumed he encountered an unexpected obstacle. Nearly all the cultures had become sterile. He attempted to revive them by sub-inoculation into broth and injection into fowls. Most of the subcultures failed to grow and the birds were not affected, so he was about to discard everything and start fresh when he had the inspiration of re-inoculating the same fowls with a fresh culture. His colleague Duclaux relates: "To the surprise of all, and perhaps even of Pasteur, who was not expecting such success, nearly all these fowls withstood the inoculation, although fresh fowls succumbed after the usual incubation period." This resulted in the recognition of the principle of immunization with attenuated pathogens (Beveridge, 1950).

Beveridge (1950) has compiled a sizable list of cases of scientific discovery, and one cannot help but be impressed with the number of them that occurred serendipitously. Taylor et al. (1959) reported on a conference in which research workers in psychology described their approach to research; here, again, the description is one of unsystematic, intuitive groping toward an only vaguely defined goal. Young (1951) has given an excellent description of the research scientist:

> One of the characteristics of scientists and their work, curiously enough, is a confusion, almost a muddle. This may seem strange if you have come to think of science with a big S as being all clearness and light. There is indeed a most important sense in which science stands for law and certainty. Scientific laws are the basis of the staggering achievements of technology that have changed the Western world, making it, in spite of all its dangers, a more comfortable and a happier place. But if you talk to a scientist you may soon find that his ideas are not all well ordered. He loves discussion, but he does not think always with complete, consistent schemes, such as are used by philosophers, lawyers, or clergymen. Moreover, in his laboratory he does not spend much of his time thinking about scientific laws at all. He is busy with other things, trying to get some piece of apparatus to work, finding a way of measuring something more exactly or making dissections that will show the parts of an animal or plant more clearly. You may feel that he hardly knows himself what law he is trying to prove. He is continually observing, but his work is a feeling out into the dark, as it were. When pressed to say what he is doing he may present a picture of uncertainty or doubt, even of actual confusion (Young, 1951).

Theories may Limit Perspective

Theories have often been charged with limiting the experimenter's perspective. During the 1940s and 1950s, too much attention was concentrated on tests of theory. Other issues tended to fall by the wayside. And the value of the research done in response to theory rests heavily on the value of the theories, which is now in grave doubt.

Theories of color vision have dominated research on color. Researchers have emphasized testing of three-pigment versus opponent-colors theory. Other equally important questions have been given the once-over-lightly. What is the use of color vision? Why do people pay large sums of money for color television sets? Can color vision be modified by experience? These and many other questions have been researched much more lightly than the theoretical questions.

A similar tendency to put on blinders when in the framework of theory can be seen in many research areas.

The Uses of Theory

Modern experimental psychologists have, to say the least, trimmed theory down to size. The conventional description greatly exaggerated the role of theories as aids to discovery (heuristic devices). Scientists succeed in making discoveries without theories, and theories may even hinder them in some respects.

Granted that theories have been overblown as heuristic tools, should we conclude that the sole business of scientists is to gather the raw facts? May we conclude that theory making is useless? This is a conclusion that suits the temperament of many experimentalists but it is unjustified. Even if we grant that theories have *no* value as heuristic devices, they may well have other uses.

Theories Can Be Mnemonic Devices

A theory may be an aid to memory—a *mnemonic device.* Scientists complain of the enormous explosion of scientific literature, and all acknowledge that they cannot begin to read, still less to remember, a large number of otherwise diverse functional relationships.

Theories Can Predict Limiting Conditions

In a similar vein, a theory can provide rules for deciding when a given set of functional relationships will apply and when they will not. Functional relationships inevitably have *limiting conditions.* That is, relationships hold only if certain other variables are within reasonable limits. Unless we have a way to decide when they hold, the statement of functional relationships becomes trivial. Such a statement boils down simply to "it holds when it holds and it doesn't hold when it doesn't hold." Then one can determine whether a given relationship holds only by observing what happens to the dependent variable when the independent variable has been manipulated. But this undermines the predictive value of the functional relationship. We are saying: "Nature will do whatever you see it do when you look." Reliance on raw experience without theoretical interpretation, when carried too far, becomes sterile.

Theories Can Make Raw Data Usable

Theories can stipulate limiting conditions. For example, Bernoulli's kinetic theory of gases implies that the variable "frequency of molecular collisions" will exert critical influence when gas pressures are high, but not otherwise. It is said that, in the Middle Ages, if a person wanted to know how many teeth there were in a horse's mouth, he or she would look it up in Aristotle rather than take a look inside a horse's mouth. In reaction to this tradition, we now regard "the facts" as almost sacred. But it is important to realize that the value of facts lies in our ability to *use* them. One might well be better able to control and understand nature with fewer facts after the information has exceeded a certain limit. In Gogol's classic (and entertaining) novel *Dead Souls,* a strategy is described whereby guilty defendants could foil the courts through flooding them with evidence. In the Russian courts of the time, defendants could present as much evidence in their defense as they wished, and there was no penalty for presenting irrelevancies. Consequently, no one who could afford to pay the lawyer's fees need ever fear conviction because they could simply supply the court with reams of written materials that could not be read and evaluated in their lifetime. Theories, by simplifying large masses of data, can reduce the information that has to be processed, while retaining its pertinent aspects. Massive data gathering without theory may place twentieth-century science in the position of the courts of nineteenth-century Russia.

Theories Can Predict Measurement in Novel Situations

Since theories can provide a rule for deciding when given functional relations apply, and because they have implications that are not always apparent from the simple original statement composing the theory, they can predict what will happen in novel situations. Predictions can be made on the basis of a theory, including predictions of what will occur in situations that have never been observed before. It is one thing to predict that what has happened previously under a given set of conditions will happen again if the same conditions are reinstated. It is another thing to predict what will occur in new, unprecedented situations, as theories commonly do.

Theories Are Sometimes Valuable Heuristic Devices

It is not at all correct to suppose that theories are of no value as heuristic devices. There have been many cases in the history of science in which theories guided research. Mendeleev's periodic table led to the search for elements to fill the gaps in his chart. Morgan's years of research on chromosomes would have been virtually pointless were it not for the gene theory. The planet Neptune was discovered by pointing a telescope in a direction in which theory predicted such a mass must be.

Why, then, do accounts of scientific discovery emphasize serendipity so much? There are a number of possible reasons. The heuristic value of a theory may simply not be one of its strongest points. Furthermore, the accounts given are nearly always accounts of outstanding discoveries. But a discovery may be remembered as outstanding largely because it was unexpected and not predicted by any theory. Thus the scientific discoveries given detailed descriptions in the history books may be strongly biased in the direction of serendipitous ones. Such examples also tend to come from the newly emerging sciences. It would be difficult for theory to guide research in a discipline where no substantial theory has been developed. On the other hand, psychology is certainly not one of the well-developed sciences, and so it might well be expected to have much in common with less advanced sciences.

Formal Theories Clarify Loose Verbal Theories

We are stuck with theory whether or not we like it. Our only choice is whether to have a loose theory or a rigorous one. My students and I have often formalized theories of ours by doing computer simulations. I quickly learned that prior to the formal modeling, I simply did not know what I was talking about. I have never known anyone to formalize a theory without getting the same feeling. How can vague, inconsistent theories be better than clear, consistent ones? Clarification of ideas deepens understanding.

Informal theories inadvertently rely on the empathy of listeners. Equations and computers do not emphathize. Even a "theory" by so rugged an empiricist as Skinner, that presented in *Verbal Behavior* (1957), would require immense clarification before a computer could have a go at it. He knows what he means, I know what he means, you know what he means . . . or do we?

The Influence of Paradigms on Selection of Problems for Research

Kuhn (1962) has pointed out that sciences tend to become dominated by what he calls *paradigms.* Certain scientific achievements, such as that of Isaac

Newton in physics, provide such a powerful model for future work and conceptualization that they become the matrix or paradigm for subsequent research. Paradigms tend to define which problems are considered to be worth investigating and which methods are thought adequate to solve the problems.

Strictly speaking, psychology is what Kuhn calls a "non-paradigmatic" science. No single great achievement has come to dominate our thinking to the extent that this has happened in physics. However, if we use the term "paradigm" in a broader sense to include a widely and firmly accepted notion about which topics are worth researching and which methods are acceptable, psychologists have something of the sort. They may in fact have several of them. For example, the present book attempts to give an account of a certain set of methods that are regarded as acceptable to psychologists who place their trust in scientific research. Other psychologists, many of them very famous, do not bother with such exacting methods. They regard their own life experiences and their understanding of other people (especially their patients) as enough to give them an understanding of psychology. They may see measurement, control, and the like as unnecessary compulsions. The scientific paradigm is markedly different from the latter, more intuitive approach.

My purpose here is not to engage in argument over which of these paradigms is to be preferred. To some extent I did so in Chapter 1. With respect to the issue of selecting research ideas, however, the paradigm is of some importance. Certain topic areas are less likely to be appreciated than others, and a loyal adherence to accepted methods will be very important in getting work to be recognized as of value. For example, researchers in the field of parapsychology usually have to conduct much more tightly controlled experiments than other researchers if their work is to have much impact. There are also methodological "folkways" characteristic of certain subdisciplines that are important in getting work accepted. For example, operant conditioners, psychophysiologists, and experimental clinical psychologists each tend to have strong feelings about certain research methods.

It is important for you to realize that you may have an uphill battle getting your work accepted in a given field unless you acquaint yourself with the topics, styles, and customs in that field. The best way to do that is probably to apprentice yourself to someone whose work is already well-regarded.

This is not to say you should never be willing to go through the uphill struggle. *Somebody* has to do it, and if you have a lot of self-confidence and persistence, it can be very rewarding. But you should make the decision to do so with your eyes open.

SUMMARY

1. A major source of ideas for research is in reading relevant literature, including textbooks, monographs, and journals. It is important to keep a log

of research ideas so the ideas can be organized and remembered.

2. When searching the literature, the following sources may be consulted:

a. Textbooks.
b. Well-informed people in the field.
c. Library card catalogues.
d. *Psychological Abstracts.*
e. Other abstracts such as *Biology Abstracts,* or *Index Medicus.*
f. Review articles (e.g., in *Annual Review of Psychology, Psychological Review, Psychological Bulletin*).
g. Articles referenced in the articles you read.
h. Computer retrieval services.
i. *Current Contents & Life Sciences.*
j. *Science Citation Index.*
k. Reprints solicited by mail from authors.
l. Phone calls to authors.

3. In reading articles in experimental psychology, go through the following steps:

a. Identify the problem and its significance. Remember that the articles are abbreviated and the significance may not be evident without background knowledge.
b. Look for inadequate controls; evaluate the methods of measurement.
c. Note the results and ask how reliable they are. Consider such things as the statistical probability values, whether the influence of the variable was apparent even without statistics, whether the correct statistics were used, and whether the study was done more than once.
d. Ask whether the experimental arrangement was sensitive enough to detect effects of the expected magnitude.
e. Consider what has been done to assure that the findings will generalize to other situations. Were the measures and subjects representative?
f. Ask, "What was the significance of the findings?" and "Did the study answer the questions posed in the introduction?"

4. Major ways of extrapolating from previous experiments include:

a. Attempting to verify them through repeating some part or all of the study.
b. Recombining components of separate, previous studies.
c. Determining whether earlier findings can be generalized to new situations, subjects, measures, and so on.
d. Determining whether a highly general phenomenon applies in certain special cases.
e. Eliminating confounded variables.

f. Improving measurement techniques by using more quantitative, representative, or varied measures.
g. Looking for causal factors underlying previous descriptive results.

5. Often the development of a new technique provides a ready source of new research problems simply by applying the technique to a variety of familiar problems.

6. Other people often have ideas they are willing to give away. It is a good idea to work as an apprentice to an experienced investigator before doing totally independent research on your own.

7. There are many widespread beliefs with little scientific support. Scientific tests of these can often make good projects.

8. A *conventional description* of science is that implications are drawn from theories. The implications are called *hypotheses* and are put to experimental test. Verification of the hypothesis strengthens belief in the theory. If results do not fit the hypothesis, the classic view was that the theory is refuted. More recently, the view has been that theories are only abandoned when a better theory is available, even though the data do not always fit.

In fact, many if not most scientific discoveries occur *serendipitously.* This means that they occurred while the researcher was looking for something else. Thus the role of theory in aiding discovery has not been as great as the conventional description indicates. Further objection to theories as a guide to research comes from their tendency to *blind scientists to possibilities* outside the framework of the theory.

Nevertheless, theories are valuable. They *clarify* loose ideas. They sometimes give us good *ideas for research.* They help us *organize* and *remember* data. They also have a *predictive power* not provided by mere generalizations of functional relations. They often make predictions about quite novel situations, and they can predict the limiting conditions under which established functional relations will no longer hold.

9. A paradigm is a model of investigation that determines which problems are worth investigating and which methods are adequate. Although psychology has not developed a single strong paradigm, there are a number of lesser ones that greatly influence attitudes toward research. You should become familiar with them and keep them in mind when deciding on a research project.

CHAPTER 3

Measurement and Observation in Psychology

Levels of Measurement

In the history of human attempts to understand nature, nothing stands out more vividly than the very special role of refining ordinary forms of observation. These ordinary methods of observation severely limit the acquisition of knowledge. Our habits of thought, our prejudices, our motives—conscious and unconscious—and all sorts of other influences tend to lead us into error unless special precautions are taken. Thus, superior forms of knowledge almost inevitably entail special procedures for making observations. Specifically, as methods of making observations improve, scientists substitute *measurements* for casual observations.

How do measurements differ from ordinary observations? The most important point of difference lies in the greater *reliability* of measurements. Observers can be consistent from one time to another when they use measurement. We call this consistency within observers *"intra-observer reliability."* Both intra-observer reliability and *"inter-observer reliability,"* which is the ability of different observers to agree with each other's observations, are characteristic of measurement. The lowest level of measurement merely involves making observations that have the properties of inter- and intra-observer reliability. This is called a *nominal scale* of measurement. The term "nominal" comes from a Latin word that means "name." When something is scaled at a nominal level, it is simply identified or named. The scale value tells nothing about the item other than the category to which it belongs. The major requirement of nominal scaling is that items must be capable of being assigned to the various categories in a reliable way. Thus, we would not have a nominal scale if there were serious dispute over which categories various items belonged to.

As an illustration of nominal scaling, let us take the example of a person's sexual identity. If we have males and females, we can, with considerable accuracy, place them in the categories "male" and "female." We could just as well call them sex number 1 and sex number 2. This would imply nothing about any rank ordering of the sexes. It would make no difference whether women or men were assigned the number "1," as long as the assignment stayed constant throughout the measurement procedure.

Although nominal scales provide the lowest level of measurement, they are widely used in psychology. When studies are done comparing such categories as "male versus female," "blacks versus whites," "liquid versus solid food," or "punishment versus reward," the scale is nominal. Note that many of these could be converted to more quantitative scales. For example, we could measure various levels of liquidity or solidity, of blackness or whiteness, of shock or reward. The fact that the items *could* be measured more elegantly does not mean that they *are* other than nominally scaled.

In the preceding chapter I mentioned the possibility of extrapolating from previous studies by improving measurement. Taking something that is nominally scaled and changing the measurement to a more quantitative scale would be a case in point. Thus, whereas "electric shock versus reward" is scaled at a nominal level, introduction of different amounts of shock or of reward would be an example of raising the level of measurement and, potentially, of gathering better and more useful information.

It is also important to realize that, although the examples given all had just two nominal categories, this is not essential. A study done to compare the effectiveness of three teaching methods, say, 1. programmed learning, 2. self-study of ordinary books without lectures, and 3. standard lecture-homework format would also be at a nominal level, but with three categories.

Although the nominal scale meets the minimal scientific requirements of inter- and intra-observer reliability, it is the lowest-level scale and has important limitations. For example, many mathematical operations cannot legitimately be performed on nominally scaled items. Suppose "female" were assigned category number 1 and "male" were assigned category number 2. That would not mean that men were in some sense twice women. Nor would it make any sense to multiply or divide the category numbers by other numbers.

A further problem with nominal scales lies in the variations permitted within the categories. Take, for example, the categories of "liquid versus solid food." Everything from milkshakes to liquid protein would fit into the liquid category, and everything from roast beef to chocolate cake would fit into the solid category. If one investigator picked cake for the solid food and another picked roast beef, the outcomes of their experiments might disagree radically.

The deficiencies of nominal scaling lead to a need for more refined levels of scaling. One form of refinement is to place the scaled items in characteristic categories and also to stipulate a rank ordering of the items. This type of scale is called an *ordinal scale.* Birth order is an example of something on an ordinal scale. Many psychologists have been interested in psychological differences between children who are first-born, second-born, and so on. If a person is named "Jennie," she has been placed in a nominal category. If a person is also labeled "first-born," she is further identified as being older than her siblings. With respect to the shock-hunger example mentioned earlier, we could vary the levels of shock and/or hunger by placing them at "High," "Medium," and "Low" intensities to make the scale ordinal. This would be an improvement over the original nominal scaling and might well improve the reliability, as well as the generalizability of the results.

A further improvement might be made by stipulating how far apart the adjacent scale values are. Notice that the ordinal scale does nothing to stipulate the relative distances between "High" and "Medium" versus "Medium" and "Low." To illustrate the problems underlying the use of an ordinal scale, consider what it would be like if rank orders were used instead of raw scores on your examinations. Suppose that you got a score of 92 percent correct but that there were 11 people above you (obviously you have an easy teacher), and you rank number 12. Suppose, further, that the next score below you is 63 percent correct. That score receives a rank of 13. Your score is really closer to the top few people than to number 13, but the numbers fail to show that.

An *equal interval* scale improves the situation by stipulating that equal numerical differences on the scale represent equal distances between the scaled items. Thus, on an equal interval scale, 1 is as far from 2 as 2 is from 3 as 3 is from 4, and so on. The equal interval scale involves the specification of a zero point and a unit of measurement. For example, the familiar scales of temperature, the Fahrenheit and Celsius scales, have stipulated zero points and stipulated units. Neither the zero points nor the units are the same on the two scales. Zero degrees Celsius is equal to 32° F, and 1 degree on the Celsius scale equals 1.8 degrees on the Fahrenheit scale. The zero points and units of measure are arbitrary (although they may be related to such familiar events as the freezing and boiling points of water). It is not uncommon, and highly desirable for psychological measurement to reach the level of equal interval scaling.

A still higher level of scale is the *ratio scale.* A ratio scale has a stipulated unit of measure and a nonarbitrary zero point. When a ratio scale reaches zero, it means that there is no more of the item to be scaled. Notice that there is some heat left at either 0° F or 0° C, since, in either case, readings can go below zero.

The ratio scale gets its name from the fact that it is the only kind of scale to use ratios of numbers on the scale. To illustrate why it is improper to use ratios on an interval scale, consider ratios of temperatures. The ratio of 25° C to 50° C is ½. But 25° C equals 77° F and 50° C equals 122° F. The ratio of 77/122 is *not* equal to ½. Nor would it make sense to form ratios with nominal or ordinal scales.

Familiar measures at the ratio level include the centimeter, the gram, the inch, and the pound. In psychology, such scales can also be obtained. For example, people can simply be asked to assign numbers to their experiences that reflect the magnitudes of these experiences. This is called the method of magnitude estimation and will be discussed later in this chapter.

Reliability and Validity of Measures

At any given scale of measurement, measures may differ with respect to their *reliability* and their *validity.* It is very important that consideration be given to these aspects of measurement, since a measure is useless if it is not reliable and valid.

The *reliability* of a measure is its repeatability. Suppose you had made a yardstick of some material that contracted over time and expanded with increases in temperature. Obviously you would not get very consistent results from day to day with such an instrument. It would be an unreliable instrument.

In psychological measurement you should check to determine whether your measures are reliable. Most well-known psychological tests have been checked extensively in this way. A major method of doing this is to give the same test more than once to the same subjects and determine the extent to which the outcomes are consistent on the different testings. This is called *test-retest reliability*.

Since there may be carry-over from the earlier experiences with the tests, we often construct *equivalent forms* of a test and measure the consistency from one form to the other. A relatively simple way to construct equivalent forms is to make up one large test, then place the items in random order and use the top and bottom halves of the now randomized items as equivalent forms. Measuring the equivalence of these forms would yield what is called the *split-half reliability* of the test.

The *validity* of a measure is the extent to which it actually indicates the thing it is supposed to be measuring, which we call the *criterion*. It is best to *validate* a measure by showing that it relates consistently to the criterion. Many popular psychological measures, such as those used in magazine articles that invite you to "test yourself" for one quality or another, have not been validated. Usually they rely on what we call *face validity*. Face validity means that the validity of the items is determined by simply looking them over and judging whether they test what they are supposed to test. Most college exams are validated in this way by the teachers.

Face validity is better than nothing, but it is often misleading. One of my former teachers was hired to devise a psychological test to predict which people would make good machinists. He asked the employers to tell him what seemed to them likely to be predictive of high-level performance as a machinist (what had face validity). One of the most strongly emphasized predictors was "mathematical ability." After systematic validation of the test, he found that high performance on mathematical tests actually predicted *poor* performance as a machinist!

A useful way to validate a test is to find separate groups of people known to be high versus low on the characteristic being measured (for example, highly successful versus failed machinists). The test is valid only if it accurately differentiates between the good and poor performers.

In summary, we have now considered certain highly important properties of measurement. These include the level of scaling, the reliability, and the validity of the measures. Three further topics require treatment: the directness of measures, their obtrusiveness, and the role of error in measurement.

Direct and Indirect Measurement

At times we can directly measure the behavior or psychological process of interest. At other times this may be very difficult, or even impossible. Then we must rely on measures that are merely indicative of the target, or *criterional,* behavior. When we talk about assessing the validity of a test by noting the relationship between that test and some criterion, we imply that the test is an indicative rather than a criterional measure.

To illustrate the difference between indicative and criterional behaviors, take the case of voting in a presidential election. Up until the actual election, there is no way to measure the target behavior—that of casting ballots. We rely instead on various other measures that we feel will predict the real behavior of interest. Pollsters have become masters at identifying responses that accurately predict how people will eventually vote. The various responses obtained on the pre-election polls are indicative measures. The voting itself is criterional. We also refer to the indicative measure as an *indirect* measure, and to the criterional measure as a *direct* measure. It is very important to be aware of the distinction between direct and indirect measurement. The importance stems from a tendency of psychologists and other social scientists to treat indirect measures as though they were necessarily valid. Actually, the validity of indirect measures is an open question. Indirect measures are widely used because it is often difficult to get access to the target behavior. When such investigators as Kinsey (1953), Fisher (1973) and Hite (1976) studied human sexual behavior, they did not generally make direct observations of sexual activity. Instead they relied on *self-reports* of unobserved sexual activity. It would have been impossible for them to observe many of the behaviors reported on in their studies (for example, early childhood sexual experiences of now grown people) and difficult to observe others. However, direct measurement was shown to be feasible for many human sexual behaviors when Masters and Johnson (1966) did their groundbreaking work on the human sexual response. Masters and Johnson brought volunteers into the laboratory and directly observed and measured sexual responses.

A major type of indirect measure is the verbal measure. Verbal measures are not necessarily indirect, but they usually are. Suppose you are doing a study of the frequency of the use of sexist language in college textbooks. Would this be an indirect or a direct measure? Since the real focus of interest is the language itself, it is a direct measure. If you were using the sexist language to indicate something else, such as the likelihood that the authors would discriminate against one of the sexes in writing recommendations, then the measure of sexist language would be an indirect one, merely indicative of the target behavior. If the verbal measures are criterional, the verbal report is the basic datum in its own right, and is, by definition, valid. If *indicative* the verbal report is being taken as a measure of something else, another verbal or nonverbal behavior. Indicative verbal measures may not be valid. They may not be good indicators of the "other" behavior.

Verbal reports may also be categorized according to the temporal relation of the report to the event being reported. They can be *retrospective, contemporaneous,* or *prospective.*

Retrospective Verbal Reports

A retrospective verbal report is one in which a person is asked to report on an event that took place in the past. A widely distributed book on the female orgasm (Fisher, 1973) relied heavily on such retrospective reports. For example, women were asked to respond to the following questionnaire item:

> Please circle the answer or answers which most nearly apply to you:
> During the menstrual cycle I notice greatest sexual responsiveness at the following times:

1. During menstruation.
2. The week after menstruation ceases.
3. During the middle of the cycle.
4. The week before menstruation begins.
5. No differences noted during the menstrual cycle.

Fisher concluded that women are most sexually responsive during the week following menstruation.

The retrospective method is notoriously invalid. A particularly striking study of the retrospective method was that of Pyles, Stalz, and Macfarlane (1935). They compared actual data to mothers' retrospective reports on pregnancy, birth, and the early life of their children. This was done when the children were only 21 months old. The inaccuracies were striking. For example, 30 mothers whose children had suffered severe illnesses during the first year of life reported that they had no illness at all. Robbins (1963) found that parents, especially fathers, were woefully inaccurate in reporting past child-rearing practices. The errors tended to be in the direction of recommendations of "experts."

Thus we have good evidence that it is unwise to rely on retrospective verbal reports. It is surprising to see how frequently they are used in spite of this.

Contemporaneous Verbal Reports

Contemporaneous verbal reports are widely used by experimental psychologists. Perceptual judgments are commonly of the contemporaneous verbal type. For example, Hilgard (1969) measured pain by asking subjects to rate the pain on a 0–10 scale, with 0 meaning no pain at all and 10 meaning a pain so severe the subject would wish to withdraw.

Contemporaneous verbal reports are usually criterional, so their validity is not in question.

Prospective Verbal Reports

A prospective verbal report is one requiring subjects to say what they will or would do or how they will or would react at some future time if the occasion occurred. Many verbal reports of attitude are prospective, in the sense that the verbal report is taken as a predictor of nonverbal behavior.

Certain studies, have shown that prospective verbal reports sometimes fail to predict future nonverbal behavior. Milgram (1965b) asked subjects how they would behave if they were asked to shock another person electrically in the setting he actually used on other subjects. There was little relationship between their estimates and the actual behavior.

Prospective verbal reports can be taken as criterional or indicative. An investigator might be interested in what people *say* they will do (criterional) or in how what they say predicts what they will actually do (indicative). For example, verbal reports may be as legitimate a measure of attitude as are nonverbal behaviors. If they are taken as indicative, then it is hard to say whether they are valid without directly checking their validity.

On the other hand, prospective verbal reports have sometimes been shown to be valid predictors of nonverbal behavior. For example, Rokeach (1960) asked subjects to range an array of religions in order of similarity to their own religion. Out of this, he obtained a scale of distances between religions (see Figure 3.1). He went on to examine church records from two churches in each of six denominations and found that the degree of similarity on the scale predicted migrations from one church to another.

The inadequacies of prospective verbal reports have probably been exaggerated in the psychological literature. A widely cited study by La Piere (1934) is often used as proof that such verbal reports do not correspond to actual behavior. La Piere traveled the western United States with a Chinese couple. Out of 251 places where they stopped to eat or sleep, they were refused service only once. Six months later, La Piere wrote to the 250 accommodating places asking whether they would serve Chinese. 50 percent of them responded; 90 percent of the respondents said "No," they would not accommodate Chinese.

On the surface, this seems to say that there is little correspondence between verbal and nonverbal behavior. But Dillehay (1973) has pointed out that the people answering the letters were probably not the same as the

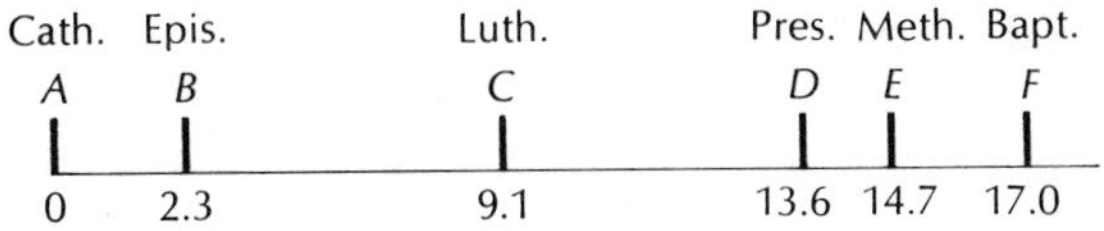

FIGURE 3.1 Relative psychological distances between religions according to Dawes (1973; based on Figure 16.1 from *The Open and Closed Mind: Investigations into the Nature of Belief Systems and Personality Systems,* by Milton Rokeach, © 1960 by Basic Books, Inc., Publishers, New York).

people who had been accommodating. The waitress in a diner or the desk clerk in a hotel are not likely to be the ones to receive and answer such a letter. Similar criticisms apply to other widely cited studies that indicate a discrepancy between prospective verbal reports and actual behaviors.

Nevertheless, there are enough valid instances of discrepancy between verbal and nonverbal behavior to make us worry a great deal about relying on the verbal reports. Until we know when the prospective reports do and when they do not work, it is best to avoid relying on them.

Psychological Scales: Direct and Indirect

Measures may also be direct or indirect with respect to how a given level of scaling is reached. For example, if you want to obtain an equal interval scale, this might be done in some direct way, or it might be done indirectly. If it is done indirectly, you start with a lower level scale and do special manipulations on the data to extract interval-level information from the original data.

For example, let's suppose you are asked to rank your four favorite foods in the order of your preference for them. Suppose your list is like this:

1. Chocolate cake
2. Pecan praline ice cream
3. Roast beef
4. Potato chips

On the surface, the rank orderings give us no way to tell how far apart the ranked items are in your preference. The rankings you gave are consistent with many possible distancings of the ranked items. The following diagrams illustrate several of those possibilities:

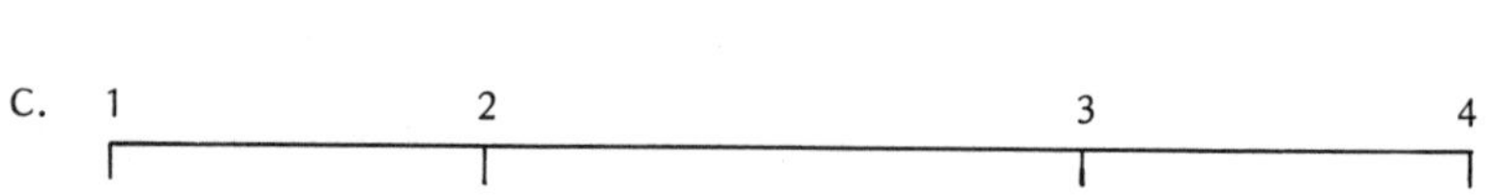

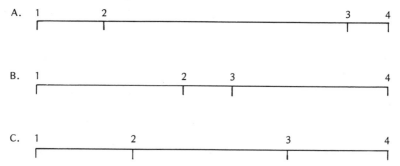

It might appear, then, that there is no way to tell from such ordinal data just how far apart the ranked items are. There is certainly no *direct* way. But indirectly we can tell by asking you to rank order the items many, many times and looking at how consistently you rank the items. Suppose you feel that chocolate cake and pecan praline ice cream are very close in palatability. Depending on your whim, you might rank one or the other of them on top. If it is hard for you to tell the difference between them, you are likely to vary their ordering a great deal. If, on the other hand, you see them as markedly far apart, such "confusions" are less likely to occur. You will consistently rank one above the other. Note, then, that things that are frequently confused tend to be close together whereas things that are seldom or never confused tend to be far apart on the scale. Thus the degree of overlap in rankings, or the frequency of "confusions," may be taken as an indirect measure of distance apart on the scale. By using some measure of these confusions it is possible indirectly to derive an equal interval scale from ordinal data. We say then that there is a *latent* interval scale in *manifestly* ordinal data.

Rating Methods

Clearly the most widely used procedure for psychometric scaling today is the method of *rating*. You have undoubtedly used rating scales many times in the past. You have probably also been rated on such scales. A very common scale is the Likert-type rating scale. With this type of scale, one is asked to indicate the degree to which one agrees or disagrees with various declarative items. For example, you might be given the statement: "The space program was a foolish waste of taxpayers' money." The categories of response might be

1. strongly agree
2. agree
3. undecided
4. disagree
5. strongly disagree

I have called this a Likert-type scale because a full-fledged Likert scale takes this form, but involves one more step. The experimenter must do an analysis of the items to be sure all items measure the same attitude (Kiesler et al., 1969). This can be done by determining which raters are in the top and bottom 25 percent for a given item with respect to their total score. Any item that fails to differentiate between people in the top and bottom 25 percent is then thrown out. In practice, experimenters often do not bother to do the analysis of items, but they use the Likert format. The resulting scales are satisfactory for most purposes.

Rating scales yield ordinal data, but we can derive interval level data from them by procedures like those already described for getting at the latent interval data. Next we will deal with a classic case of the derivation of interval from ordinal data.

The Method of Pair Comparisons

A classic indirect method of interval scaling was the method of pair comparisons. It was honed and polished by Thurstone (1927). With this method, items are presented two at a time. Usually, all possible pairs are given. Suppose, for example, you wanted to know how people value various parts of the body. You might have "hands," "feet," "eyes," "tongue," and "ears" as stimuli. The various possible pairings would then be composed; for example, "hands-eyes," "feet-tongue," "eyes-ears."

At any given time, a subject would receive a single pair and be instructed to concentrate on that pair alone and decide which of the two was more valuable. This process would be repeated with the various pairs, and each pair would be judged many times. For close decisions there will be some proportion of judgments in which a given member of a pair is judged more valuable.

Essentially, Thurstone's argument was based on the notion that items are further apart on the scale if they are less easily confused. In fact, the *degree* of their confusion can be taken as a *measure* of their distance apart on the scale. Suppose, when choosing between "hands" and "tongue," that "hands" are rated more valuable 55 percent of the time. This implies that "tongue" is rated more valuable than "hands" 45 percent of the time. The decision must be a close one, and the two items must be close on the scale of value. In contrast to this, if one item were ranked more valuable than another on 90 percent of the choice trials, we would argue that the two items must be far apart.

The principles behind Thurstone's reasoning are easily understood, but considerable effort is needed to work out the details. We will not describe them here. They actually took a variety of forms depending on whether various simplifying assumptions were made. Such details, and a clear treatment of the steps in getting actual scale values, may be found in Engen (1971).

The method of pair comparisons is a bit more cumbersome to use than many other methods of scaling. The number of possible pairs grows quite large as the number of items grows, so that it becomes impractical to work with more than 10 or 15 items. The calculations are also somewhat burdensome. Most researchers seem content to use simple rating scales and settle for measurement at an ordinal level.

Ranking Methods

If judges are asked to place the items to be measured in order on the dimension of interest, it is called *ranking*. People sometimes confuse ranking with rating. To see the difference, suppose you want to evaluate the teaching of Professor John Smith. First you *rate* him on a Likert-type scale. Your alternatives are to rate him as

1. Outstanding
2. Above average
3. Average
4. Below average
5. Poor

Let's say you rate him 1, outstanding. Now suppose someone asks you to rank him along with ten other professors under whom you have taken courses. Even though you regard Smith as outstanding, you might find there are three other professors you feel are better. Thus Smith *ranks* number 4 in 10. Differences between rating and ranking can be marked.

You can see that ranking forces you to make discriminations you might otherwise avoid. On the other hand, it is necessary to keep the whole stimulus array present, at least mentally, in order to do ranking. Thus, it may not be a feasible method if there are large numbers of items to be ranked or if judges are not familiar with all of the items.

Ranking provides ordinal data directly. But it may also be used indirectly to get data on an interval scale. The degree to which judges "confuse" rankings of items can be taken as an index of closeness on an interval scale (see Engen, 1971).

Direct Methods of Psychological Scaling

We need not derive high level psychometric scales from actual measurements done at a lower level. It can be done directly. Even in the nineteenth century, Plateau used direct methods of scaling. In recent times, Stevens has developed remarkably simple but highly effective methods for obtaining ratio scales directly.

The Method of Magnitude Estimation

As a prime example of direct psychometrics, let us consider the method of magnitude estimation. In its simplest form, this method merely involves asking people to give a numerical value to some experience so that the resulting number reflects the magnitude of that experience. The numbers can range from very large ones to decimals or fractions. For example, a person might be asked to rate the seriousness of such crimes as burglary, robbery, murder, failure to observe a stop sign, speeding, rape, and child-molesting. With the method of magnitude estimation, each person would simply associate any number with each crime, as long as the number reflected how serious the crime seemed to them. Someone might estimate "child molesting" at 166,722 and jaywalking at 0.01.

This method is so flexible that it hardly seems possible that it would give a good reflection of actual psychological values, but it does. This can be seen most clearly when the dimension rated has a clear physical counterpart, as it does in so-called "psychophysical" scaling. For example, we might ask people to estimate the lengths of lines. In this case we can see the relationship between the psychological estimates and the actual physical measurements, whereas we have no actual physical measurements of the seriousness of crimes. When we have an opportunity to draw comparisons between the psychological and the physical, the method of magnitude estimation yields results that are a very simple mathematical transformation of the physical scale. This indicates that the psychological measure is quite orderly, as are physical measures.

Sometimes observers are given a sample with an associated number in order to provide them with a point of reference. For example, we might tell them that "murder" equals 100 and that they are to assign numbers to the rest of the crimes on the basis of a scale on which murder has that value. Such a reference point is called a *modulus.* For one who has not worked with the method of magnitude estimation it might seem highly valuable to have a modulus, but in fact it is not at all necessary. The method of magnitude estimation works remarkably well without it.

One problem we face when using the method of magnitude estimation stems from the fact that certain individuals tend to use much larger numbers than others. For example, we have done research in which people were asked to rate the erotic pleasure they got from the various parts of their body. If a given male assigns 1,000,000 to his penis and most others use numbers like 100, 86, or 212, the individual using the very large number can, when the data are averaged, have more influence than all the other people combined. It is therefore necessary to correct for the use of extreme numbers. This is generally done by avoiding the use of the arithmetic mean in favor of the geometric mean. We will discuss these two different types of average in Chapter 7.

Direct Behavioral Measurement

Many psychologists dislike even the best of verbal measures of behavior. They prefer direct behavioral measurement. Given the difficulties we have noted with verbal measures, it is easy to see why they would have such a preference. It is often very *easy* to get a verbal measure of what people did or felt or would do or intend to do, but it is very difficult to be certain that the resulting verbal measure reflects nonverbal behaviors. Though it is commonly more difficult to get actual behavioral measures, it may well be worth the extra effort.

Identification of Behavioral Units

If a psychological researcher decides to use direct behavioral measures, it will be necessary to identify clear behaviors that represent the phenomenon of interest. This is basically a problem of operational definition (see Chapter 1).

For example, if one is interested in studying factors influencing marital satisfaction, it might seem easy to measure that satisfaction simply by asking people to scale their level of satisfaction by one of the typical verbal methods of scaling. But the method of direct behavioral measurement requires that we select behaviors that are themselves components of marital happiness. For example, frequencies of sexual intercourse, arguments, or shared social activities have been used as behavioral targets in studies of marriage (Edwards & Edwards, 1977).

Sometimes behavioral targets clearly reflect the overall topic of interest, as when number of bites of food per day is recorded in a study of control of overeating. At other times, as in the case of a complex concept like marital happiness, it may be difficult to identify fully satisfying behavioral targets. Some of the directness of behavioral measurement may be lost if the pinpointed behaviors fail to give an adequate reflection of the psychological phenomenon of interest. The most direct case is that in which the phenomenon of interest and the targeted behavior are identical.

Types of Behavioral Measure

Even within the category of "behavioral measures" there is considerable leeway as to which aspect of behavior will be selected for measurement. At a very simple level we can simply record whether or not a certain behavior occurred in a given sample of subjects. For example, did they vote for a given political candidate or not? Did they cross the street when the light was red or not? Such results are usually tabulated as percentages of people engaging in a certain behavior.

Often we wish to know not only whether a behavior occurred but also something about the strength of that behavior. One widely used measure of strength of behavior is the *latency* of that behavior. The latency of a behavior is the amount of time elapsing from the instant when there is an opportunity to engage in the behavior until the behavior actually occurs.

Another measure of strength of behavior is the proportion of times an organism engages in the behavior over a series of opportunities. When the response options are to respond or not respond, this sort of measure would take the form of "proportion of 'trials' on which the response occurred." For example, a dog conditioned to salivate to a bell might salivate on *x* percent of the presentations of the bell.

Strictly speaking, we could call this the "percentage of correct responses" and regard the trials during which the response failed to occur as "errors." Normally, however, the latter terminology is reserved for cases in which we have clearly circumscribed correct *and* incorrect responses. For example, turning to the right might be correct and turning to the left incorrect. Then we would commonly speak of such measures as percentage of correct responses or percentages of trials on which an error occurred.

If we wanted to measure the rate of learning the correct response we might count the number of errors or trials until the correct response was learned. In order to do this, we would, of course, have to set up an operational definition of "learned" (for example, reached a criterion of 90 percent correct responding in 20 consecutive trials).

Rate of Behavior as a Dependent Measure

Many psychologists feel that the best measure of behavior is its *rate.* The rate of a behavior is its frequency divided by the amount of time it took to emit the behaviors. In real life we are commonly interested in the rates of behaviors. For example, we are usually not as interested in whether a person has ever had an alcoholic beverage as in how many such beverages are consumed per day.

Behavioral rates often reveal behavioral differentiations not apparent with simpler measures. Suppose we merely record the age at which a child first crawls, stands, walks, or talks. Two very different children might have identical records. One of them might walk at a very high rate and jabber constantly while the other engaged in the targeted behaviors on only one or a few occasions.

The significance of measuring rates of behaviors may be seen very clearly if we consider that normal children engage in the same general behaviors that highly disturbed children do, but at vastly different rates. Both types of children may pull out their own hair, pinch themselves, bite themselves, rock back and forth, and the like. But the normal children do so only rarely whereas the disturbed children may do so at menacingly high rates.

Obtrusiveness of Psychological Measurement

The act of taking measurements has a tendency to change the thing being measured, and this is especially true in psychology. When a person enters a psychological laboratory as a subject, she or he will probably expect to be studied, manipulated, and even deceived. Even outside the laboratory, awareness of being observed, or even a dim awareness that something "peculiar" is taking place may change the behavior of the observed subjects.

If a measurement changes the system being measured, we say that it is obtrusive. *Obtrusiveness* is a major and often neglected problem, especially in experimental psychology. Therefore it is highly important to give serious attention to minimizing obtrusiveness. Two major errors creating problems of obtrusiveness are using obviously inauthentic variables and research settings and failure to control for "demand characteristics" of experiments.

Authenticity of Manipulated Variables

Many of the variables of interest to those who study complex human behavior are difficult to manipulate at will. If we want to study willingness to intervene in an emergency, how are we to produce an emergency? If we wish to study willingness to obey malevolent commands, how are we to produce authentic malevolent commands?

This is a problem that should be given very careful attention by experimenters. It is not enough to have ill-trained actors produce a caricature of the real situation. In fact, even trained actors might not be able to produce the desired impact, since the simulations that are effective on stage may not work in a closer setting. Staub (1974), who wished to study the willingness of passersby to help someone under distress, went to considerable lengths to assure credibility. One technique used in the study of helping behavior involves making a tape recording of an emergency, then playing the recorded emergency while the subject is in an adjacent room. Staub pointed out the importance of having very high-quality recordings that were tested for their capacity to appear real.

Staub (1974) also went out onto the streets with some of his tests. This is likely to make subjects far less prone to suspect they are part of an experiment. Unfortunately, even Staub fell into the use of an implausible situation when he had a college student go into a lower-middle-class neighborhood and feign a heart attack by grabbing his chest and collapsing. It is unlikely that a healthy young college student would be having a heart attack in the streets. Far more likely that such a healthy young man might be a practical joker or be trying to lure someone near in order to take a wallet or purse!

In a later experiment Staub (1974) corrected this error to a degree by having an overweight student play the role. In this more plausible situation, the behavior of passersby was somewhat different. More people intervened.

It is not always easy to create plausible situations, but there is little point in doing such experiments without having given this matter very careful attention.

Demand Characteristics of Experiments

Experimenters who deal with human subjects are currently plagued by concern over the influence of demand characteristics on the outcomes of experiments. The idea of demand characteristics goes back to at least 1933 (Rosensweig, 1933, cited in Silverman & Shulman, 1970), but the major impetus for concern came from a very important paper by Orne (1962).

Orne found that human subjects were remarkably compliant with various requirements imposed on them by experimenters. He was interested in testing the influence of hypnosis on performance of various tasks, and he sought to find a task at which subjects in the waking state would balk. Such a task would act as a control for evaluating the influence of the special hypnotic relationship. But Orne found himself hard pressed to find any task subjects would refuse to do.

He had subjects add pairs of numbers taken from sheets with random numbers printed on them. There were 224 additions to be done for each sheet, and subjects were placed in a room with 2000 sheets! The experimenter assigned them the task, explaining that he would come back later. Says Orne, "Five and one-half hours later, the *experimenter* gave up!"

The task was made even more obviously meaningless by having the subjects tear up each sheet after completing the additions, but subjects still persisted. Interviews revealed that the subjects gave meaning to the task by conjecturing that the experimenter must have in mind various hypotheses that would make sense of it. For example, some subjects thought that it must be an endurance test.

Out of these and other observations, Orne derived the concept of *demand characteristics.* The demand characteristics of an experiment are various cues that give the subject a notion of the experimental hypothesis. Orne stressed the idea that human subjects often are controlled by the wish to comply with the experimenter's expectations. Subsequent writers have suggested that even when subjects choose not to comply with the experimenter's expectations, even when they choose to defy them, their awareness of the demands may have an important influence (Page, 1971, 1973; Rosenberg, 1965). Subjects may suppose that the experimenter expects them to do a certain thing but that they will look bad if they do it. So they do something else. They are said to have "evaluation apprehension" and to engage in "impression management." In order to give a good impression of themselves they may, given their notion of the experimental demands, comply or do something quite contrary to their notion of compliance. They are less likely to comply when the demand characteristics are obvious.

The influence of demand characteristics is a grave problem. In fact, we are becoming increasingly aware only very recently of just how pervasive their influence might be. Orne (1962) showed that much of the effect of perceptual deprivation occurs when a number of the demand cues are provided without the deprivation. An important role for demand characteristics has been proposed, and in some instances demonstrated, for such diverse areas as the classical conditioning of attitudes (Page, 1969, 1971), the operant conditioning of verbal behavior (Page, 1970, 1971, 1972; Page & Lumia, 1968; Patty & Page, 1973), attitude change (Page, 1973; Silverman & Regula, 1968), obedience to authority (Orne & Holland, 1968), hypnosis (Barber, 1969), and many others.

Measuring and Controlling for Demand Characteristics

Now that we know about the influence of demand characteristics, it has become important that they be taken into account in designing, conducting, and interpreting studies involving human subjects. Much research of this kind done in the past will have to be reexamined with demand characteristics in mind. It would be dangerous to ignore demand characteristics, but let us not be tempted to use them as an explanation for observed results unless proper evidence for such effects has been obtained. It would be easy to fall into using demand characteristics as a pseudoexplanation (see Chapter 1). Remember, a functional explanation is not adequate unless at least two separate measures have been taken, one for the dependent variable and one for the independent variable. Thus, experimenters must measure demand characteristics if such cues are to be used to explain observations.

Unfortunately, adequate measures of demand characteristics are just beginning to be developed. For the most part, experimenters have relied on verbal reports from subjects. Most common has been *postexperimental questioning.* Subjects are merely asked how they perceived the situation. This may not be as simple and straightforward as it sounds. Verbal reports are always suspect. In some cases the questioning itself may provoke subjects to say that they perceived the experiment in a certain way. In particular, subjects might tell an inaccurate story if, after the fact, they perceived their behavior as putting them in a bad light. We cannot assume that whatever subjects *say* is true, since they may be rationalizing or trying to create a good impression.

Page (1971) has provided evidence that the way the postexperimental interview is conducted can have a heavy influence on the results. He showed that single, open-ended questions missed many individuals who were aware of the demands of his experiments. A multiple-question technique was necessary to detect many of them. So it may be necessary to do a great deal of probing in order to identify subjects who are aware of the demand characteristics of the experiment. Unfortunately, in so doing, the risks of influencing subjects by suggestions go up.

Questioning should include inquiry about *when* the subject became aware of the demands. This may detect some of the subjects who became aware late, or even during the postexperimental inquiry. Subjects often may think it makes them look better if they say they knew what was really going on in an experiment. In some instances their behavior may seem reprehensible once they understand the real nature of the experiment, and they use the classic ego-defense mechanisms of rationalization to account for their behavior. Thus, it is hard to tell whether or not they really knew the nature of the experiment on the basis of verbal reports obtained after the fact.

A further problem with postexperimental questioning lies in what the experimenter does with the subjects who indicate that they understood the experimental hypothesis. Typically one eliminates them from the analysis of data. However, in so doing one creates a biased sample of subjects. It is hard to say how subjects who do catch on to the hypothesis differ from those who do not, but it might be the case that in throwing out the aware subjects, the experimenter is eliminating the more intelligent, perceptive, sensitive subjects. If subjects are only eliminated from the group receiving the experimental treatment, this creates a confounded variable.

Preexperimental inquiry may have the advantage over postexperimental questioning. With preexperimental questioning, a control group of subjects is submitted to all of the experimental procedure up to the point of actually taking them through the procedure. At that point, they are asked to describe their perceptions of what is expected of them. A limitation on this method is that some discovery of demand characteristics might take place during the actual conduct of the experiment.

An interesting alternative to the preexperimental interview is to direct subjects to behave in a manner opposite to that which they perceive as expected of them. Page (1973) showed that subjects so instructed in an experiment on the conditioning of attitudes produced results opposite to those normally obtained in such experiments, indicating that the process controlling their behavior was not conditioning, but compliance with demand characteristics.

Another method of dealing with demand characteristics is to ask subjects to simulate or role play in a situation lacking the independent variable (Orne, 1962). For example, subjects can be asked to act as though they were hypnotized in order to see whether there is anything unusual about subjects who are actually hypnotized. It proves to be very difficult to find any differences (Barber, 1969). The simulation procedure may not always work, however. In certain types of experiments, the simulation procedure may be effectively identical to the real treatment procedure because subjects may suspect a trick and perceive other demand characteristics.

A second objection to the simulation procedure is that we cannot conclude from duplication of a phenomenon under a given set of conditions that those same conditions normally control behavior. There is typically "more than one way to skin a cat," and it might happen that a phenomenon can be produced either by simulation or authentically, the underlying processes being quite different.

Silverman and Shulman (1970) have argued that we might deal with demand characteristics by using indirect, unobtrusive measures in laboratory settings, thus minimizing the likelihood that demand characteristics will be perceived. A second alternative they suggest is to experiment in naturalistic settings, once again minimizing or eliminating demand characteristics. In general, increasing the authenticity of an experimental setting should reduce the likelihood that demand characteristics determine the behavior.

Probably the most important test of the role of demand characteristics in experiments is the extent to which experimental findings generalize. If experiments lead to concepts or models of human behavior that work in accounting for what goes on in the real world, we need not concern ourselves over demand characteristics. The reason for worrying about demand characteristics is that they might create results that are not applicable to the nonlaboratory environment.

The Problem of Errors in Measurement

We have now discussed a fair range of the important features of measurement. A final topic, to be dealt with at this point, is probably the most basic. It is the problem of errors that occur in the process of measuring things. Here, I will give a general classification of errors, including the kinds specifically discussed earlier in this chapter.

There is no way to avoid making *some* errors while taking measurements. This is true in all fields, not just in psychology and the social sciences. Although we cannot eliminate errors entirely, our task is to reduce errors to a level that leaves us with useful measures. Thus, it is important to be aware of the major sources of error.

There are errors inherent in the measuring instrument itself. The term *error of measurement* is often reserved for errors inherent in the instrument. Any measuring instrument (and a human being may be such an instrument—we are not just talking about inanimate devices here) has limits to its powers of discrimination. An instrument that makes very small discriminations is said to be *precise.* Errors will occur as a result of limitations in the precision of the measuring instrument, and, though these errors may be small, they can accumulate into important errors.

Errors of measurement, whether or not inherent in the instrument can be subdivided into *systematic* and *unsystematic* or *random* errors. Examples of systematic errors inherent in an instrument would be errors of accurate calibration, so that the instrument systematically under- or over-estimates measures. Some years ago it was found that the carbon-dating method for determining the age of archeological materials systematically underestimated the age of those materials. This is a classic case of systematic instrument-error.

Even after careful and accurate calibration of the instrument, random errors will persist. Fortunately, random errors, by definition, lead equally often to over- and under-estimation. Thus these errors will cancel each other out if enough measures are taken and averaged. However, in the short run, small, random errors may accumulate into significant errors, simply on the basis of chance.

There is another broad class of errors that we might call *circumstantial* or *ambient* errors. These are not inherent in the instrument itself, but have to do with the circumstances under which the measures are taken. They, too, may be either systematic or random. An example of a systematic ambient error is the case of the obtrusive measure with demand characteristics that tend to influence responses in a certain direction. Various other factors, such as fluctuation in sounds, small shifts in temperature, and so on give rise to unsystematic, random errors.

You can see that systematic errors are likely to be something we can deal with through care in taking measurements, calibrating instruments, introducing careful controls, and so on. It should be possible to reduce these to a minimum, though, as in the case of the carbon-dating method, even the most careful scientists will have to endure them from time to time.

Random errors can also be reduced to a minimum, but they are always with us. We can never get a perfectly precise measuring instrument, nor can we completely control the circumstances under which measures are taken. We must be aware that errors, especially random ones, are inherent in all our measures. A given raw measure has a component due to error. We can conceive of observations as "signals" from nature that are always somewhat obscured by "noise" (errors). I will elaborate on this analogy at length in subsequent chapters.

SUMMARY:

1. Improvement of observations through *measurement* is probably the most striking feature of science.
2. *Reliability* between and within observers is the most important characteristic of measurement.
3. There are four major scales of measurement: *nominal* which provides reliable categorizing of scaled items; *ordinal,* which categorizes and places items in order; *equal interval,* which involves stipulation of an arbitrary zero point as well as a unit of measurement; and *ratio,* which has a nonarbitrary zero point and a specified unit of measurement.
4. The repeatability of measures is called their *reliability.* This may be assessed in various ways, basically by comparing outcomes on the test with outcomes on the same or an equivalent test.
5. The extent to which a test measures what it is supposed to measure is its *validity.* This is assessed by determining the relationship of scores on the test to performances on some accepted *criterion.* Tests are often not well validated. Face validity, which is not uncommonly used, means that we merely look at items to see the extent to which they appear to measure the right thing. Face validity is better than nothing, but not really adequate. It is best to show that the test accurately predicts performance on an accepted criterion of the tested behavior.
6. *Direct measures* are those made on criterional behavior, whereas *indirect measures* are merely indicative of criterional behavior. *Verbal measures* are usually taken as indicative of some nonverbal responses. Indicative verbal measures are often unreliable. This is especially true if they refer to past behavior (retrospective verbal reports). There is also evidence that verbal reports of future behavior (prospective verbal reports) are often, though not always, unreliable. If interest is in the verbal behav-

ior as such, the verbal behavior is criterional. This is often the case with verbal measures of current psychological experiences (contemporaneous verbal reports).

7. A given level of scaling may be obtained either directly or indirectly. In the latter case, higher level scales are derived from data originally obtained with lower order scales.

8. *Rating scales* yield ordinal data and are often used in psychology. A common example is a *Likert-type scale.* With a Likert-type scale, degree of agreement with a statement is rated.

9. With the *method of pair comparisons,* a pool of items to be rated is converted to pairs, with judgments being made of which of the pairs is rated higher than the other. The frequency with which ratings of pairs are confused (one changes ones mind as to which is first) is taken as an indicator of the distances between items. From this an equal interval scale may be developed.

10. With *ranking methods* judges must place items in order on some dimension. This may force finer discrimination than the typical rating scale.

11. The *method of magnitude estimation* is a method of scaling that directly yields ratio scales. The judge is merely asked to assign any numbers to the scaled item, as long as the numbers reflect item magnitude.

12. Many psychologists feel that *direct behavioral measurement* is preferable to indicative verbal measurement. To do so, one must find an adequate set of operational definitions of the target psychological phenomenon.

13. Several different aspects of behavior may be used in direct behavioral measurement. The latency is the time elapsing between first opportunity to respond and the occurrence of the response. The proportion of times the organism engages in the behavior over a series of opportunities may also be used. The numbers of errors or trials until some behavioral target is reached is a common measure. Many psychologists argue that the **rate** of occurrence of a response (number of responses/unit of time) is the best measure.

14. The obtrusiveness of a measure refers to the tendency of measurement to change the measured behavior. It is a major problem in psychology. Artificially manipulated variables must seem authentic or subjects will change their normal responses. *Demand characteristics* of experiments are the various cues that give the subject a notion of the experimental hypothesis. They may lead to conformity with the experimenter's expectations or to *impression management.* The latter refers to doing whatever the subject thinks will look good, in view of her or his ideas of what the experimenter has in mind (not necessarily conforming to the experimenter's expectations).

15. Various techniques have been devised for measuring demand

characteristics. Most of these involve varying degrees and times of interviewing (for example, postexperimental = after the experiment, preexperimental = before the experiment but after they have been given the experimental instructions). A very good method is to direct a control group of subjects to behave in a manner opposite what they think is expected of them. Some other methods are discussed in text.

16. Measurement always entails *errors.* Errors may be *systematic* or *unsystematic* (random). Systematic errors can, in principle, be controlled for, but we always are left with a residuum of random errors. Errors may also be attributed to the imprecision of the measuring instrument or to various aspects of the circumstances under which the measures are taken (*circumstantial* or *ambient errors*). Any raw measurement has a component due to error.

CHAPTER 4

Sampling and the Generality of Data

Once, after a well-known psychologist had finished delivering a lecture on some very socially relevant research in human social psychology, a colleague of mine threw up his hand and snarled, "What's this got to do with the behavior of rats?!"

He was only joking. He is a long-time student of both animal and human behavior. But his one-liner illustrates a prevalent objection to the work of psychologists. Does it apply beyond the particular subjects used by the experimenter? This is one facet of the problem of the generality of data.

Types of Scientific Generality

There are many types of scientific generality—as many as there are facets of an experiment. Does a functional relationship determined with rats apply to pigeons and to people? Does the relationship at certain values of the independent variable still hold at other values? Will a relationship calculated from data obtained by using one kind of apparatus, hold for a different kind? Do principles induced from small group interaction observed in a laboratory also hold in a business organization? All such questions pertain to generality.

If a finding (functional relationship) holds in situations other than the one in which it was discovered, we say it has generality or can be *generalized.* The situations may differ with respect to subjects, apparatus, measures of the variables, or any of the many facets of the original experiment. Without generality, conclusions drawn from scientific data would be of little value.

If all functional relations held only under the exact conditions under which they were obtained, science would be in real trouble. Virtually every situation would be novel and the ability to make predictions would be limited almost to the point of incapacity. Scientists could hardly be motivated to do experiments if they believed that functional relationships had such limited application. They are far more inclined to believe that observed functional relations will survive many modifications of the original experimental situation.

Given the obvious importance of scientific generality, it is odd that researchers pay relatively little attention to generality of data—the basis of valid extrapolation of findings. They are very conscientious about the stability or reliability of their findings, but take little interest in identifying the generality of these findings. Such attitudes prevail largely because of the commonly accepted rationale for assuring the generality of data. That rationale is virtually impossible to reconcile with what scientists actually do, so they tend to ignore the problem entirely. The rationale I am talking about is the one that says experimenters must assure generality of data through random sampling procedures.

Population and Sample

A scientist who does an experiment wants to make statements about some target group of interest. This target group is called the *population.* If one wants to make statements about alcoholism, one's target population is "all alcoholics." If one wants to make statements about mental illness, one's population is "all the mentally ill." If one wants to make statements about learning in general, one's population is "all creatures capable of learning." You can see that experimenters usually could not bring the entire population into the laboratory. Instead, they must settle for a part of that population. The part of the population they actually study is called the *sample.* So the problem of generality of data boils down to a problem of making statements about a population on the basis of observations made on a sample from that population.

Avoid getting the impression that the problems of scientific generality apply only to the matter of extrapolating from a subset of experimental subjects to a larger set. They include generalization from one setting to another, from one measure to another, and so on. However, extrapolation across subjects is a particularly important and subtle issue in experiments with human subjects.

Representative Sampling as a Basis for Data Generality

It is a common belief among experimental psychologists that the generality of data is founded in *representative sampling.* With representative sampling, experimenters make sure that the sample of subjects used in their experiment has essentially the same composition as the general population to which they hope to extrapolate. They make sure that the sample is *representative of* the general target population. So experimenters who wish to study the opinions of college students (and thus wish to generalize any relationships found to the college student population as a whole), should try to be sure that the sample of students they study is typical. If it is typical, then they can be confident of the generality of their data.

Suppose someone interested in sampling the opinions of college students were foolish enough to inquire only at a campus lecture on meditation or only at a right-wing political meeting. In each of these cases the interviewer could have an unrepresentative or *biased sample,* and the study would likely run into trouble if its conclusions were generalized to college students as a whole.

Most of us are not likely to be so silly as the hypothetical experimenter just described, although more subtle sampling biases can find their way into an experiment. Experimenters doing brain lesion experiments might select their subjects by going to a rat colony and grabbing the first rat they can catch. This practice might lead to their having a sample biased in the direction of sluggish rats. Masters and Johnson (1966) had great trouble with sample representativeness in selecting subjects for their work on human sexual response. At first, they tried using prostitutes. Not only was this an unrepresentative sample, but there was definite evidence that the subjects' sexual physiology had certain peculiarities stemming from the practice of their profession. Masters and Johnson then sought volunteers. Here, again, there is trouble with respect to sample representativeness. The investigators were well aware of this difficulty and discuss it in some detail (Masters and Johnson, 1966, pp. 9–23).

A particularly striking case of overgeneralization from a biased sample was described by Hoffman (1968) in his book on male homosexuality. In considering whether homosexuality is a mental illness, several psychiatrists decided that homosexuals are indeed mentally ill. The psychiatrists based this judgment on the fact that all the homosexuals they encountered were mentally disturbed. But, as Hoffman points out, their experience with treatment of homosexuals was restricted to those who sought psychiatric aid. Presumably, all their heterosexual patients were also disturbed! Hooker (1957) did a study in which she obtained 30 homosexuals who seemed well adjusted. She matched them with 30 heterosexuals for age, education, and IQ, and submitted all 60 subjects to a battery of psychological tests. Several of her colleagues were then asked to evaluate the test results, without knowing the sexual preferences. They were unable to distinguish homosexuals from heterosexuals. Thus, the generalization that all homosexuals are mentally disturbed was due to sampling bias.

Instances of overgeneralization from biased samples are easy to find in popular science articles, and even in many technical ones.

Methods of Sampling

What do researchers do about the problem of sample representativeness? They try to see to it that each member of the population of interest has an equal opportunity of being selected or that the probability of being selected is proportional to the real representation of subjects of that sort in the population. With *random sampling with replacement,* each subject in the population has an *equal* and *independent* chance of being selected. One has as good a chance as anyone else, and one's selection at a given time has no influence on future selections, for one is as likely as any other subject to be selected for future samplings.

Random Sampling Without Replacement. Sometimes it would be a mistake to sample with replacement. A subject, once used, may be changed in some way so as to become ill-suited for future use. For example, an experiment might include a test that would be easier if taken a second time. Or there might be some gimmick in the experiment that is exposed to participants who are then irrevocably knowledgeable about it. In animal research there may even be permanent bodily changes, such as modifications of the brain.

Thus it is common to sample without replacement. Does this mean that the sample must necessarily be unrepresentative? No. The experimenter can make sure that the fundamental *sampling unit* is randomly selected. The sampling unit can be an individual subject, but it can also be a group of subjects. If you consider all the possible samples of a certain size that could be taken from the population, you can treat "samples of size n" as the sampling unit. Then the sampling unit can be selected randomly. In *random sampling without replacement,* each sample of size n has an equal and independent chance of being selected.

The Use of "Rational Procedures" in Sampling. Some experimenters do not rely entirely on the chancy process of randomization in making sure that they get a representative sample. They use their knowledge of the population and simply see to it that the sample has the correct composition. Opinion pollsters commonly do that sort of thing. They usually make sure that the various regions of the country, which they know to be important determinants of political opinion, are represented in their sample in a proportion like that found in the population as a whole. They often do the same thing with age, race, and declared political party affiliation. You should realize, though, that within these imposed limits randomization is generally used. These samples are merely placing what are called *constraints* on randomness.

If you rely on your knowledge of the population and take control of the sampling to assure that it is representative, rather than relying entirely on randomization, you are using "rational procedures" in sample selection. The rational procedure I just described is called *stratified sampling.* With stratified sampling, care is taken to assure that the proportions of certain key elements in the sample are the same as those in the population. For example, in selecting human subjects for an experiment, the experimenter might see to it that the proportion of women selected is the same as that found in the population as a whole, or might attempt to assure that whites and blacks are represented in accord with their proportional representation in the population. Selection is otherwise random. We must, of course, have certain information about the population in order to do this.

It might seem to you that rational procedures are better than randomization procedures. People are usually inclined to be uncomfortable about leaving things to chance when they can have control over them. But keep in mind that rational procedures depend on the accuracy of knowledge about the population. If you make a mistake about this, you may fail to get a representative sample.

Problems in the Practical Use of Sampling Theory. If experimenters use the sampling procedures described, generality of data across subjects is assured, but it is hard in practical situations to adhere to the principles of sampling. If you want to study human memory, a random sample of the population to which you wish to generalize will require that every human being be included in the potential sampling population. Clearly, you would be hard-pressed to fulfill the conditions of the sampling procedure under such conditions.

In practice, experimenters typically use a kind of "catch as catch can" sampling procedure. A human learning study is done on a selection of volunteers from among students enrolled at a given university, rats are selected from a colony of albino rats available in the experimenter's laboratory, or other convenient sources are used. The conditions required by sampling theory to assure representativeness are simply not feasible in the typical psychology experiment.

Another problem in the use of sampling theory as justification of generality of data is that it applies only to generality across *subjects.* There are many other aspects of generality. How can an experimenter apply sampling principles across experimental designs, types of apparatus, and the like? Little attention is given to problems of this type, yet they are problems as important as those involved in subject sampling.

Despite the failure of sampling theory to justify most of what is done by experimenters, there is a tendency to adhere to it as a rationale for statements of generality. For example, a scientist may object to the use of rats because they are a species unrepresentative of the population to which we wish to generalize, yet fail to apply the same arguments to other features of the experimental setting.

Special Problems for the Experimental Psychologist: The Volunteer Subject and the Albino Rat

Experimental psychologists have most commonly conducted their studies on nonrandomly selected subjects. Those experimenters interested in human research have largely worked with college students, commonly sophomores who volunteer or are more or less "drafted" from the pool of those enrolled in introductory psychology. Those who experiment with animals have typically utilized rats, especially albino rats. By no stretch of the imagination can either college students or albino rats be thought of as representative of organisms in general. With respect to the sampling of human subjects, eminent statistical psychologist Quinn McNemar (1946) made the remark that "The existing science of human behavior is largely the science of the behavior of sophomores." In a similar vein, Lockard (1968) has argued that the use of the albino rat is more of a "bad habit" than a judicious choice. Indeed, it is well known that albinos of various species have a number of neuroanatomical, neurophysiological, and biochemical characteristics that make them notably different from normally pigmented individuals (see, for example Creel, 1971).

Human subjects who participate in psychological experiments may be pressured in various ways to do so, but, at least in recent times, ethical procedures of the American Psychological Association do not permit coercion as a method of recruiting subjects. Thus, volunteers are mainly used in psychological experiments. Unfortunately, there is a great deal of evidence that volunteer subjects constitute a strikingly unrepresentative sampling of people. Rosenthal and Rosnow (1969) reviewed a wide range of studies indicating peculiarities of volunteers. For example, volunteers tend to be better educated, have higher occupational status, have a higher need for approval, have higher IQs, be less authoritarian, and be better adjusted than nonvolunteers. It might seem that experimenters could correct for the selective effects of volunteering merely by taking these known characteristics into account. Unfortunately, these characteristics cannot be relied upon to occur in any given sample of volunteers. For example, Zimmer and I recently found that a sampling of volunteers for an experiment involving autogenic training (a kind of self-hypnosis) were very far *above* norms in authoritarianism. The difference between this finding and those reviewed by Rosenthal and Rosnow might be due to any number of factors (such as regional variations in the United States, differences between the kind of people who volunteer for certain *types* of experiment, differences between people who volunteer early versus late in a semester, and so on). Indeed, Rosenthal and Rosnow themselves point out that most of the studies on "volunteer-effects" are flawed, in that they compare people who *say* they will participate in an experiment to those who *say* they will not. Since many people say they will participate, then fail to show up, this method does not provide an adequate comparison between true volunteers and nonvolunteers. It is likely that the method leads to underestimation of the differences since those who fail to show up are probably more like nonvolunteers than like volunteers. The upshot of all this is that the typical method of getting subjects for psychological experiments does not provide representative samples, nor do we have any adequate way of determining just how to limit generalizations based on data gathered from such subjects.

As I pointed out earlier, similar problems plague us with respect to the use of rats, especially albino rats. Many investigators have pointed out the genetic peculiarities of these animals. One eminent psychologist, Neal

Miller, who is famous for having done many incisive experiments using rats as subjects, has even suggested that there may have been a "genetic drift" in the rats available from standard suppliers (Miller & Dworkin, 1974). He provides some evidence that it may not be possible to generalize, in certain respects, from rats obtained several years ago to rats obtained today!

General versus Specific Laws of Behavior

Difficulties inherent in the use of volunteer subjects and albino rats might well lead us to wonder at the adequacy of many, if not most, of the findings in contemporary experimental psychology. This is a severe problem, and practical limitations on the availability of types of experimental subjects other than those already in wide use make it difficult to solve that problem. However, the situation is not quite as bad as it might seem, since many psychologists are looking for very basic, highly general psychological laws. When we deal with the most basic principles, we can expect that they will be shared by a very wide range of subjects. Both a rock and a human being share in common their domination by the law of gravity. Similarly, highly general laws of psychology must apply to all human beings, to all mammals, or even to all organisms. If we are looking for such principles, it makes little difference which subset we sample from the population.

The attitude that science should first seek the most general principles, and only later proceed to the more specific ones, has largely been responsible for the willingness of experimental psychologists to tolerate nonrandom sampling of subjects. Unfortunately, some psychologists went on to look for more specific laws without changing the sampling procedures.

In recent times there has been increasing emphasis on the study of specific laws. For example, experimental psychologists interested in the study of learning long placed emphasis on the study of highly general principles of learning. This led to the selection of arbitrary species (usually albino rats) and arbitrary responses. In recent years, work in the area of *specific hungers* has resulted in increased recognition of the specificity of laws of learning. Operationally, the term "specific hunger" refers to the fact that many organisms can select foods that contain substances for which they have a deficiency. Sometimes, as in the case of deficiency for sodium, the preference requires no learning at all! Commonly organisms immediately prefer foods containing sodium if the diet has been sodium-deficient (Rozin & Kalat, 1971). In other cases, for example, thiamine deficiency, some learning may be required before they make appropriate selections. Rozin and Kalat (1971) point out that rats mainly learn an aversion for the deficient food. This occurs despite the large time gap between dietary deficiency and the development of ill health. Of all the possible stimuli that occur prior to sickness, rats select the *diet* as the one to which they develop an aversion. They are not averse even to such things as the familiar food dish.

The selection of a particular stimulus to avoid seems to be specific to given species. A similar case has been reported of taste aversions in rats learned from associating tastes or odors with malaise induced by X rays or apomorphine (Garcia & Ervin, 1968). There is a special readiness to associate specific stimuli with specific responses. Wilcoxon et al. (1971) have shown that whereas rats tend to associate induced illness with taste cues, quail associate it with visual cues. There seems to be a preparedness of the nervous system to develop certain kinds of conditioned response, and the preparedness depends on adaptations that make evolutionary sense (Rozin & Kalat, 1971).

A related phenomenon is called "instinctive drift." It was described by Breland and Breland (1961) in a classic paper on the "misbehavior" of organisms. While trying to develop operant responses in a variety of species, they found them sometimes quite resistant to the contingencies of reinforcement. For example, raccoons tend to wash their food before eating it, and they will persist in doing so even if the food is sugar that dissolves when washed!

Seligman (1970) argues that organisms may be *prepared, unprepared,* or *counterprepared* to associate certain events. He cites many experimental examples, and speculates that the laws of learning may vary with the preparedness of the organism for the association. If experimental psychologists are going to shift their emphasis to "specific" laws, it will be necessary to improve sampling procedures and to devise tactics for strengthening the generality of data. To that end, we will next consider procedures for arranging experiments with maximum likelihood of generality. In particular, we will discuss the selection of settings and of subjects.

Selecting a Setting

Experimenting in the Target Setting

Selecting the setting of your experiment is a critical step. The first possibility is to do the experiment directly in the target setting of interest. Experiments are seldom done in natural settings, but this can be done to considerable advantage. Some advantages are that:

1. It maximizes generalizability to the target setting.
2. It may minimize the artificiality and the intrusiveness of experimental settings.
3. It permits the full range of natural behaviors to occur.

The main disadvantages are:

1. It may make the exercise of experimental control difficult.
2. It may be logistically, including ethically, difficult.

Keep in mind that there are important distinctions between a *naturalistic experiment* and an experiment in a natural setting. In a naturalistic experiment, the experimenter does not have control of the independent variable, but waits for natural changes to occur in the independent variable. In contrast, the experiment done in a natural setting involves *manipulation* of the independent variable by the experimenter. The latter arrangement permits more complete isolation of the controlling variables.

It is also important to recognize that an experimenter working in a natural setting must still select behaviors to be measured. It is not enough to give a general description of what occurs in that setting. Behaviors must be measured if we are to have a scientific experiment. Mere casual description like that done by nature lovers and people watchers is not enough.

Experimenting in a Model Setting

If the disadvantages of experimenting in the target setting outweigh the advantages, it will be necessary to find or devise a setting that is a good model of the target setting. I use the term *model setting* to refer to anything that, when manipulated, can be expected to produce effects that can be generalized to those found in the target setting itself. When an experimenter brings people into a laboratory and arranges for group pressure to be placed on them to make distorted perceptual judgments, the experimenter is using a model of natural conformity in the expectation that its results can be generalized. An experimenter who memorizes lists of nonsense syllables and measures the decline in recollection of them is using a model of verbal learning and memory. The range of potential models is great. Obviously, model settings can range from close imitations of the target setting to settings that are thought to be similar to it only in a functional sense.

What do we mean by "similar in a functional sense"? Two behaviors may appear to be quite different, but the functional relationships underlying them may be alike or even identical. When Reedy the rat presses a bar for food, he may be executing a behavior functionally identical to little Georgie's saying "Mik" at the table when he wants more milk. If Janie's parents were alcoholic, she may engage in self-destructive behavior that merits her being considered a "dry alcoholic." Without drinking at all, Janie might imitate the essential self-destructive behavioral characteristics of the alcoholic parents. Her and their behaviors are functionally similar despite the surface differences.

Selecting the Subjects

Subjects from the Target Population

Here again, you can use subjects directly from the target population. If your question is about people, you can use human subjects; if it is about a given nonhuman species, you can use subjects of the kind involved directly in the question. This has the obvious advantage of strengthening the generalizability of the findings.

Model Subjects

If you cannot sample from the target population, you may have to use model subjects, in particular animal subjects. The selection of animal subjects will depend on how available they are and on certain strategic decisions which will be discussed here.

Selecting Convenient Subjects Such as Rats. If you are doing an experiment in which you seek broadly general, basic behavioral principles, the nature of the animal subjects may matter little. If you look for the most general laws of behavior, any organism displaying behavior will serve your purpose.

It is a misconception to suppose that animal subjects must be *representative* in the sense of being like human subjects or like higher mammals to a special degree. Lockard (1968) has argued against the use of rats as subjects in psychology on the grounds that rats are not sufficiently representative. But general laws are often discovered on species that are convenient, and by no means ordinary or typical.

When geneticists spent many years studying the genetics of the tobacco mosaic virus, they were dealing with a rather exceptional kind of organism. But it happened to be convenient for the procedures they wanted to use. Many Nobel Prizes were won, and ultimately the genetic code was understood as a result of such work. Neurophysiologists made the first direct measures of conduction in individual nerve fibers on a downright freakish preparation, the giant axon of the squid. With the geneticists and the neurophysiologists the preparation used was technically convenient, and the principles sought were of the most general kind.

Selecting Apt Model Subjects. Another approach is to attempt to select model subjects that are particularly representative with respect to some property of the target population. Physiologists commonly do this sort of thing. If they are interested in kidney function they will use humans if this is not threatening. If they cannot use human subjects, instead of just taking the subjects at hand, they will find an animal model that has a kidney as similar as possible to that of humans. When psychologists insist on using primate subjects for potentially harmful experiments, they are taking an attitude similar to that of the physiologists. When students of alcoholism move away from the use of rats and monkeys, which species display a singular lack of enthusiasm for alcohol, and shift to a special kind of pig that takes readily to drink, they are selecting apt subjects.

Investigators like those mentioned are usually studying specific complex phenomena that may only exist in a limited number of species. Their strategy is different from that of experimenters interested in broadly general basic principles.

Generality of Data as an Empirical Question

The best way, even better than representative sampling, to find out whether data are general is to demonstrate by experiment. If you run an experiment with one pigeon as the subject, and someone suggests that the finding might be unique to that particular pigeon, the best answer is to run another pigeon. If you run an experiment on social behavior in a small group in the laboratory, discover regular behavioral patterns, and wonder whether similar patterns of behavior occur in comparably structured small groups in factories, the best approach is to repeat the experiment in a factory. If you have evaluated prejudice by means of a questionnaire and wonder whether different measures such as heart rate, pupillary dilation, or behavior when offered the opportunity for an actual act of discrimination will yield the same results, nothing could be more convincing than actually doing experiments to find out whether data are general.

Unfortunately the empirical approach to generality of data has its limitations, just as sampling does. If we are limited in our statements of generality to conditions identical with those situations we actually observed, our science will be virtually useless. Even if you show that a finding obtained in your laboratory can also be obtained in a factory, what about other laboratories and other factories? To make truly general statements based solely on actual observations, it would be necessary to experiment in every conceivable setting, using every conceivable method. Even if this could be accomplished, generality with respect to future situations would have to be based on something other than direct observation.

The Complexity of Bases for Affirming Generality

Judgments of generality are founded on a variety of considerations. When it is argued that future pigeons may not be like past pigeons, most experimenters react to the argument as a parent might react to a tedious child. Their tendency is to treat such objections lightly and to go on insisting that generality is an empirical question. They overlook the fact that there is a reason for their unwillingness to take seriously the possibility that the laws of nature will change today. In fact, there is a whole assumptional system within which scientists work, and one of the assumptions seems to be that nature displays some degree of stability.

Another point that is seldom mentioned is that the assumption of generality, in the absence of evidence to the contrary, is simply a *good strategy*. This is essentially what the *principle of parsimony* is about. The principle of parsimony states that scientists should not add new explanatory principles unless the evidence requires them. Thus, the simplest possible explanation, the one with the fewest parts, is preferred. At the very heart of science is the urge to reduce the complex world to a few basic principles.

Since scientists want to keep explanatory principles to a minimum, they are inclined to expect that a principle that applies in one situation will also apply in similar situations. Thus they tend to generalize first and ask questions later. There is an apocryphal story that the physicist Isaac Newton, who had been sent home from school to his farm during the spread of bubonic plague over Europe, was sitting under an apple tree and was struck on the head by an apple. He immediately had an "Aha" experience, and went on to discover the universal law of gravitation. He *observed* an apple falling on his head, but he intuitively concluded that there must be a certain law of attrac-

FIGURE 4.1 The relationship of Newton's population and sample. Should he generalize?

tion between all physical bodies on earth or in the heavens. He assumed that what occurred in one small place applied everyplace.

A similar parsimonious leap occurred when it was first discovered that a magnetic field is generated whenever electric current flows. There is always a magnetic field perpendicular to the direction of flow of any electric current. When the French physicist Ampère (after whom the unit of electrical current "ampere" is named) learned of this, he immediately supposed that *all* magnetism, even that found in permanent magnets, was due to the flow of electric current. This went far beyond the observations, since no one had observed current flow in permanent magnets. It was in accord with the principle of parsimony in that it assumed that only one set of principles explained both the properties of permanent magnets and those of electromagnets. And it proved to be a correct supposition, for we now know that there is indeed a net movement of electrons in those materials that are permanently magnetized.

We generalize unless given evidence to the contrary. For example, given a single observation from a population, the best guess about the character of the remaining observations is that they will be the same as the first one. A simple example will illustrate the point. Suppose you are asked to reach into a box and draw out an item. The item withdrawn is a black sock. If you are now asked, in the absence of any other evidence, to guess the nature of the next item you will draw, what will you say? Many people will simply say, "I haven't got the foggiest notion," but that strategy is not a good one. It would be better to guess and say, "a black sock." Why? Because the items most frequently represented in the box are the ones that were most likely to be drawn in your one attempt. Thus, by guessing that future items will be the same as the one you drew, you can do better than by failing to guess at all, or by guessing "at random." Similarly, it seems preferable to assume that observations have generality than to assume that they do not or that there is no way of guessing.

Notice that the argument just given is couched in terms of *guessing.* This sort of thing will certainly not make anyone certain that a finding has generality. It simply means that, lacking anything better, generality is a good guess. Verifications that the guess is correct will strengthen our conviction of generality and falsifications will weaken it. Empirical evidence is always the most compelling source of information. To assume that guesses, even strategically good guesses, are absolute truths is to be guilty of hasty generalization—an error that has often caused scientists a great deal of trouble.

SUMMARY

1. The *generality* of an experimentally determined relationship is its applicability to situations other than the one in which data were obtained

(for example, with different subjects, in a new setting, with a new experimenter, and so on).

2. We usually wish to apply research findings to a larger set of subjects and situations than we actually measure. The measured set is called a *sample* and the set about which we wish to generalize is called a *population.*

3. *Representative sampling* is one basis for assuming generality of data. If the sample used is representative of the population, generality of data will be assured.

4. There are various methods of making it likely that a sample will be representative. *Random sampling with replacement* means that every subject in the population has an *equal* and *independent* (that is, selection of one subject has no influence on selection of any other subject) chance of being selected. In order to maintain independence of sampling, subjects who are selected must be replaced in the pool for the next selection. In *random sampling without replacement* they are not so replaced. In this case any given sampling unit (for example, $N = 10$) has an equal and independent chance of being selected.

Sometimes *constraints* are placed on randomness. This is when we want to be sure the composition of the sample is consistent with a known composition of the population (for example, a certain percentage of males and females, blacks and whites, and so on). *Stratified sampling* stipulates that the sample must have a given composition, known to exist in the population. In other respects, this kind of sampling is random.

5. Experimental psychologists have tended to limit themselves to two kinds of subjects: the *volunteer subject* and the *albino rat.* There is evidence that neither of these is particularly representative of the populations of interest. The use of such subjects makes sense if the psychological laws of interest are of a highly *general* kind but not if they are of a more *specific* kind.

6. Experimenters should consider experimenting in *target (natural) settings,* since this maximizes generalizability to such settings, minimizes obtrusiveness, and permits the full range of natural behaviors to occur. However, this may be difficult in practice and may make it hard to get experimental control.

7. A second option is to experiment in *model setting.* This is any situation that, when manipulated, can be expected to produce effects that can be generalized to the target setting.

8. *Subjects* may also be either from the *target population* or *"models."* Researchers tend to select convenient subjects, but should try to select *apt* models.

9. The bases for affirming generality are complex. Flaws in representa-

tive sampling do not necessarily mean that data will not ultimately be useful. Generality can be demonstrated empirically by showing directly that a finding applies in a new situation. The *principle of parsimony* says that we assume generality of data until we have evidence that new laws are needed. Scientists have long used this principle as an effective strategy.

CHAPTER 5

From Testimonial to Experimental Design

The Purpose of Design

There is a very old story about a character known as the Mulla Nasrudin who was found throwing food on the street in front of his house. Nasrudin was by no means a wealthy man, so a friend who saw this ran up to him, extremely puzzled, and yelled "Nasrudin! Have you gone mad? Why are you throwing this precious food on the ground?" Nasrudin looked up and somewhat matter of factly answered, "To keep the tigers away." His friend exploded "But there *are* no tigers around here!" Nasrudin smiled and said "You see! It works, doesn't it!"

Nasrudin's fallacy is a prime example of the problems faced by people who want to find out whether a given variable is potent. It is surprisingly easy to believe that something works when it either has no effect at all or even produces undesirable effects. Throughout human history, people have invested their time, their energy, and their goods in efforts that were worthless or harmful. A major reason for doing research is to find out which efforts really pay off.

There are many ways to make mistakes in doing research, and these mistakes may have consequences that leave us no better off than we were before conducting the study. Primarily what we want to do is learn whether certain phenomena occur, in what quantity they occur and under what conditions they occur. Nasrudin could not say under what conditions tigers stay away because he had not tried just doing nothing (running a control condition). Nasrudin's hypothesis was that throwing food on the ground keeps tigers away. His friend's hypothesis was that tigers stay away even without the food. Nasrudin's method does not permit him to dismiss this alternative hypothesis.

A major function of research is to permit us to dismiss plausible alternatives to our main hypothesis. In order to do this we must design our study with great care. We must assign the various treatments to our subjects in ways that render various plausible alternative hypotheses untenable. In this and the following chapter we will deal with a wide range of methods commonly used when studying psychological phenomena. Some of the methods are no better than Nasrudin's. Others are of maximal sophistication and permit rather precise targeting of the real controlling variables. This chapter deals primarily with the methods that are most open to criticism on the grounds that they fail to render certain alternative hypotheses implausible.

Some Preexperimental Procedures

With experimental design, treatments and control procedures are arranged in a way that tells us which variables actually control changes in levels of outcome variables. There are many procedures in wide use that fail to reach the full level of *experimental* design. This is because they lack the full array of controls, and therefore fail to allow us to dismiss certain alternative hypotheses. Using these procedures, we see changes occur with varying degrees of accuracy. But we cannot say with certainty whether the treatment procedures we are interested in evaluating actually *produced* those changes. You may wonder why anyone would use such a procedure, so I will try to explain the advantages and disadvantages of some of these methods.

The Testimonial

One widely used method of determining the effectivess of procedures is the testimonial. This method is often used with treatments for various physical and psychological disturbances, though it is almost unheard of in the scientific community. In a testimonial, someone communicates, either spontaneously or upon request, about the personal impact of a certain treatment. Though testimonials are potentially very great sources of inaccuracy, even *they* have certain uses and advantages. The data are readily available, requiring little effort on the part of the inquirer. The data may also provide a source of hypotheses to be evaluated later in more systematic research projects. Finally, testimonial data may be all that we can get under some circumstances.

The disadvantages of using testimonials are very great. There is likely to be a problem of sampling bias. The people who give testimonials may be enthusiasts who are unrepresentative of the bulk of people taking the treatment. This problem may be compounded if the inquirers also select out their "best cases," not bothering to present information concerning their failures.

A second problem with testimonials lies in the method of measurement. Earlier, the inadequacy of verbal reports was discussed, and testimonials are a case in point. Those giving the testimonial may have various motives for doing so (for example, to please the inquirer), and the kind of response they give may be influenced by those motives. In any case, verbal reports, especially retrospective ones, are often poor reflectors of nonverbal realities.

A third problem is that the testimonial typically lacks proper control procedures. Those people who happened to take the treatment just before a period of spontaneous change will likely attribute the change to the treatment. Many disorders such as depression and the common cold are known to go away spontaneously. Even those things that do not go away spontaneously are likely to have variations that, when caught at a certain phase, will give the impression of an effect of the treatment.

The Case Study

Unlike testimonials, case studies have been used widely in the studies of professionals. For example, Freud relied heavily on certain case studies in developing his interpretations of the human mind. In more recent times the well-known work of neurosurgeon Wilder Penfield which gave rise to the Transactional Analysts concept of "tapes," was based largely on his case studies. Bolgar (1965) states that "The case study method is the traditional approach of all clinical research." On the other hand, Campbell and Stanley (1963) speak of the use of case studies as "well-nigh unethical."

The term "case study" refers to a range of possible procedures.

Baselines

There is usually no direct measure of behavior prior to treatment. However, various case studies may involve greater or lesser degrees of gathering information concerning baseline behaviors prior to treatment. In addition to retrospective verbal reports such as the results of interviews and questionnaires, confirming evidence may be gathered from diaries, old letters, autobiographies, verbal reports of various people such as family and friends, officially recorded documents, and so on. At the most casual level, such evidence may be extremely unreliable, but at its upper limit a very large amount of converging evidence may be gathered for a particular account of baseline behavior, even though the evidence is retrospective. In those cases in which strong information concerning baseline has been gathered, the case study bridges into the somewhat more advanced pretest-posttest design, which is to be discussed later. Most typically, baseline measures taken in case studies are not up to scientific standards.

Follow-up

Case studies often differ in the extent to which follow-up observations are made. This is an important consideration, since there are certain general improvements that tend to occur with any treatment ("placebo effects"), and these are generally thought to be only short-term. To some extent, persistence of effects for long periods can be used as evidence against the alternative hypothesis that only placebo effects are taking place. However, there *may* be long-term placebo effects.

Generality

A common form of the case study involves the use of a single, perhaps unique individual. No serious effort may be made to ensure generality of the findings. Indeed, Allport (1955) has proposed the idea that the case study is well suited for identifying the unique influences on a particular human life. This is called an *idiodynamic* approach to psychology, as contrasted to a *nomothetic* approach, in which generally applicable principles are sought.

Besides the single case study, there may be multiple case studies. In this case, the same treatment may be given to several individuals, and the generalizability of the effects may be assessed.

Control and Confounding

Case studies may involve anything from introduction of a single, identifiable treatment to a kind of "fly by the seat of your pants" approach in which a variety of treatment procedures are introduced according to the best judgments of the therapist. Inevitably, there is a serious lack of control in case studies. It is therefore impossible to determine which variables are responsible for any observed changes in outcome.

Overall Advantages and Disadvantages

Case studies are not without their advantages. The information is often readily available—a spontaneous by-product of treatment procedures that are being given for clinical or other purposes. The case study permits study of real-life situations to a greater extent than is typical in contrived experiments. The case study method can readily be used in situations where ethical principles forbid withholding treatment from subjects. Allport has argued that only the case study can give us information about the enormously wide array of variables actually influencing a given person's life. However, since we cannot attribute causality to variables without proper control procedures, we cannot really conclude that *any* of the variables actually influenced the person. We are left with interesting hypotheses. However, the case study can be a very useful source of hypotheses to be evaluated subsequently by better controlled research. Some major disadvantages of the case study method are that this method usually involves poor measurement, especially of baseline behavior, control is usually poor, and generality not well established.

Though common sense may seem to tell us that accurate understanding of controlling factors might be obtained from case studies, the history of human inquiry shows otherwise. For example, take the case of bloodletting. This was a procedure used for centuries to "cure" a variety of physical disorders. Large amounts of blood were drawn from a sick person to get rid of "vile humours."

The people dealing with these cases were by no means stupid—at least many of them were not. Their ability to observe and interpret what they observed was no doubt as great as ours. Yet case after case failed to make them realize that the procedure was at best ineffectual and at worst harmful. It was not until the British anatomist and surgeon John Hunter ran a control group that did not receive the treatment that people were able to see the deficiencies of the technique.

The One-Group Pretest-Posttest Design

With the one-group pretest-posttest design, a group of individuals are first observed and their baseline behavior measured, then the treatment is given and changes from baseline recorded. Note that the baseline is in this case adequately measured. Changes that occur from pre- to posttest are attributed to the treatment condition.

The fundamental problem with this type of design is that a variety of intervening factors may be confounded with the treatment, making it impossible to dismiss the rival hypothesis that one of these factors created the changes in outcome. For example, taking of the pretest might itself cause changes in the subjects that make them react differently to the posttest. An external event might also intervene and produce the observed changes. For example, the assassination of a public figure, the change in seasons, or the occurrence of holidays can cause significant changes indistinguishable from effects of the treatment. Spontaneous changes might also occur. For example, if we are studying depression—the "common cold" of psychiatric disorders—it is well known that depression tends to lift spontaneously. Such spontaneous changes might be attributed to the treatment.

An example of what is needed in order to render these rival hypotheses implausible is a control group in which the treatment is not given and perhaps a placebo condition is introduced. All of the changes mentioned above as due to extraneous factors should occur in the control group as well as in the treated group. Thus the effects of the treatment will be reflected in such things as differences between the amount of change from pre- to posttest in controls versus in treated subjects. Once we have arranged a study in this way, we have a full-fledged experimental design. But we will postpone the fuller discussion of experimental designs until later.

You might reasonably wonder why anyone would use a design with clearly inadequate controls. Often it is impractical to have a control group. The researcher may feel that it would be unethical to run such a control, or access to the subjects may be contingent on giving all subjects the treatment. Sometimes running the control group is not impossible, but difficult. The researcher may prefer to establish that important changes occur at all before honing in on final identification of the controlling variables.

Many important studies have been done with this type of preexperimental design. For example, the original study that showed the potential usefulness of electromyographic biofeedback (giving people signals that tell them how tense their muscles are) in alleviating tension headaches was designed in this way (Budzynski, Stoyva, & Adler, 1970). The investigators subsequently did better controlled studies (Budzynski & Stoyva, 1973).

The Static-Group Comparison

The static-group comparison is one in which naturally formed groups that differ with respect to the treatment condition are compared. For example, we might want to assess the influence of a new teaching procedure by comparing students enrolled in two different sections of a particular course, one group of which received the new procedure. The treatment procedure might be already in use in one of the sections, or be actively introduced by the investigators.

The static-group comparison appears to have a control group, but it is open to confounding because people have been placed (or placed themselves) in groups nonrandomly. Many extraneous factors might influence whether students enroll in a given section, and there might also be factors influencing their tendency to drop out of a given section. Thus, differences in outcomes of the two groups cannot rightly be attributed to the treatment condition. It is quite plausible that these results might be due to differences in composition of the groups that are independent of the treatment. This design can be converted to a fully adequate one by assigning membership in the two groups on a completely random basis. If people are put in the groups at random, there is no plausible reason to expect that there will be stable differences in the outcomes of the two groups, except as a result of the influence of the treatment. When the static-group design has been replaced by one in which group membership is determined randomly, we have a true experimental design, called a completely randomized design. Such designs will be discussed later.

Correlational Designs

A final type of preexperimental design to be discussed here is the *correlational design.* There are several noteworthy characteristics of correlational designs. One is that they attempt to show that there is a relationship between two or more variables, with little or no emphasis on determining which are the controlling variables. To say that there is a relationship between, say, two variables is to say that the levels of the "outcome" variable can be, at least to some significant degree, predicted from knowledge of the levels of the "predictor" variable. But such predictability does not imply that the predictor variable *controls* the levels of the outcome. We can exchange predictor and outcome variables without modifying the correlation. Thus, if we show that skirt lengths predict the Dow-Jones Stock Market Average, no causality need be implied. We could as well say that the Dow-Jones Average predicts skirt lengths.

With mere establishment of correlations between variables, we must accept the possibility that control of the relationship is exerted by either the outcome or the predictor variable, or even by some other variable or set of variables. Correlational designs do not attempt to distinguish between these various possibilities. Such distinctions are made by experimental methods.

Essentially, correlational designs are characterized by an attempt to show a relationship between variables while taking little or no interest in identifying controlling variables. By these two criteria, many of the designs discussed previously in this chapter could be considered correlational. However, we usually do not refer to them in that way, partly as a simple matter of custom and partly because the designs described earlier are usually intended to identify controlling variables. They simply do an incomplete job of it. With correlational designs it is common for the investigator to have no intention of demonstrating control or causality. Sometimes researchers erroneously claim they have demonstrated causal relationships when they have only demonstrated correlations.

One very common characteristic of correlational designs is an emphasis on showing the *degree* of relationship between variables. There is an important difference between showing *that* a relationship exists and showing *how much* of a relationship there is. There is a relationship between hair loss (even one hair!) and how much one weighs, but the magnitude is so slight that few people would think of it as worth including in a weight-reducing program. The typical correlational design is primarily intended to show that there is a relationship between variables, to indicate the magnitude of that relationship, and to do so without determining the controlling variables.

Uses and Dangers of Correlational Designs

Correlational designs are highly useful. Certain sciences, such as astronomy, reached very high levels of sophistication by showing reliable relationships between the variables of interest. Many scientists feel that the early stages of investigation in any field should be given over to *description* of relationships without experimental manipulation. Excessively early attempts at experimental manipulation may lead to manipulation of the wrong variables, or may lead us into studying unnatural situations that fail to bring out the full range of normal behaviors.

Even in later stages of study, correlational designs have an important place. For example, demonstration of correlations is the major method of showing the reliability and validity of measures. To illustrate, one group of investigators was interested in identifying a set of conversational behaviors that people use in defining a good conversationalist (Minkin, et al., 1976). They first reviewed videotapes of conversations and noted, quite unsystematically, that certain behaviors were *related to* the impression of conversational skill. These included certain types of commands such as "Tell me more about it," asking questions either directly ("How long have you gone to school here?") or indirectly ("So you are a student"). They also included positive conversational feedback indicating approval, agreement with, or comprehension of what the other person has said.

Having rather unsystematically identified certain relationships, the investigators then went on, more systematically, to show that these behaviors could be identified reliably. They did so by showing that there was a high correlation between judgments of independent observers who were asked to identify the behaviors. They also demonstrated the validity of the measures by showing that the prevalence of the behaviors proved to be a very strong predictor of how conversationally skilled the speakers were in the eyes of other people. The focus of attention throughout this study was on the demonstration of correlations.

This study not only illustrates the use of correlation to establish reliability and generality, but also provides a good starting point for discussion of the temptation to infer causality on the basis of correlations. When we hear about a relationship between skirt lengths and the Dow-Jones Average or between breast size of women and IQ (Smith, 1968 claims there is an inverse relationship) we are not likely to be tempted to believe that one factor controls the other. But when we see that there is a relationship between certain conversational behaviors and observers' judgments of conversational skill, it is very tempting to conclude that the behaviors cause the judgments. I will discuss the nature of causal inference from correlational findings in a later section of this chapter.

Establishment of reliability and validity of measures is certainly not the only use we have for correlational studies. Sometimes there are phenomena occurring in nature that we cannot manipulate. Our inability to manipulate these phenomena might be either due to a technical inability or to ethical limitations. In such cases we might only be able to do correlational studies. In other instances, experimental manipulation might be possible but difficult. It may be practical to determine whether a relationship exists and how strong it is before investing great effort into determining which variables control that relationship.

Can "Causality" Be Inferred from Correlational Data?

The presence of a correlation, no matter how strong, does not imply that one of the variables controls or "causes" changes in the other variable. Sometimes this is obvious, as when the relationship makes no sense. At other times, as when there is a correlation between certain conversational behaviors and observers' tendency to judge one as conversationally skilled, it is tempting to assume a causal relationship.

It is remarkably difficult to amass really good evidence for causality from correlational data. Neale and Leibert (1973) point out that there are two basic classes of problems blocking us from deducing causal from correlational relationships. For one thing, the *direction* of the control is often difficult to assess. If high blood pressure (hypertension) and atherosclerosis ("hardening of the arteries") tend to occur together, we cannot tell whether high blood pressure causes atherosclerosis or atherosclerosis causes high blood pressure.

A second barrier to causal inferences is that it is hard to tell whether some further variable or set of variables is responsible for the observed relationship. The relationship between the Dow-Jones Average and length of skirts is presumably a case in point. Neither of the two variables is at all likely to control changes in the other. Something else must be responsible.

Despite these problems in identifying causal influences from correlational data, many very interesting and important relationships are difficult to show in any other way. When strong relationships between cigarette smoking and various cancers, heart disease, and so on are found, there are good reasons for wanting to know whether the relationship is causal. If it is causal, at least in a contributory way, then control of smoking will decrease the risk of the diseases. When we can find few cases of long distance runners with heart disease, there is a good reason to wonder whether running will prevent heart disease. When high blood pressure is related to hardening of the arteries, it is important to know whether controlling the blood pressure will also alleviate the atherosclerosis and its many deadly concomitants.

The ideal way to determine whether the predictive variables are also controlling variables is by experiment. But we commonly cannot study such phenomena experimentally. Imagine requiring a randomly selected half of a sample of adolescents to smoke and the other half not to smoke, and to keep it up for years! Think of the difficulties entailed in getting randomly selected people to become long distance runners while preventing the control subjects from doing so.

Experimental work on such topics is often restricted to research done with animal models. Recently an investigator was forcing pigs to run on a tread mill. The experimenter's purpose was to determine whether a regular regimen of running prevents heart disease. You may say, "Of course it does! People who run don't get heart attacks! You said so yourself." However, there are other possibilities to consider. What if the only people who stick to a regimen of running are those who already have superior cardiovascular systems. Maybe the rest feel such difficulties in running because they start out with a less efficient system. Then the low rate of heart disease in runners might be due to a bias of sampling.

On the other hand, objections could be raised about the limitations on generality of data obtained with animal subjects, such as pigs, instead of people. Such objections are behind the serious attempts made to infer causality from correlations.

Information Relevant to Causal Inferences

Although fully satisfactory evidence of causality from correlations is usually not obtainable, many factors influence a decision in favor of a causal hypothesis rather than one of the alternatives. These factors may be placed in two broad classes: (1) What are the various costs and payoffs for making wrong or right judgments about causality in a given case? and (2) To what extent can plausible alternative hypotheses be dismissed?

To illustrate the issues involved under the heading of payoffs and costs, consider the contrast between the relationship of cigarette smoking to lung cancer versus the relationship between intelligence and size of breasts. The latter is largely in the category of trivia, perhaps somewhat annoying to large-breasted women. Little can be done about it in any case. But people have the potential to stop smoking. Even relatively modest evidence might be enough to lead a person to take the causal hypothesis seriously in such cases.

Several lines of evidence influence the plausibility of alternative hypothesis. For example, if there are many instances of a correlation in a variety of settings where most other factors vary, the alternatives to a causal hypothesis may become quite weak. To illustrate, a Japanese study indicated that there was a relationship between drinking soft water and having high blood pressure. At that point, the basis for causal inferences was flimsy. However, later work in the United States, England, Finland, Canada, Sweden, the Netherlands, and Ireland independently confirmed the relationship (Galton, 1973). This certainly does not provide a definitive case in favor of the causal hypothesis, but it leads us to think of that hypothesis as more likely.

We are also influenced by having an understanding of an underlying causal mechanism that would account for an observed correlation. The breast-IQ relationship mentioned earlier suffers from lack of a familiar causal pathway to make sense of it. The relationship between drinking of soft water and getting high blood pressure, on the other hand, can be explained by familiar chemical and physiological principles (too complicated to explain here).

The temporal ordering of the related variables also influences our willingness to accept a causal hypothesis. Causes cannot come later in time than their effects. Thus we are more willing to accept a causal hypothesis if the purported controlling variable precedes the "controlled" variable in time. However, temporal ordering alone is not a sufficient basis for inferring causality. There is a logical fallacy known as the fallacy of *"post hoc ergo propter hoc"* ("after this, therefore because of this"), which is based on asserting causality just because one thing follows another in time.

However, Matheson, Bruce, and Beauchamp (1978) have pointed out that one type of causal inference can be made with confidence on the basis of correlational evidence. This is the inference that *no* causal relationship exists. If a correlational design fails to show any relationship, there is little point in going to the greater effort of conducting a fully controlled experimental investigation. Therein lies one of the most important uses of correlational design. We can do preliminary work of a correlational type in order to decide whether the evidence merits further experimental investigation.

A full discussion of correlational designs requires that we deal with descriptive measures of the degree of relationship between variables. Correlation coefficients are used to indicate how much relationship there is between variables. That topic will be discussed in Chapter 8. Here, I will discuss in a highly general way, methods for identifying controlling variables. By introducing controls of various kinds in order to eliminate the influence of confounding variables, we make the transition to full-fledged experimental methods.

Experimental Methods

The main purpose of an experiment is to identify *factors* that predict and control outcomes of interest to the experimenter. We use the term "factor" here in the same sense as the term "variable." For example, if we are interested in the effects of electric shock on escape from an electrified area, we often speak of the independent variable, electric shock, as a "factor" with varying *levels.* The term "levels" refers to the various values the factor may take. For example, shock may be high, medium, or low. It may also be .1, .2, .3, .4, . . . milliamperes. In each case, we would speak of the "levels" of the shock factor. The term "levels" in ordinary English seems to imply some kind of rank ordering of the values. However, in the technical jargon of experiments it is used also with nominally scaled factors. Thus the levels of a "sex" factor might be "male" and "female," even though there is no rank ordering implied.

Thus we can speak of the goal of experiments as one of identifying those cases in which knowledge of the levels of some predictive factor or factors permits us to state, reliably and ahead of time, something about the levels of outcome-factors. The major way experimenters do this is by determining which manipulated variables actually control outcomes. In order to make such a determination, it is necessary to identify ineffectual variables as such (to dismiss plausible alternative hypotheses). Experimenters achieve that goal by introducing various control procedures.

Controlling Extraneous Variables

Suppose we are setting out to answer a question experimentally. We have to analyze our question and find measurement operations for the concepts of interest. We can then go looking for a reliable functional relationship. What we really want is to find independent variables that work. Our major adversary in this quest is the uncontrolled variable. If uncontrolled variables interfere, we won't know what, if any, potency independent variables have. We have two major weapons to use against the uncontrolled variable. They are *technology* and *chance.* If we want to get rid of an uncontrolled variable, we may seek the technology to do so. If we lack the technology, we may arrange things so that the uncontrolled variable will be evenly represented in the various treatments. Chance will work for us because random processes tend to distribute themselves evenly in the long run. But we have to be sure that chance gets an opportunity to operate. We have to look out for systematic errors. In so doing, we are engaging in experimental design. Experimental design is discussed in Chapter 6, but some underlying principles will be discussed here.

What can we do about an uncontrolled variable? First, we might consider *allowing it to influence your results.* If so, we are working at a preexperimental level. At times, this is not a bad idea, but it limits our understanding of controlling variables. On the other hand, since real-life variables are complex, it may give us a more authentic variable. We discussed preexperimental methods in more detail earlier, and so will stop with it here.

The most common way of coping with a confounded variable is to try to *hold it constant.* We can do this through technology or chance. Technologically we might *reduce it to zero,* eliminate it. This is holding it constant at zero. Or we might *hold it constant at above zero.* For example, if we want to find out whether a certain breed of dogs can discriminate color, we cannot reduce brightness to zero. The dogs couldn't see anything. But we could make each color equally bright. (Technically this is hard to do. This is because apparent brightness depends on the visual system of the perceiver. We cannot assume that what is bright for us is also bright for a dog.)

Often, we cannot hold a variable perfectly constant, but only *approximately* so. This goes for reducing it to zero, too. But although physicists cannot make a perfect vacuum, nevertheless they still use vacuums. Approximation is often used in science.

Now let us suppose we want to hold a variable constant by taking advantage of the effects of chance, statistically. One way to do this is to rely entirely on chance. Another is to introduce partial technological control and then rely on random processes to take care of the rest. For example, suppose we are worried that the time of day when subjects participate in an experiment is important. We cannot make the day stand still. We lack the technology. But if we determine randomly which treatment each arriving subject will get, any given time of day will, in the long run, occur as often as any other time of day. Thus, chance provides for the holding constant of the variable "time of day."

But maybe we do not want to trust to chance. Chance will rarely turn up things in some systematic order. But sometimes it will. Sometimes poker players get a royal flush. In the long run, this is not worth worrying about. But in the short run, it may be smart to distrust chance. So we may want to use a deliberately planned procedure for averaging out the variable of concern. Going back to concern over the time of day, we could always conduct our experiment at the same time each day or deliberately see to it that each time of day was equally represented in each treatment. We could just schedule subjects so that each treatment was given equally often at each running time. Whenever you reach the limits of deliberate planning, the remaining variables can be dealt with by randomization.

Randomization is good if we have a large number of things to randomize. Randomization may even out variables we have not thought about. But randomization can only be expected to hold variables constant in the long run. If we have a small number of observations, deliberate procedures may well be better.

A final way to deal with uncontrolled variables is to *manipulate* them. Students in one of my laboratory courses were doing an experiment on the two-point threshold. They were trying to find the smallest detectable separation between two points on the skin. If the two points are close enough together, they are perceived as one. Moved apart further and further, they will eventually be perceived as two. Several students got widely scattered, unreliable results. They felt that variations in the pressure of the points might have caused the nonuniformity. What were they to do? They could have used any of the methods for dealing with uncontrolled variables. But one group decided to rig up a device to vary the pressure systematically. This would show whether this variable was important. If so, the two-point threshold should be different at different pressures. Manipulation is a good way to deal with uncontrolled variables. It not only gives us control, but also shows limitations on when the functional relationship holds.

SUMMARY

1. The major purposes of the design of research studies is to identify a correct hypothesis and render alternative hypotheses implausible. Experimental design does this most completely, but, for various reasons, many research studies are done with preexperimental designs that achieve this goal only partially.
2. With the *testimonial* someone communicates about the impact a certain treatment had on her or him. Testimonials provide *easy access* to data and can be a good *source of hypotheses* for more systematic studies to be done subsequently. At times the testimonial may be *all that is available.* However, testimonials tend to suffer *sampling bias,* since testifiers are usually selected nonrandomly, measurements are usually *retrospective verbal reports,* and *control procedures* are usually lacking.

3. *Case studies* involve reporting of the responses of a treated person, usually by the person doing the treating. Though there are strong feelings for and against them, no simple statement about them can be made because there are so *many types of case study.* They must be evaluated on several of their features, including the *adequacy of baseline data* and *follow-up,* and the presence of attempts to assess *generality* (for example, by reporting multiple cases). Case studies inevitably suffer a serious *lack of control procedures.*

Case studies have the advantages of providing *readily available* data; providing data from *real life;* and permitting collection of data on the influence of *highly complex,* maybe even *unique sets of variables.* Major disadvantages are that *measurement* is usually poor, *baselines* are often not well measured, *control* is poor, and *generality* not well established.

4. With the *one-group pretest-posttest design,* baseline measures are taken, treatment introduced, and changes from baseline observed. Observed changes are attributed to the treatment. This design fails to permit us to dismiss the rival hypothesis that *changes might have occurred even without the treatment.* This type of design is nevertheless used, since it may be *ethically questionable to have a control group,* and the researcher may want to find out whether the changes occur under less controlled conditions *before investing heavy efforts into running the controls.*

5. With the *static-group comparison,* naturally formed groups that differ with respect to the treatment condition are compared. The flaw in this kind of design is that *groups are formed nonrandomly,* and observed differences might be related to variables other than the one under study.

6. With *correlational designs* the researcher typically has a primary intention of *measuring the relationship between two variables,* including the *magnitude* of the relationship. However, the intention is *not to identify the controlling variables.* This may be an excellent method during the *early stages* of investigation, and even in the later stages such research is useful in *establishing the reliability and validity of measures,* and in studying phenomena that occur in nature but are *difficult or impossible to manipulate.*

In general, it is *very difficult to infer causality from correlations.* However, many factors influence the reasonableness of a decision to accept a causal hypothesis. The two major classes of factor are the various *payoffs* and *costs* for making wrong or right judgments about causality and the extent to which evidence can be amassed to *dismiss alternative hypotheses* to the causal one. If no correlation exists between variables, a strong inference can be made against the causal hypothesis.

7. The designs discussed so far tend to deal with confounded vari-

ables by allowing them to vary. This is useful, but it limits our ability to identify controlling variables. To identify controlling variables we have to introduce controls. There are *various ways of controlling for extraneous variables.* This may be done either *deliberately,* through our technology, or *statistically,* by letting chance work for us. Another approach to control is *systematic manipulation* of the potentially confounding variable.

CHAPTER 6

Experimental Designs

CHAPTER 6

Experimental Designs

Purpose of Experimental Design

The major purpose of research design is to reveal relationships between variables. If we know relationships between variables, we can improve our prediction of future events, simply by taking into account our knowledge of the levels of the independent variable. If obesity is related to high blood pressure, our ability to predict whether a given set of people will have high blood pressure is improved.

But it is not enough to be able to predict future events; we want to control them. The first step in controlling outcome variables is to know which variables exert control over them. (Will losing weight lower blood pressure?) Then we have to find out how to manipulate those controlling variables. The main virtue of experimental methods is that they provide clear information about controlling variables. No other methods have comparable ability to allow rejection of alternative hypotheses and permit us to conclude what the controlling variable is in the situation under study. Thus the primary purpose in introducing experimental methods is to gain knowledge of controlling variables.

It is not easy to design studies that will result in findings that permit exclusion of all alternative hypotheses. Identifying all the potentially confounding variables is a painful process that can be dealt with in two ways. One is to "fly by the seat of our pants" and put together a design that is perhaps unique to a given study. This approach has been a common one for those whose method is called the experimental analysis of behavior. I will discuss this approach in Chapter 11.

A second option is to take advantage of certain "canned" experimental designs. These help assure us that we have not left any inadvertent gaps—that is, missing controls—in the research study. Experimental designs also help us inform other people about what we did. It is much easier to label our design by a standard nomenclature than to describe it piece by piece. A third useful feature of standard experimental designs is that there are standard methods of statistical analysis worked out for them. Thus we do not have to be terribly imaginative, nor do we have to be particularly mathematically inclined in order to analyze the data successfully. Standard statistical procedures can be used.

Experimental design tells us how to *assign treatments to subjects* so that we can draw clear conclusions about whether the independent variables under study predict and control the levels of the outcome variables. Notice that the method of assigning treatments to subjects differs from the method of getting the subjects in the first place. The latter is sampling. With sampling we select, say, 40 college sophomores to participate in our experiment. Now that we have the 40 sophomores, how shall we assign the various levels of the factor or factors under study? That is a matter of experimental design.

Classification of Experimental Designs

Methodologists classify experimental designs in a variety of ways. These different systems of categorization depend on such variables as what the methodologist thinks is logically sound, which dimensions of design she or he regards as most important, what can be communicated most easily, and so on. Some major dimensions along which experimental designs vary are the following:

1. How are treatments assigned to subjects? For example, are treatments assigned randomly or according to some deliberately planned pattern?

2. How many factors (independent variables) are there? Some experiments have only one factor, but most contemporary ones have many factors.

3. How many levels of the factor(s) are there? The relevant variation here is whether there are two or more than two levels. This is relevant because the method of statistical analysis varies markedly depending on whether there are more than two levels.

4. Were factors manipulated directly or by selecting subjects of certain classifications? For example, if one factor in a study is sex of subjects, this cannot be manipulated directly (even sex-change operations wouldn't quite do). The interpretation of data based on such *subject* or *organismic variables* is complicated because many other factors vary along with the factor on which they were selected. The strikingly different upbringing of men and women is a case in point. Any differences due to "sex" of subjects might be attributable to any one of many different factors that cluster around "sex." Fortunately, although the interpretation of data based on subject variables is complicated, the method of analysis is unchanged (Campbell & Stanley, 1963).

5. Were all levels of the factors represented, or was there just a random selection from the population of levels? To use sex as an example again, we can readily represent all levels in a study (women, men, and, technically, "other"). But if we were studying, say, "techniques of relaxation," we might have to select only a few from the wide array of available ones.

When all the levels of the factors are represented in our experiment, we are working with *fixed factors*. as opposed to a random selection of levels *(random factors)*.

The scope of this book does not permit a complete account of all the possible combinations of these "dimensions" of experimental design. I will emphasize the first three. Since the analysis of data will not be influenced by introduction of organismic variables, it will be enough to admonish against interpreting results as though the variables were manipulated ones. With respect to the issue of fixed versus random factors, I will assume that we are dealing with fixed factors, as psychologists most often are. The presence of a random factor *does* make a difference in analysis of the data. The reader is referred to higher level texts for more details (see, for example, Keppel, 1973).

Major Classes of Experimental Designs

Completely Randomized Designs with Two Groups

A completely randomized design has two characteristics. Each treatment (experimental or control) is given independently to a different group of subjects. Subjects are drawn independently and are assigned randomly to experimental and control conditions.

What is meant by "subjects are drawn independently"? In some types of design, assignment of a given subject to one of the conditions *determines* that another particular subject (for example, a twin) be assigned to the opposite condition. In the completely, randomized design, placing a given subject in one condition of the experiment has *no influence* on the placement of any of the other subjects. Figure 6.1 illustrates this type of design. Let's consider an example.

Suppose you wonder whether people can learn to see the world correctly when they have distorting prisms placed over their eyes. Experimenters have been curious about this kind of question for a long time. Originally they thought it might tell us why we see the world upright despite the fact that the image on the retina is upside down. You might also want to know the conditions under which relearning occurs. There is evidence that it makes a difference whether subjects are active or passive (see, for example, Held, 1965). So suppose you decide to compare the effects of active or passive movement on adaptation to distorting prisms.

All subjects could be placed in a visual environment with distorting prisms over their eyes. One group could be composed of subjects allowed to move around on their own initiative. The other group could be moved about passively in a wheelchair. Some measure of adaptation to the prism-induced distortion could be taken. The experimental and control group adaptation-performances could then be compared.

There may be some advantage in going over this type of experiment in some detail, step by step. First, you obtain a group of subjects by one of the various means available to experimenters. Typically they draft students enrolled in introductory psychology courses, hire subjects through an advertisement, or something of this sort. Theoretical problems of finding subjects have to do with *sampling procedures,* and I have said that these are distinct from experimental design.

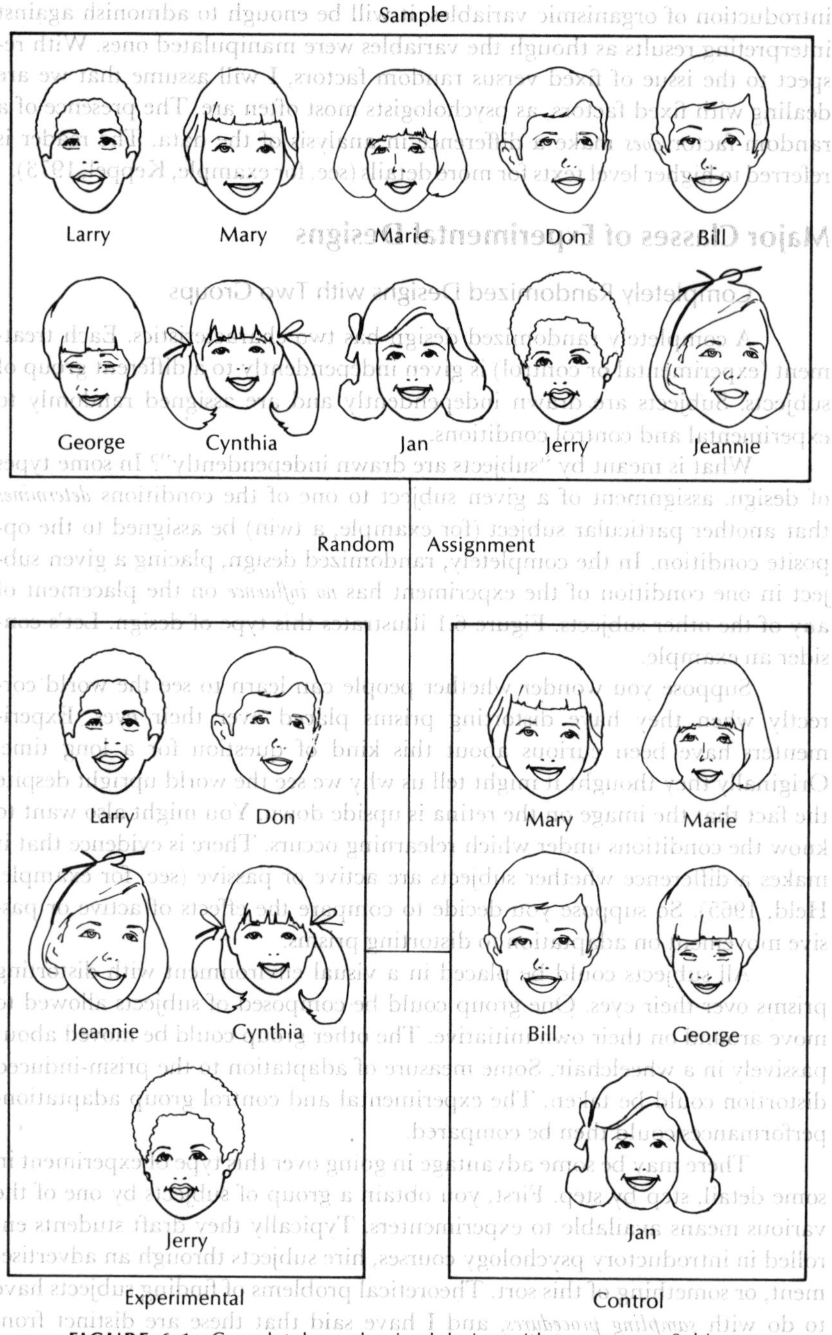

FIGURE 6.1 Completely randomized design with two groups. Subjects are randomly assigned to conditions.

You must decide whether a given subject will be assigned to the active condition or to the passive wheelchair condition. There are a number of ways you can do this. Haphazard methods tend, inadvertently, to produce systematic patterns. One effective way would be to compile a list of the subjects' names, placed in any order at all, and to assign subjects to conditions by way of random numbers.

Randomizing by Way of a Table of Random Numbers

The best way to randomize subjects, treatments, or what-have-you is to use a table of random numbers. You will find one in the Appendix, Table A. Start with a list of the subjects in any order. Assign each subject a random number by entering the table at a haphazard starting place, and taking the numbers in order after that. You must make up a rule for deciding which numbers belong in which group. You might say that even-numbered subjects go in the experimental group and odd-numbered subjects go in the control group. Any other property of the numbers that would give you a two-way split would be all right.

Experimenters use tables of random numbers often. The tables are useful with types of experimental design other than those using independent subjects. You should get used to working with such tables.

The following is a list of imaginary subjects. Next to each subject is a random number I found by entering the table in a haphazard way and moving straight down the column thereafter.

Cynthia	3	Experimental
George	8	Control
Larry	9	Experimental
Mary	2	Control
Jerry	1	Experimental
Don	5	Experimental
Jeannie	7	Experimental
Jan	2	Control thereafter
Marie	7	
Bill	3	

The third column shows the subject's assigned group. Notice that after five subjects had been assigned to the experimental group by chance, the rest had to go in the control group. This constraint was imposed by the wish to put equal numbers of subjects in each group. The process was random with that constraint. We could tolerate unequal numbers of subjects in each group, but it would make the analysis all the more difficult. Also, with small samples, serious inequalities might occur. One of the groups might be too skimpy to provide a good estimate of the real effect for that condition.

The design ends up looking as follows (see Figure 6.1):

Experimental Group	Control Group
Cynthia	George
Larry	Mary
Jerry	Jan
Don	Marie
Jeannie	Bill

Purpose of Randomization

Experiments are designed to detect effects of the independent variables and to detect only those effects. It might seem that the best way to control for other variables would be to identify them and eliminate their effects. But to identify all variables that might conceivably influence an experimental outcome would not be easy. By randomizing, we arrange an experiment so that extraneous factors tend to be equally represented in experimental and control groups. Coin tossing will tend in the long run to yield equal numbers of heads and tails. Random assignment to conditions in an experiment will tend to produce equal representation of variables requiring control.

Analyzing Data from a Completely Randomized Design with Two Groups

A specific kind of experimental design calls for a particular method of statistical analysis. Rationales for certain major statistical tests are given in Chapters 9 and 10. Here, I will tell which types of analysis are appropriate for each type of design. Simple descriptions of how to compute the statistics are in Appendixes E, F, and G. None of this is a substitute for a good statistics course.

Various methods of analysis could be used with this kind of design. Most often you would use a *t* test for independent subjects (Appendix E1). If possible, you *should* use the *t* because it is the uniformly most powerful test. This means that it is the most sensitive instrument for detecting real effects.

Certain assumptions were made in devising the *t* test. The variances of the experimental and control groups were assumed to be equal. This means that variability due to error is the same whether the independent variable is present or not. The data were also assumed to come from a population having a normal (Gaussian) distribution.[1] Recent studies have indicated that the *t* test remains accurate despite sizable violations of these assumptions. It can be used unless the violations of assumptions are fairly large.

There is a test almost as powerful as the *t* test that is not based on these assumptions. And it is very easy to compute. It is called the *Mann-*

[1] A normal distribution, also called Gaussian after Gauss, who discovered it, is bell shaped and symmetrical about its mean. It is discussed further in Chapter 9.

Whitney U *test* (see Sheridan, 1976, or Siegel, 1956).

Incidentally, statistical tables are sometimes based on one-tailed and at other times on two-tailed probabilities. A one-tailed alpha merely takes into account one possible direction of difference between the treatment conditions (either greater or less but not both). Two-tailed probabilities take into account both possibilities. You will rarely want other than the two-tailed figure, since readers tend to be suspicious of the more lenient one-tailed test even when it is logically justified. In general, two-tailed values can be obtained from a one-tailed table simply by doubling the associated alpha level. For example, a one-tailed p of 0.01 yields a two-tailed p of 0.02.

The appropriateness of a statistical test depends on the type of measurement of the dependent variable. With the t test we assume that the data are measured on at least an interval scale.

Completely Randomized Designs with More Than Two Groups

So far the discussion has centered on experiments with only two groups of subjects, an experimental and a control group. The completely randomized design can also be used for a greater number of groups. In fact, it can have n groups of subjects. For example, students could be independently and randomly assigned to three procedures for teaching introductory psychology. One group could receive a standard lecture course. A second group might get an opportunity to learn the same material with a teaching machine. A third group might be given a regular text, but simply study it at home. The assignment of subjects to conditions is essentially the same whether two or n groups are used.

Randomization with Three Groups

Again, let's illustrate the assignment procedure with imaginary subjects. We will start with 15 subjects and require that there be 5 subjects in each group. This time we cannot use oddness or evenness of numbers as a basis for assignment. We need to divide the numbers into three equally likely categories. I chose to use the numbers 1 through 9 in the table of random numbers. The numbers 1, 2, and 3 represented assignment to the lecture method. The numbers 4, 5, and 6 indicated assignment to the teaching machine method. The rest of the subjects would then have to get the home study method.

First, we arrange a list of the subjects. I used the following list:

Cynthia	Don	Ruth
George	Jeannie	Donna
Larry	Jan	Lilly
Mary	Marie	Sam
Jerry	Mike	Gordon

This list is not randomly arranged. It is in the order in which the names came to my mind. People cannot generate random processes unaided. Going into the table of random numbers I got: 5, 0, 9, 5, 7, 8, 9, 0, 7, 7, 8, 3, 4, 5, 8, 8, 1, 9, 5, 9, 1, 5, 2, 2.

The first number is a 5, so the first subject, Cynthia, goes in the Machine group. The second number is zero. It is not from 1–9, so ignore it. The next number is 9, so the second subject on the list goes into the Home Study group. I continued this process until, at the ninth random digit, all the Home Study slots had been assigned. After that I ignored, besides 0, the numbers 7, 8, and 9. By the digit third from the end, all the Machine slots were assigned. The remaining subjects were assigned to the Lecture method.

To be sure you understand how to do this, it would be good practice to finish up the assignment of the listed subjects and arrange them under the headings: "Lecture," "Machine," and "Home Study."

Analysis of the Completely Randomized Design with More Than Two Groups

The most common statistical method for analyzing data from completely randomized designs with more than two groups is the simple, one-way analysis of variance. This is based on the *F* statistic.

The analysis of variance assumes that data are on an interval scale. It also assumes they are selected from a Gaussian distribution of measures. Finally, it assumes that the variances of the different groups are equal. However, here as with the *t* test, studies indicate that the statistic works well despite sizable deviations from the assumptions, provided sample sizes in the different groups are equal (see Keppel, 1973).

If data are only on an ordinal scale or if you are concerned about extreme deviations from assumptions, a Kruskall-Wallis one-way analysis of variance is appropriate. For data on a nominal scale (frequencies), a chi-square test for *k* independent samples will do. These two analyses are explained very clearly and simply in Siegel (1956).

Designs with Matched Subjects and Two Groups

We assess reliability by looking at a ratio of

$$\frac{\text{signal} + \text{noise}}{\text{noise}}$$

If this ratio is near one, we assume that there is just

$$\frac{\text{noise}}{\text{noise}}$$

If it is sufficiently greater than unity, we decide there is a signal. If there is a signal, this means the independent variable had an effect, and if it had an effect it will have one in the future as well, all else being equal.

Anything we do to reduce the bottom part of the ratio makes us better able to detect effects. Technically we would say that decreases in the estimate of error increase the power of our design or test. In practice, a major source of noise is the tendency for individual subjects to differ from each other. We have very different backgrounds; we come from very different genetic pools. Some people have stomachs many times the size of other people's stomachs. This is bound to influence their eating behavior. Some people get agitated when given drugs that sedate most of us. The many such individual differences are likely to inflate the noise factor.

Designs with matched subjects are used in an attempt to reduce the influence of individual differences. Subjects are not assigned to groups randomly. They are matched on some factor that is positively correlated with the dependent variable. Figure 6.2 illustrates this type of design.

As an example of the procedure of matching, suppose we are interested in the effects of caffeine on memory. We might match our subjects prior to the experiment according to their grade-point average (GPA). Our assumption would be that GPA and memory are positively correlated. We would then give one member of each matched pair the experimental treatment and the other the control treatment. An experimenter interested in the effects of marijuana on chess playing might be fortunate enough to get sets of identical twins closely matched in chess-playing performance. One twin could be given the measured dose of marijuana, while the other received

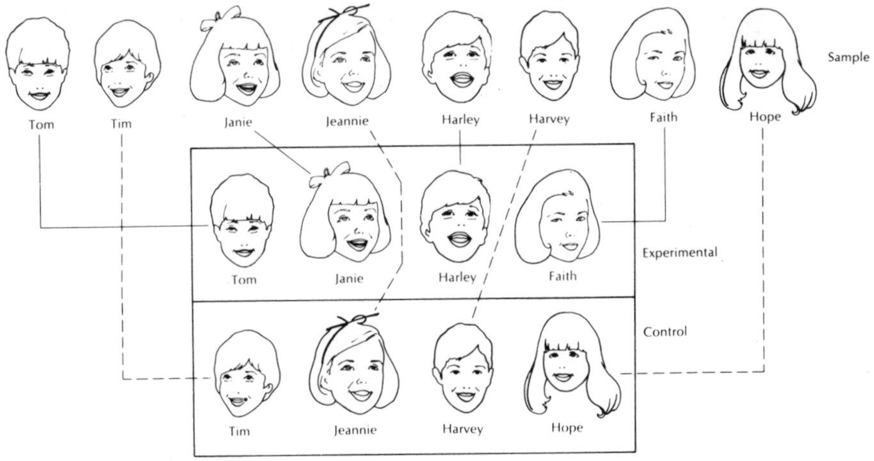

FIGURE 5.2 Matched subjects design with two groups. One each from matched pair is assigned to experimental and control groups.

some sort of placebo. A third common example of matching is the use of littermate controls in animal experiments. For example, Held and Hein (1963) were interested in measuring the effects of active versus passive rearing on later visuomotor performance. Pairs of kitten littermates were selected; one of each pair was randomly assigned to the active condition and the other to the passive.

Notice that randomization is used even with this type of design. Assignment to the experimental or the control treatment is random, with the constraint that no more than one of each matched pair can be in a given treatment condition.

Setting Up a Design with Two Groups of Matched Subjects

Suppose we set out to conduct the experiment on the effects of marijuana on chess playing. We obtain a group of identical twins with each pair evenly matched for ability in chess. They are:

Tim	Tom
Janie	Jeannie
Harvey	Harley
Faith	Hope

For each pair, we want one of them assigned to the experimental group, which receives a measured dose of marijuana just before playing. The other goes into a control condition with a placebo. First, let's decide on a rule for deciding which of each pair gets the marijuana. Let's say that we will select four random numbers. If the number is even, the subject listed first gets the experimental treatment. If it is odd, the subject listed second gets the treatment.

Entering the table of random numbers, I got 5, 6, 3, 6. Five is odd, so Tom gets the treatment. Six is even, so Janie gets the treatment. By the same rule, Harley and Faith get the treatment (see Figure 6.2).

Disadvantages of Using Designs with Matched Subjects

For matching to be of help, it is essential that the variable used as a basis for matching actually be predictive of levels of the dependent variable. In fact, the degree of predictability should be fairly high. Further, the relationship between levels of the matching variable and levels of the dependent variable must be a positive one. (that is, both go up together and both go down together). If the relationship is an inverse one, the result will be an inflation of the noise level, instead of a reduction.

A second problem is that the matching of subjects may require a high degree of selection of subjects. For example, suppose matching were done by using identical twins, identical twins might not be representative of the average person. Even without using identical twins, many subjects might have to be left out of the study because they lacked another subject that matched.

Analysis of Designs with Matched Subjects and Two Groups

The statistic used most often for designs with two groups of matched subjects is the t test for correlated means (see Appendix E2). This test is much like the t test already discussed, except that it corrects the estimate of error for the reduction of noise due to matching.

For ordinal data a simple, but not very sensitive, test is the *Sign Test.* An alternative to the t test for correlated means that is more sensitive than the Sign Test is the *Wilcoxon Matched-Pairs Signed Ranks Test.* It is designed to be used with ordinal data, since it is based on the rank ordering of scores. The method of computing both of these alternatives to the t test may be found in Siegel (1956).

Designs with Matched Subjects and More Than Two Groups

Randomized Blocks Design

We can use the matching principle on any number of groups. The *randomized blocks design* illustrates this. It is also called a "treatments by levels" or "stratified" design. Subjects are categorized prior to the experiment on some measure that is positively correlated with the dependent variable. They are then arranged in two or more blocks. Similarity of subjects within blocks is thus greater than similarity of subjects between blocks.

Suppose you are interested in the ability of people to control their heart rate voluntarily. You decide to manipulate the type of feedback they get while trying to learn such control. You have a control group, a group receiving points on a counter for correct control (this is simple biofeedback), a group receiving 1¢ per beat for correct control, and a group receiving 5¢ per beat.

Let's say you have read Luria's *Mind of a Mnemonist* (Luria, 1968). In this book Luria describes his many years of studying a man with seemingly flawless photographic memory, who could control his heart rate markedly by picturing himself running down a street. Exceptional visual imagery seems positively related to voluntary control of heart rate. Variations in the ability to make visual images might well be an important source of variance in your study.

You could use a completely randomized design, but the variable of "imagery" would contribute to your estimate of noise. Why not measure ability to make visual images prior to the experiment, and then put subjects into three blocks with high, medium, and low imagery?

The impact of this blocking procedure will be to permit the removal of the variability due to "imagery" from the "noise" component of the statistic (F ratio) used to evaluate the results. Thus the design will be more likely to detect real influences of the variable under study. However, we gain sensitivity only if there is a noteworthy positive relationship between the blocking variable and the dependent variable. As a rule of thumb, this correlation should probably be at least +.2 (Feldt, 1958).

Analyzing Data from the Randomized Blocks Design

Analysis of variance is used to analyze data from the randomized blocks design. The type of analysis of variance (Appendix F2) is more sensitive than that used for the completely randomized design. The reason is that variability due to individual differences is reduced since the "noise" level is estimated from the relatively homogeneous blocks. The variability due to error is also reduced by isolating any variability due to interactions between treatments and levels of the blocking variable. Although this point is probably not clear now, it should become so later when we discuss the concept of interaction.

Designs with Repeated Measures on the Same Subjects

Matching one subject with another can never be perfect, although it can be very good in some cases. The most thoroughgoing extension of matching procedures can be realized by giving the same subject more than one treatment. In such cases, repeated measures are taken on the same subjects. It would be difficult to imagine a more satisfactory "matching" procedure, since subjects are certainly more similar to themselves than to any other subject, even an identical twin.

Just as in the case of the matched-subjects design, the goal of a same-subject design is to reduce error variance ("noise") by reducing intersubject variability. If variability between subjects can be reduced, the noise level of the experiment will be lowered. Thus the effects of a given independent variable will be more readily identified. The same-subject design is very powerful. A further advantage of this sort of design is that it permits observation of data from individual organisms.

Designs with Repeated Measures and Two Treatment Conditions

Each subject can get both the experimental and the control treatment (see Figure 6.3). The design is otherwise like a design with matched subjects. But care must be taken to deal with effects of order. We will postpone discussing the problem of such effects until after we have dealt with designs having repeated measures on more than one group.

The t test for correlated means (Appendix E2) is appropriate for data from this type of design, as are the other tests for designs with matched subjects.

Designs with Repeated Measures and More Than Two Treatment Conditions

If more than two treatment conditions are used with repeated measures on the same subjects, the design is usually called a *treatments-by-subjects design.*

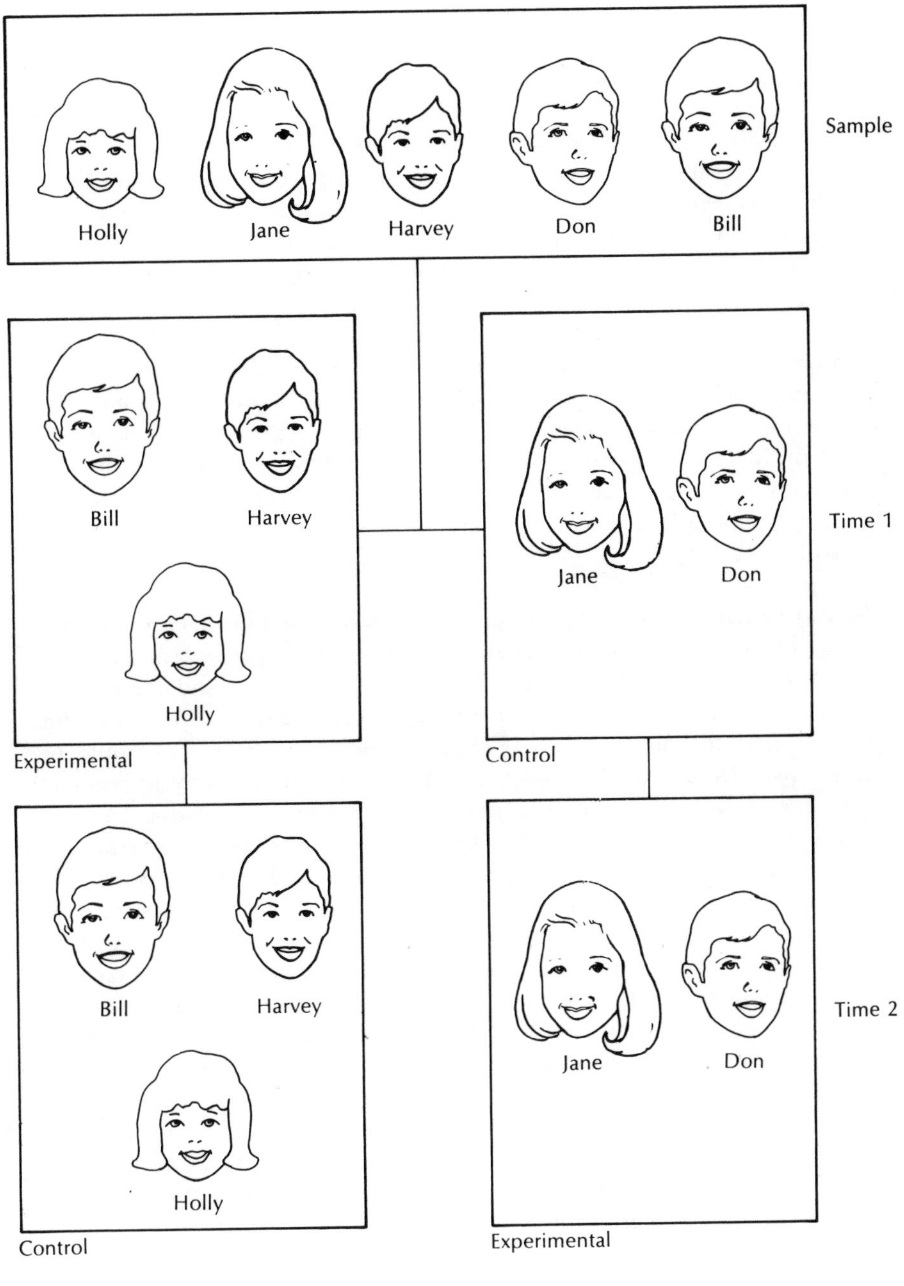

FIGURE 6.3 Design with repeated measures. The same subjects receive all treatments, but in different order.

The analysis of variance for treatments by subjects designs is explained in Appendix F3.

Methods of Dealing with Effects of Order

Order-effects must be dealt with when repeated measures are taken on the same subjects. Suppose you wanted to compare the effects on hand steadiness of large doses of alcohol with the effects of equally large doses of milk. You have a device permitting accurate measurement of hand steadiness. You might give the alcohol on Day 1 and then measure hand steadiness; and you might give the milk on Day 2 with the hand-steadiness measure repeated again. If alcohol and milk were administered in that order, the result might be that milk impairs hand steadiness more than alcohol. But the really important disrupter of hand steadiness might well be a hangover from the alcohol. The order of presentation of the two treatments, milk and alcohol, is likely to make a great difference in the experimental outcome. If milk were presented first we would hardly expect it to impair hand steadiness.

Randomization There are various control techniques for determining the effects of the order of presenting treatments. For example, we can *randomize* order of presentation. In the alcohol versus milk example, randomization of order of presentation would mean that the experimenter would decide for each subject by some random process whether milk or alcohol would be given first. Randomization means that treatments are as likely to occur in one order as in another. It also means that presenting a treatment in one position for a given subject (say, milk first) has no influence on whether the same treatment occurs in any other position (say, milk second) for another subject. This means that the experimenter does not follow a "balancing" rule that milk must be given first a certain proportion of the time. We assume that a truly random process will lead in the long run to a fairly even balance of the various orders of presentation. Randomization thus has the disadvantage that imbalances in order of presentation might occur simply on a chance basis. This is so especially if the number of treatment presentations is small. Randomization will even things out in the *long run,* but only if the experiment is very extensive. It is even possible that a purely random procedure will lead to a situation in which a given experimental treatment always comes first, just as it is possible for someone to draw four aces in a row from a deck of cards without cheating.

Counterbalancing In order to avoid such imbalances, *counterbalancing* is often used instead of randomization. Counterbalancing means that the experimenter makes sure that the various possible presentation orders occur equally often. With two treatments, an experimental and a control treatment, the design would be counterbalanced if the experimenter required that the experimental treatment come first on half of the occasions and that the control condition occur first on the other half. By counterbalancing, any effect of either treatment's coming first will be present equally in the experimental and control conditions. By looking at the results when a treatment comes first and comparing it to the results when the same treatment comes second, effects of order can be seen.

Procedures like randomization and counterbalancing permit us to *assess* the effects of order in an experiment. They do not *eliminate* such effects. Suppose you find that order of presentation has an important influence on the outcome of your experiment. It may be worth your while to learn how to manipulate those effects directly through experimental techniques. Ideally, you should learn how to *reverse* the effect of whatever treatments are presented early in the experiment. Reversal of the effect would permit returning the experimental subject to the original baseline before presenting any subsequent treatment. If the subject has been truly returned to baseline, order-of-presentation effects will indeed have been eliminated. However, we often do not have a technique at our disposal for returning a subject to baseline. Some treatment effects are irreversible, or virtually so.

Equivalent Tests Since we cannot always return an experimental subject to the original state, experimenters must rely on approximations to the ideal. For example, an experiment sometimes requires that tests, such as IQ tests, be given twice to the same subject, before and after a treatment. Since a previous single test may influence the score when the subject takes it the second time, there is great danger of an order effect. Psychologists have no practical way of erasing a subject's memory of a previous test. But they can offset its effect by using a device known as an *equivalent form* of the test. A large test is devised and then half of the items are selected randomly for deletion. Those taken out can be expected to be equivalent to those remaining. This is because the deleted items were selected randomly without bias. In this way two equivalent tests are available. A subject can be given one form before the experimental treatment and the other after the treatment. Strictly speaking, the subject is not brought back to baseline. For example, there might be some similar features in the two equivalent forms. But the result is a good approximation to the ideal of returning the subject to baseline.

Running subjects to asymptote Sometimes subjects will show progressive changes in behavior only up to a certain point. They eventually level off. For example, you generally can only go so far in improving accuracy of basketball shots. Then you stabilize at a certain level of accuracy. Sometimes the progressive growth in performance can show up as an order effect. But if subjects are first trained until little or no further progress occurs, then the order-effect is eliminated.

Providing Rest Intervals Many variables have effects that go away by themselves over time. Fatigue is like that. So are the effects of many drugs. By spacing out the various treatments appropriately, we can eliminate the effects. In a repeated-measures design, this can mean the elimination of an order-effect. It would prevent confounding in the study of the effects of alcohol versus milk mentioned earlier.

The Use of Stimulus Control Effects of order can often be minimized by bringing behaviors under stimulus control. A subject may be placed on a *multiple schedule of reinforcement.* Let us say we wish to compare a rat's bar-press behavior under continuous reinforcement (a reinforcement for every bar press) with its behavior under extinction (no response reinforced). The nonreinforced periods might have their effect on behavior during the reinforced periods, and vice versa. But a specific stimulus can be associated with each of the two states of reinforcement. "Light on" might indicate continuous reinforcement, and "light off" might indicate extinction. In time the behaviors typical of continuous reinforcement and extinction will tend to occur only in the presence of their appropriate stimuli. The behavior is then said to be under stimulus control. When there is more than one schedule of reinforcement and more than one stimulus, the procedure is called a multiple schedule of reinforcement. Schedules of reinforcement are discussed in more detail later.

The Use of Stable Baselines Another method is to develop baseline behaviors that resist order effects. Guttman and Kalish (1956) used this technique in their experiments on stimulus generalization. First organisms were trained to respond in the presence of a given stimulus. Guttman and Kalish wanted to measure response rates in the presence of that stimulus and several other more or less similar stimuli. They wanted to do this in the absence of reinforcement. Since the behavior tends to deteriorate in the absence of reinforcement, stimuli presented late in the series would likely be associated with lower response rates. Guttman and Kalish coped with this order effect by using a schedule of reinforcement that is known to result in behavior that disrupts very little in the absence of reinforcement (a variable interval schedule). Thus, by using a baseline behavior that resisted disruption, order effects were minimized.

The Use of Probes Our last example will be that of *probing.* This technique resembles the spot-checking procedures most of us have used from time to time. In this instance, behavior is maintained by some stable technique, and the behavior of interest is sampled only periodically. For example, a sensitive baseline behavior might be brought under stimulus control and the controlling stimulus introduced only periodically. It is essentially a probing technique when sleep researchers awaken individuals periodically during the night and ask them whether they were dreaming. The ongoing silence supports sleep but does not allow access to verbal reports of dreaming. Waking and asking is a stimulus that probes the state of this sleeping behavior by eliciting verbal reports.

Multifactor Designs

In discussing the various things you can do about uncontrolled variables, I mentioned that a good thing is to *manipulate* them. Students measuring the two-point threshold in their experimental psychology laboratory often worry over the effects of pressure. Some of them choose to manipulate pressure. They still work with the original independent variable (distance between the two points of the stimulus). Thus, they have more than one independent variable in a single experiment. This is called a *multifactor* design. Factorial designs are one kind of multifactor design.

A factorial design can be illustrated as follows:

Loading on Apparatus	Distance between the Two Points (Millimeters) 2 4 6 8 10 12 14 16
5	
10	
15	
20	
25	

Notice that with this design every level of the first factor is paired with every level of the second factor. Five grams is presented with each and every distance between the points. So is 10 grams, and so is every other level of pressure. Furthermore, the 2 mm distance is tried at each and every level of pressure. So is the 4 mm distance, the 6 mm distance, and so on. When all the possible pairings are used in an experiment, it is said to be *completely crossed. A factorial design has more than one independent variable and it is completely crossed.* Factorial designs permit us to study the effects of *limiting conditions.*

Functional relationships inevitably have *limiting conditions.* This means that a given functional relationship will only hold when certain other variables are within specific limits. For example, room temperature must be within certain limits if most behavioral functional relationships are to hold. If the temperature is low or high enough, the organism's behavior will be disrupted, and at certain extremes it will even die.

Normally, we simply take it for granted that there are limiting conditions on our functional relationships. But the fact that there are such limiting conditions implies that variables do not function in isolation but act together to produce an effect. If this is so, there might be some value in seeing how they interact, by manipulating more than one independent variable at a time. By determining whether and to what extent such *interactions* occur, an experimenter gets a good estimate of robustness or generality of observed functional relationships.

Suppose we are interested in testing the effectiveness of a given experimental method for producing neurosis in animals. We will naturally run subjects with the experimental treatment and control subjects without the treatment or with some placebo treatment. In assessing the reliability of our results, we will replicate, perhaps by using several subjects under each of the conditions of the experiment. Now the question is whether we should replicate under the same conditions for all subjects. That would certainly seem to fit customary scientific procedures.

An experimenter choosing this strategy would keep the treatments as similar as possible across subjects. But suppose we think that the relationship between experimenter and experimental subjects helps to determine whether experimental neurosis will occur? There actually *is* evidence that techniques that normally produce neurotic behavior in animals may fail to produce the neurotic patterns when an experimenter has been very friendly with the animal. It may be that the relationship of experimenter and subject is a limiting condition on the functional relationship.

Why not do some of the replications with a neutral experimenter and some with a friendly one? This would be a factorial design.

In outline form, the experimental design would look like Figure 6.4. It would be called a 2 × 2 factorial design. This indicates that there are two independent variables *(factors)* and two levels of each of the factors. If we add a condition in which there is a hostile experimenter, it becomes a 2 × 3 factorial design. There are still two factors, but now there are two levels of one factor and three levels of the other. The magnitude of the numbers indicates the number of levels of the factors.

We indicate how many factors there are by having more numbers. For example, adding a drug versus saline treatment as a third independent variable makes the design a 2 × 2 × 2 factorial design. (This assumes that we are leaving out the "hostile experimenter" level of one factor. Including it would give us a 2 × 2 × 3 factorial design.)

When an interaction occurs, this means that the effect of one variable differs as a function of the level of another variable. A good example of interaction came from an experience of mine. When radial steel-belted tires first came to my attention, I went out and bought the best I could find. The promised superior handling properties and wear seemed to make it a worthwhile expenditure. Later, I read in a newspaper article that radial steel-belted tires wear better than regular tires only provided wheels are kept in good alignment; they do not hold up at all well when wheels are out of alignment. Unfortunately, I rarely take care of my car, and the wheels are often out of alignment. Thus, radial steel-belted tires were a poor investment for me.

	Neurosis Treatment	Placebo Conditioning Treatment
Friendly Experimenter	A	B
Neutral Experimenter	C	D

FIGURE 6.4 A 2 × 2 factorial design. See text for explanation.

To state the case in terms of interaction, we would say that there is an interaction between wheel alignment and the performance of radial steel-belted tires. At one level of the alignment factor, the "out-of-alignment" level, the radial steel-belteds do poorly. At another level of the alignment factor, the "in-alignment" level, they do well.

Main Effects and Interactions

A major advantage of multifactor designs is that they permit us to differentiate between *main effects* and *interactions*. A main effect is an effect of one of the factors, ignoring levels of the other factors. In the previously given example of radial versus bias ply tires, an effect of radial versus bias tires without regard to the alignment of the wheels would be a main effect. For example, if radial tires were in general superior to bias ply despite the effects of alignment, this would be a main effect.

Interaction was explained in the previous section. It refers to a change in the effect of levels of one factor that depends on levels of another factor. So differences in the effectiveness of radial versus bias tires as a function of whether the wheels are in or out of alignment constitutes an interaction.

The usefulness of differentiating between main effects and interactions has to do with showing something of the range of conditions under which a given functional relationship holds—of indicating limitations on its generality.

Knowledge of interactions may also make it possible to see effects of variables that might otherwise be obscured. Suppose, for example, that you were studying methods of alleviating anxiety and happened to choose a method that lowered the anxiety of the highly anxious while increasing the anxiety of those with little anxiety. If your study pooled together people of high and low anxiety, you would conclude that the treatment did not work. This is because the therapeutic changes in the highly anxious subjects would tend to be canceled out by the undesirable changes in the less anxious subjects.

By doing the very same study while taking into account the initial

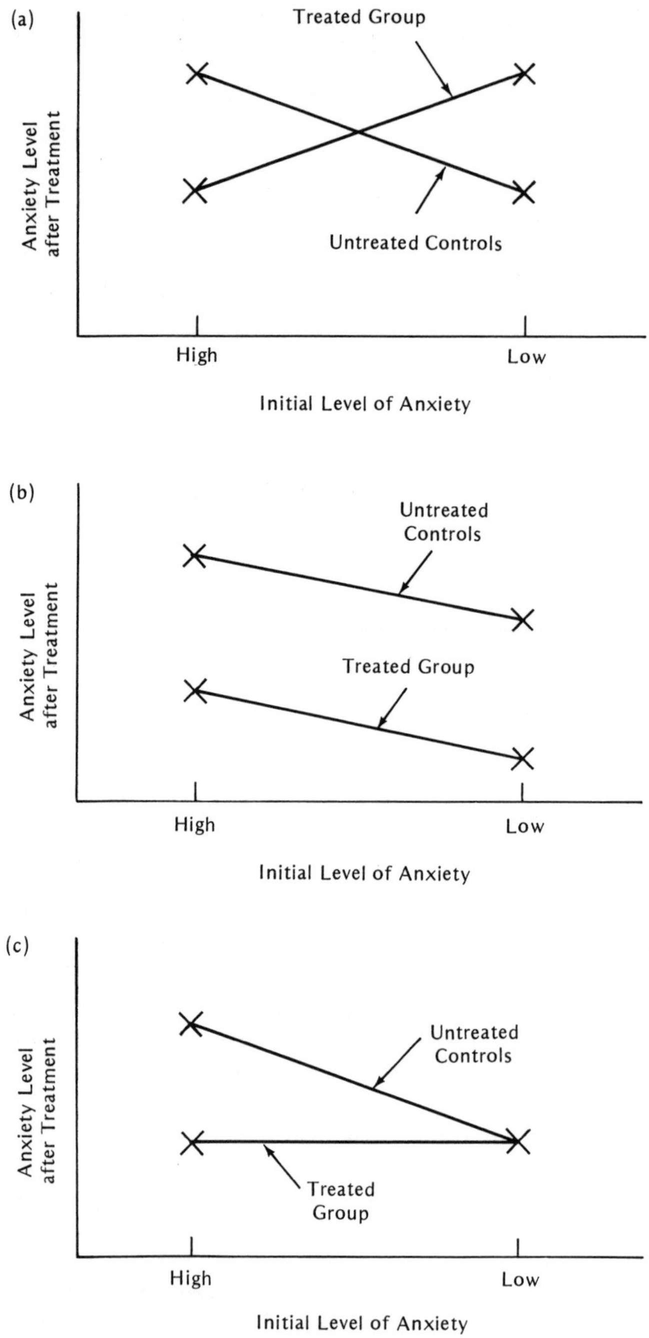

FIGURE 6.5 Graphic representation of main effect and interactions.

TABLE 6.1 Completely Randomized Factorial Design

Neurosis Treatment		*Placebo Treatment*	
Friendly Experimenter	*Neutral Experimenter*	*Friendly Experimenter*	*Neutral Experimenter*
Gordon	Blacky	King	Jennifer
Daisy	Mortimer	Pushkin	Bella
Sissy	Fido	Spot	Vic

level of anxiety and treating that level as an additional factor, you would conclude that there was no main effect of the treatment, but that there was an interaction. Analysis of the interaction would soon show that the treatment worked only for the highly anxious and had untoward effects on those low in anxiety.

Notice that the lack of a main effect need not mean that your findings are valueless. Certain interactive effects, like the one just described, tend to reduce main effects. Graphically, this interaction would be represented somewhat as shown in Figure 6.5(a). In general, nonparallel lines in this sort of graph indicate that an interaction is occurring.

Now let's examine Figure 6.5 (b). What is happening as a function of the factors? Regardless of initial anxiety level, the treatment is resulting in a decrease in anxiety. The lines are parallel. What we have in that case is a main effect, but no interaction. Ignoring levels of initial anxiety, the treatment is working, and that is a main effect. However, since the effect of the treatment does not differ as a function of the initial level of anxiety, there is no interaction.

Nonparallel lines indicate an interaction even if the lines do not cross each other. Suppose, for example, you found that the treatment helped those who were initially high in anxiety but had no effect on those who were ini-

TABLE 6.2 Completely Repeated Factorial Design

Neurosis Treatment		*Placebo Treatment*	
Friendly Experimenter	*Neutral Experimenter*	*Friendly Experimenter*	*Neutral Experimenter*
Gordon	Gordon	Gordon	Gordon
Daisy	Daisy	Daisy	Daisy
Sissy	Sissy	Sissy	Sissy

TABLE 6.3 Mixed Factorial Design

Neurosis Treatment		*Placebo Treatment*	
Friendly Experimenter	*Neutral Experimenter*	*Friendly Experimenter*	*Neutral Experimenter*
Gordon	Gordon	Blacky	Blacky
Daisy	Daisy	Mortimer	Mortimer
Sissy	Sissy	Fido	Fido

tially low in anxiety. The resulting graph would be like Figure 6.5 (c), which is nonparallel. Again, the effect of the treatment differs as a function of the "initial anxiety" factor, and that is an interaction.

TABLE 6.4 Summary of Experimental Designs

Name of Design	Method of Assigning Subjects	Number of Conditions
Completely Randomized (Independent Subjects)	Subjects assigned randomly to conditions. No Subject in more than one condition.	2-*n*
Matched Subjects Randomized Blocks	Matched subjects assigned to conditions. Assignment random within the constraint that they be matched.	2-*n*
Repeated Measures Single Subjects; Within Subjects; Treatments by Subjects	Same subjects given each treatment with order of presentation controlled.	2-*n*
Completely Randomized Factorial	More than one independent variable. All possible combinations of levels of the variables represented. Each subject randomly assigned to one combination.	4-*n*
Completely Repeated Factorial	More than one independent variable. All possible combinations of levels of the variables represented. All pairings of levels given to each subject.	4-*n*
Mixed Factorial	More than one independent variable. All possible combinations of levels of the variables represented. Completely randomized on some variables and repeated measures within subjects on others.	4-*n*

Some Types of Factorial Design

We have said that the number of levels of factors can be as large as the experimenter wishes. The number of factors can also be extended indefinitely. Limitations on how large these numbers can be are practical, not

	Typical Analyses	
Characteristics	Two Groups	More than Two Groups
High noise level due to the individual differences' inclusion in error of measurement. Needs larger number of subjects than less noisy designs.	*t* test for independent means; Mann-Whitney *U*	Analysis of variance; Kruskall-Wallis one-way analysis of variance.
Reduced noise due to matching on pre-measure. Pre-measure must be positively correlated with dependent variable.	*t* test for correlated means; Wilcoxon Matched Pairs Signed Rank test; Sign Test.	Analysis of variance; Friedman 2-way analysis of variance.
Reduced noise due to eradication of individual differences in error estimate. Must cope with effects of order of presentation, carry-over from one treatment to the other.	*t* test for correlated means; Wilcoxon Matched Pairs Signed Ranks test; Sign Test.	Analysis of variance; Friedman 2-way analysis of variance.
show variations in functional relationships of one variable when levels of another variable change (interactions), establish generality.	——	Analysis of variance.
show variations in functional relationships of one variable when levels of another variable change (interactions), establish generality.	——	Analysis of variance.
show variations in functional relationships of one variable when levels of another variable change (interactions), establish generality.	——	Analysis of variance.

theoretical. They have to do with the massiveness of the experiment and the difficulties an experimenter might have in comprehending the meaning of an extremely complex design.

The number of factors and the number of levels within factors are important in identifying a given factorial design. But these designs can also differ in another way. They may have repeated measures within subjects on one or more of the factors, or they may be completely randomized. Some factorial designs are *completely randomized.* Some are *completely repeated.* Others are *mixed,* with independent subjects on some factors and repeated measures on others.

Let's go back to the experiment on inducing neuroses in dogs. A completely randomized factorial design would resemble Table 6.1. Here all possible pairings of the two factors are included. There are two levels of the "friendliness" factor and two levels of the "neurosis treatment" factor. Thus there are four possible pairings. These are at the head of the table. Look at Gordon. He receives the neurosis treatment and a friendly experimenter. He does not receive any of the other possible pairings of levels. This is true of every dog in the experiment. Each receives one and only one pair of levels of the two factors.

Contrast this with the design shown in Table 6.2, which is completely repeated. Each subject receives every possible pairing of levels of the two factors.

A mixed factorial design might be as shown in Table 6.3. Consider Gordon again. This time he receives both levels of the "friendliness" factor. He gets both the friendly experimenter and the neutral experimenter. But he receives only one level of the "neurosis treatment" factor. He is not repeated on that factor.

Incidentally, we would say that with the completely repeated design, subjects are *completely crossed.* If you think of subjects as another factor, every level of it is paired with every level of the other factors. Also notice that far fewer subjects are needed for the completely repeated design. The number of subjects required in complex nonrepeated designs can become extremely large, even impracticably so. Despite the problems of dealing with effects of order, this provides strong motivation for experimenters to select at least partially repeated designs.

Analysis of Data from Factorial Designs

The method of analyzing data from factorial designs depends on such things as the number of factors and whether the design is completely randomized, completely repeated, or mixed. Computational procedures for such analyses are given in Appendix G. A more detailed computational handbook has been provided by Bruning and Kintz (1977). It contains "cookbook" accounts of analyses for various other statistics as well. For a deeper understanding of the methods, I suggest the handbook by Keppel (1973).

SUMMARY

1. The main purpose of experimental design is to reveal relationships between controlling independent variables and the levels of dependent variables.
2. Experimental design is defined as the method of assigning treatments to subjects.
3. Formalized designs are useful for (a) helping us identify the needed control conditions, (b) communicating what we did, and (c) providing standard designs with equally standard methods of analysis.
4. There are many properties according to which experimental designs may be classified. Some major ones are (a) the number of factors, (b) the number of levels of the factors, (c) the method of assigning treatments to subjects, (d) whether treatments are manipulable or can only be introduced by using subjects of the right classifications (such as men versus women or obese versus nonobese), and (e) whether all levels of the factors are represented in the design (fixed-factor design), or only a random selection of the available levels (random-factor design).
5. The major types of experimental design and their characteristics are summarized in Table 6.4.
6. Designs with repeated measures on the same subjects require controls for carry-over effects from one treatment to the other (effects of order). A partial list of control methods follows. With *randomization* different orders of presentation are assigned randomly to different subjects. This will balance out effects of order in the long run. With *counterbalancing* the different orders are deliberately arranged to be represented equally often in the experiment by varying the order systematically across subjects. *Experimental reversal of effects* is ideal if within the capabilities of the experimenter. It eliminates carry-over. The use of *equivalent tests can reduce the carry-over that would result if the same test were repeated. Sometimes running subjects to asymptote* (the point where their behavior has advanced until there are no further systematic changes) is helpful. For effects that dissipate over time, *rest intervals* between treatments eradicate their carry-over. Effects that might normally carry over can be brought under *stimulus control,* so that they only occur in the presence of a given stimulus and no longer spread to other conditions. Establishment of *stable baselines* may reduce carry-over, since they replace variations in behavior over time with stability. *Probing* means that the subjects' ongoing behavior is disturbed minimally by taking brief behavioral samples under the test conditions. This improves stability and can thereby reduce carry-over.
7. *Main effects* are effects of one factor that appear despite ignoring levels of other factors. *Interactions* are differential effects of one factor as a function of the levels of other factors.

CHAPTER 7

Description of Data

Graphing Data
- Geometric representation of distributions

Numerical Description of Distributions
- Measures of central tendency
- The dispersion of distributions

Corrections and Transformations of Data
- Corrections
- Linear transformations
- Nonlinear transformations

Describing Degrees of Relationship

A great deal remains to be done after measures have been taken on a properly sampled set of subjects in a well-designed experiment. Important functional relationships may be concealed in a mass of raw data. A critical step in manipulating data is reducing them to a form in which these relationships are exposed and susceptible to evaluation for such properties as reliability and generality. The data must be reduced and presented in a way that brings home to the experimenter as well as to others the full import of the findings. Here we will discuss various useful procedures for so reducing and representing data.

Graphing Data

Let's assume that you have gathered a set of data. It is most unlikely that the numbers obtained from different subjects or from the same subjects at different times will all be identical. Instead, there will be a degree of scatter of the scores. We call the scattered set of scores a *distribution.* Experimenters describe distributions according to their geometry, so it is important to start by describing the relationships among geometry, numbers, and equations.

Each number obtained from experimental observations can be represented as a location or point on a line, as in the following illustration:

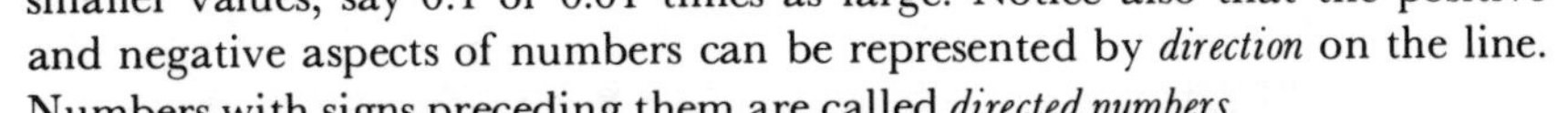

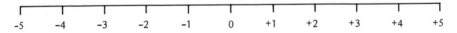

Obviously the ability to represent numbers on a line is not limited to small whole numbers. It would work as well if we were to represent numbers 10 or 100 times as large as those in the illustration, and this applies as well to smaller values, say 0.1 or 0.01 times as large. Notice also that the positive and negative aspects of numbers can be represented by *direction* on the line. Numbers with signs preceding them are called *directed numbers.*

Our thinking about numbers today is thoroughly blended with geometrical concepts, so much so that we take it for granted that numbers can be represented geometrically. But points on lines are not numbers, and it is by no means trivially obvious that numbers can inevitably be represented as points on lines. It was René Descartes, above all, who explored the possibilities of an interchange between numerical, algebraic, and geometrical representations.

Descartes fell upon the idea of representing geometrical figures on what have come to be known as "Cartesian coordinates." If, instead of taking one line as we did above, we take two lines, one perpendicular to the other, we have a system of Cartesian coordinates. Each of the two lines can represent a set of numbers, and a point on a two-dimensional figure can be expressed as two numbers, one for the horizontal coordinate line and one for the vertical coordinate line. For brevity, let us call these two numbers the *H* value and the *V* value.[1] In Figure 7.1, when $H = +2$ and $V = +2$, the equivalent geometrical representation is point B. When $H = +4$ and $V = +4$, the corresponding point is D. Since a line can be viewed as a set of points, we can represent a line as a set of *H* and *V* values.

We can get greater generality in our statement by shifting from particular numbers to a general expression such as *x*, which means "any number." The advantage of algebraic over numerical expressions is that the algebraic expressions are *general.* They save the impossible labor of listing

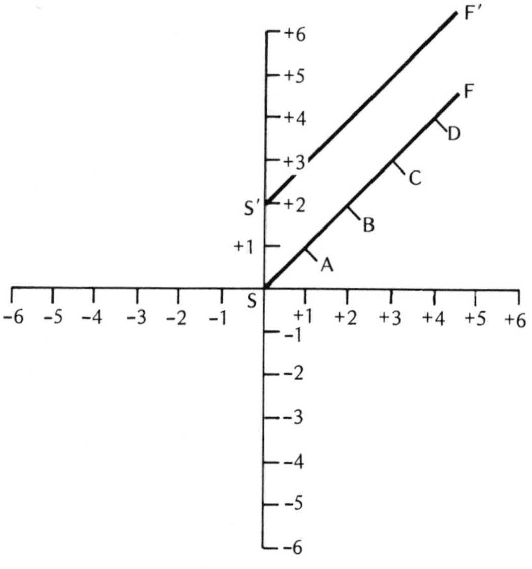

FIGURE 7.1 Graph of the equations $V = H$ (line S-F) and $V = H + 2$ (line S′-F′). Adding a constant changes the point of interception.

[1]Typically the letter *X* is used for the horizontal axis (abscissa) and *Y* is used for the vertical axis (ordinate). I have used *H* and *V* because they help us to keep track of which is which. But be ready for the translation to the system used in other books. Nonlinear of the equations $V = H$ (line S–F) and $V = H + 2$ (line S'–F'). Adding a constant changes the point of interception.

every individual number that might fit. Thus, in the present instance the general statement

$$V = H$$

tells us that, for *any possible value of H,* if V is equal to it, any graphing of several values will result in a straight line. And it will intersect the V and H coordinates at zero (when $H = 0$, $V = 0$). Straight lines that intercept the coordinates at different places will have slightly different corresponding equations. For example, if

$$V = H + 2$$

the resulting line will be the top line in Figure 7.1. Adding a constant changes the point of interception.

Other, more complex figures can be represented on a system of Cartesian coordinates. In experimental work, normally we place values of the *independent variable on the horizontal axis* and values of the *dependent variable on the vertical axis.*

Geometric Representation of Distributions

The set of numbers gathered in an experiment can be represented geometrically on a system of Cartesian coordinates. A simple representation of a distribution of numbers can be given by dividing the scores into classes, which are ranged along the horizontal axis, and then representing the frequencies of scores of the classes on the vertical axis. The result is called a histogram. Several histograms are shown in Figure 7.2.

The distribution represented by the histogram in Figure 7.2(a) is symmetrical, or evenly distributed about its center. The other two distributions are *skewed,* or unbalanced to one side. A distribution is said to be skewed in the direction of its long, skinny tail. Thus, the distribution in Figure 7.2(b) is positively skewed (tail at the right, toward higher positive values on the H axis) and the distribution in Figure 7.2(c) is negatively skewed.

If the number of categories of a histogram is increased, the bars become more and more slender. In principle the process of increasing categories and producing increasingly narrow bars could go on until the distribution would appear to be an area bounded by a smooth curve. A histogram thus approaches a smooth curve as the number of categories increases. Distributions are often expressed as curves rather than histograms.

Another way to create a curve instead of a histogram would be simply to place a dot on the system of coordinates representing the central value of each bar on the histogram and then connect the dots together. Figure 7.3 shows how this might be done.

Like the histogram, this representation of the distribution can vary in a number of ways that make visible certain properties of the underlying data. Whether for histogram or curve, the main features of interest are: (1) The location of its center, which is called its *central tendency*. (2) The degree of its scatter around the center (that is, is it narrow or is it broad). This is called its *dispersion* and indicates how variable the measurements are. (3) Its *skewness* or tendency to be shifted to the right or the left. (4) Its *kurtosis* or the extent to

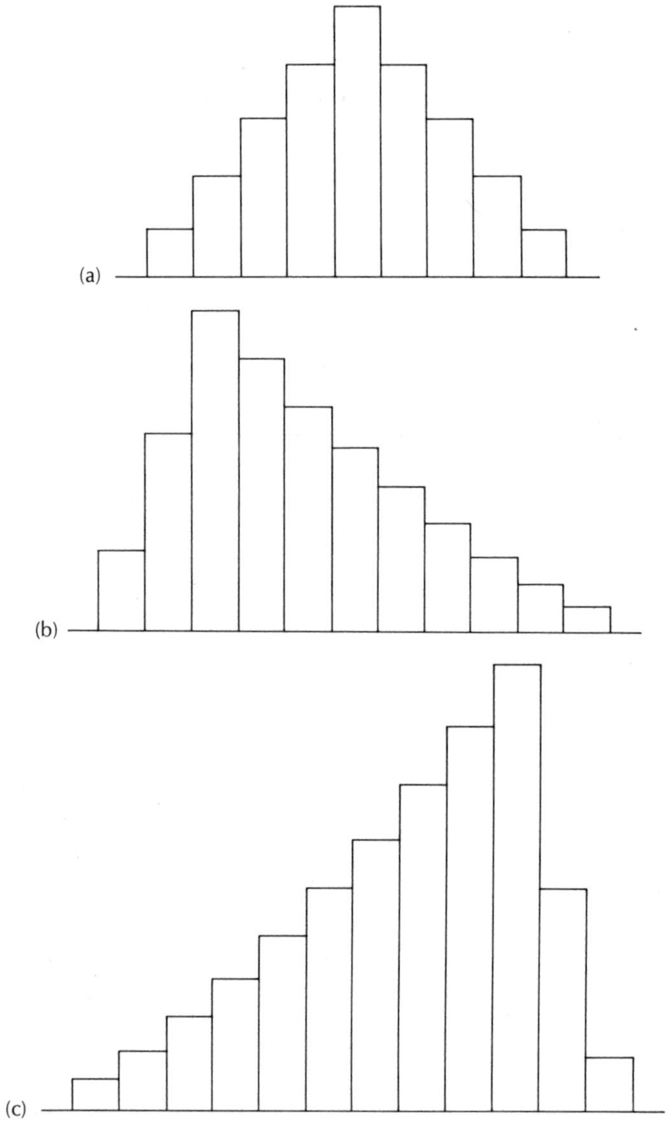

FIGURE 7.2 Histograms showing (a) symmetrical distribution; (b) Positively skewed distribution: note that it has a long, thin tail to the *right;* and (c) negatively skewed distribution: note that it has a long, thin tail to the *left.*

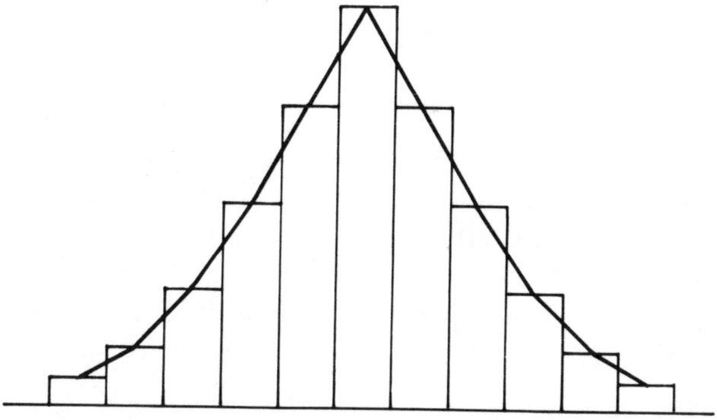

FIGURE 7.3 Formation of a curve by connecting the centers of each bar on a histogram.

which it is peaked or flat. All of these geometrical properties represent more or less important characteristics of the underlying data.

Sometimes we need to have a geometrical representation of the data and at other times we need a numerical representation. Both of these help us to understand our data and to present them to others.

The Normal or Gaussian Distribution

Figure 7.4 shows a "normal" or "Gaussian" distribution. It is bell shaped and symmetrical about its high point.

Approximations to the Gaussian distribution in sets of observations occur often, especially when many random factors are each having a small influence on the observations, some positive and others negative in direction. This means that the data from well-controlled experiments, from which systematic errors have been taken out, might well be expected to take on a Gaussian distribution. For this reason, scientists and mathematicians dealing with errors of measurement or random errors in general have commonly assumed observations to follow a Gaussian distribution.

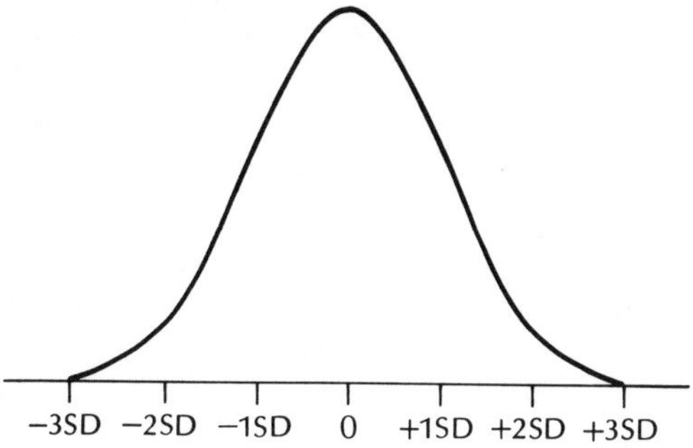

FIGURE 7.4 A Gaussian distribution. The markings on the horizontal axis indicate standard deviations (SD), which are explained later.

Numerical Description of Distributions

An experimenter can easily miss features of a distribution if he or she tries to look at it as a whole. We have a number of measures to summarize major characteristics of a distribution. These include measures that indicate where the center of the distribution is located, how scattered the scores are around that center, the degree to which the distribution is flat or peaked, and the extent to which it is symmetrical about its center rather than shifted to one side. We will discuss the most important of these measures here.

Measures of Central Tendency

Experimenters probably attend more to the central tendency of their data than to any other of its features. This stems from the belief that the measure of central tendency best represents the scores. We will treat four different measures of central tendency here. These are the arithmetic mean, the geometric mean, the median, and the mode.

The Arithmetic Mean

The arithmetic mean is the sum of all the observed values divided by the number of observations. This is the familiar "average" taught in grammar school. The mean of 2, 3, and 4 is simply 2 + 3 + 4 divided by 3 (= 3). Stated in general terms, the arithmetic mean is

$$\frac{\sum_{i=1}^{n} X_i}{n}$$

What do these symbols mean? Let's go through them step by step. The Σ means "the sum of," and the symbol X_i means the set of observed values, from first to last. The letter X is used to indicate an observed value, and if there are numerical subscripts, such as X_1, X_2, and X_3, they indicate *which* observation we have in mind, the first, second, third, and so on. When a letter such as the i in the formula is used as a subscript, it indicates that we have in mind the scores in general, no one in particular. So ΣX_i says simply "sum the scores." On top of the Σ we place a letter indicating when to stop summing. When the letter n occurs at the top of Σ, it means to sum until the last score is included. At the bottom of the Σ we indicate where to start summing. The indication in the formula says to start at the first score. So the top part of the formula says "sum the scores, starting from the first one and going all the way through the last one." The bottom of the formula says to divide by the number of observations.

The arithmetic mean is surely the most widely used measure of central tendency in science. It is so widely used that when someone refers to the "mean" without indicating what kind of mean, we take it for granted the arithmetic mean is intended. Accordingly, we will drop the adjective "arithmetic" in most cases and understand the term "mean" to refer to the arithmetic mean unless otherwise stipulated.

Individual scores typically vary around any measure of central tendency, including the mean. If the mean of 2, 3, and 4 is 3, two of the scores deviate from the mean; only one of them is right on it. If you determine how much the scores deviate from the mean (in this case 2 deviates by −1 and 4 deviates by +1), the sum of the resulting "deviation scores" will always equal zero. The deviations above it always equal the deviations below it. In this sense it is clearly "central" to the distribution.

Mathematicians often get rid of + and − signs by squaring numbers. A positive number times a positive number yields a positive number, and a negative number times a negative number also yields a positive number. Hence any number multiplied by itself will result in a positive number. In describing and analyzing data we commonly work with squared deviation scores. The mean has a special property with respect to these squared deviation scores. It is this: the sum of the squared deviations from the mean is equal to or less than the corresponding expression with any other measure of central tendency. Put another way, the sum of the squared deviations from the mean is at a minimum.

The Geometric Mean

The geometric mean is not used often with psychological data, but you will encounter it from time to time. For example, it is typically used on data obtained by the method of magnitude estimation (see Chapter 2). It is particularly useful when a distribution is skewed. To get the geometric mean, you find the product of all the n scores, then take their nth root. Thus, in comparison to the method of getting the arithmetic mean, we substitute multiplication for addition, and we substitute taking a root for the operation of division. The geometric mean of 2, 3, and 4 is

$$\sqrt[3]{2 \times 3 \times 4} = \sqrt[3]{24} \approx 2.9$$

It would be very laborious to calculate the geometric mean in this way for large numbers of observations. But we know how to do it indirectly and quite simply by using logarithms. The operation of multiplying numbers is equivalent to the operation of adding the logarithms of the numbers, and the operation of taking the *n*th root of a number is equivalent to dividing its logarithm by *n*. It is easy to convert numbers to logarithms, to add, and to divide, so the geometric mean is not hard to find. We use the geometric mean in the same situations in which we use logarithmic transformations. We deal with logarithmic transformations later.

The Median

The median is also useful for skewed distributions. The median of a number of observations is that value which has an equal number of observations greater than and less than itself. It is the point above and below which half of the observations lie. If there are an uneven number of observations, we find the median by placing the scores in order of magnitude, enumerating them, and taking the middle item. Since there is no middle score when we have an even number of observations, we use the arithmetic mean of the middle two observations as the median in such cases.

When the distribution of scores is symmetrical, the mean and median are equal. They deviate from each other when the distribution is skewed because the mean is highly sensitive to extreme scores, whereas the median is insensitive to them. For example, the median of 2, 3, and 4 is 3, and so is the mean. But the median of 2, 3, and 1000 is also 3, whereas the mean is 335.

The Mode

The mode is the most frequent score value in a distribution, or the most frequent class of score values. It is rarely used as a measure of central tendency in experimental psychology because sample sizes are commonly not great enough to provide large numbers of repeated scores.

The Dispersion of Distributions

A second feature of distributions is their scatter around the center, their *dispersion.* We represent this by using the deviation scores about the mean as an index of dispersion. The sum of the deviation scores about the mean always equals zero, so it provides a poor basis for indicating dispersion. We need to get rid of the + and − signs. This can be done by simply dropping them. The resulting numbers are the absolute deviations from the mean. Customarily we take the mean of the absolute deviations, so that we have an indication of the average amount of deviation per score.

The *mean absolute deviation* is an adequate measure of dispersion but happens to be seldom used. The second method of getting rid of the directional signs on numbers, that of squaring, has been adopted as the preferred method. We take the deviation from the mean for each score in the distribution and square it. Next we take the mean of these squared deviations. This gives the *mean squared deviation,* which is called the *variance.* Symbolically we can express it as follows (d = deviation):

$$\text{Variance} = \frac{\sum_{i=1}^{n} d_i^2}{n}$$

This says: "Take the sum of the squared deviation scores and divide by the number of scores." You can see that the formula is the one for the arithmetic mean, but deviations scores are used instead of raw scores. To represent how the deviation score is derived, we could rewrite the equation this way:

$$\text{Variance} = \sum_{i=1}^{n} \frac{(X_i - M)^2}{n}$$

with X_i representing "the scores in general," M representing the mean of the scores, and n representing the number of scores.

Since the variance has been inflated by the operation of squaring, we may want to deflate it again by taking its square root. The square root of the variance is called the *standard deviation*

$$\text{Standard deviation} = \sqrt{\frac{\sum_{i=1}^{n} d_i^2}{n}} = \sqrt{\frac{\sum_{i=1}^{n} (X_i - M)^2}{n}}$$

In practice, both the variance and the standard deviation are used as measures of the dispersion of distributions.

If a distribution has the symmetrical, Gaussian shape, about 68 percent of the distribution will be included between plus and minus 1 standard deviation, about 95 percent will be included between $\pm$ 2 standard deviations, and about 99.73 percent will be included between $\pm$ 3 standard deviations.

There are many measures of the dispersion of a distribution. The ones already described are most commonly used. Experimenters often use a cruder measure, the *range,* as a rough indicator of dispersion. The range is merely the difference between the lowest and the highest score in the distribution. It is a cruder measure than the three already described because it is influenced only by two of the scores in the distribution, whereas all of the scores are taken into account by the mean absolute deviation, the variance, and the standard deviation.

Corrections and Transformations of Data

Corrections

Raw data are not necessarily the best representation of reality. Errors are included in any recorded datum. These errors are of two basic kinds: variable errors and systematic errors. We will deal with variable errors later. The most usable datum may be one that has been corrected for various systematic errors. This is true for hard sciences as much as for psychology. For example, observed measurements of the positions of the sun and stars are thoroughly contaminated by systematic errors due to such factors as the capacity of air to bend light. The sun can still be seen when it is below the horizon. Consequently, astronomers must introduce corrections before treating measurements as basic data.

Psychologists often correct data according to "baseline" scores obtained in previous behavioral observations. For example, Besley and Sheridan (1973) trained rats to do diametrically opposed visual discriminations, one with each half of the brain. They were interested in the effects of tiny areas of brain damage made in one hemisphere of the brain. The idea was to see whether the balance of evenly matched opposing discriminations mediated by opposite brain halves might be shifted by small areas of damage, not behaviorally detectable by ordinary methods. They could have simply used the numbers of errors made by the damaged hemisphere after surgery. But even before surgery there were sizable variations in the numbers of errors. The occurrence of a large number of errors after surgery on the part of an animal that had made a large number of errors prior to surgery might not mean as much as a similarly large number of postoperative errors by an animal that had done very well before surgery. Consequently, Besley and Sheridan (1973) subtracted for each animal the number of errors prior to the operation from the number of errors after the operation. The resulting "corrected" or "difference" scores gave a more meaningful measure.

Linear Transformations

Whether or not we correct data for known sources of constant errors, we may want to transform them. Linear transformations are done when the experimenter wishes to change the zero point of a set of measures or to change the units of measurement. One may want to do this in order to make computations easier, as when the data include both positive and negative values. For example, adding a constant $+7$ to the following set of numbers converts them to uniformly positive numbers:

$$-4, 13, -3, 4, 7, -7 \quad \text{(original)}$$
$$3, 20, 4, 11, 14, 0 \quad \text{(transformed)}$$

Linear transformations are done by adding, subtracting, multiplying, or dividing all the scores by the same thing. The common procedure of going from one unit of measurement to another through multiplying by a constant number is an example. If I want to convert a certain set of measurements from feet to inches, I multiply all the measurements in feet by 12.

Linear transformations permit us to convert a distribution of scores in such a way as to achieve a desired mean and standard deviation. Multiplying a set of numbers by a constant will increase the standard deviation by the same ratio. This means that doubling each score doubles the standard deviation, tripling each score triples the standard deviation, and so on. This operation will also increase the mean by the same ratio. If you want to increase the mean without affecting the standard deviation, you do this by adding a constant to each score. The mean will be increased by that same constant, but the standard deviation will be unchanged. An application of these maneuvers to the Z_i score is discussed later in this chapter.

Nonlinear Transformations

There are various types of nonlinear transformation that experimenters make on data for various special purposes. The *logarithmic transformation* is one of the most common. The logarithm of a number is the exponent indicating the power to which another number must be raised in order to get a result equal to the original number. The "other number" to which the exponent is applied is called the *base* of the logarithm. Familiar bases are 2, *e* (2.71828), and 10. Logarithms to the base *e* are called *natural* or *Napierian logarithms.* Logarithms to the base 10 are called *common logarithms.* We usually indicate which base we are using by a subscript; thus $\log_2$ means that the base is 2, and similarly $\log_e$ and $\log_{10}$ indicate logarithms to the base *e* and to the base 10, respectively. If there is no subscript, this means that the base is 10.

An impression of the relationship between logarithms and their corresponding numbers (called *antilogs*) can be obtained from the following list:

Number	Equivalent in terms of 10 raised to a power	Common logarithm
10	10^1	1.0000
100	10^2	2.0000
1000	10^3	3.0000
10,000	10^4	4.0000

The logarithm is merely the power to which 10 is raised. Notice that the logarithm grows much more slowly than the number itself. In fact, the numbers in the list are in *geometric progression*—each successive number is a constant multiple of the preceding number. In this case, each successive number is 10 times the one preceding it. The list of logarithms is in *arithmetic progression.* This means that each successive logarithm adds a constant unit (in this case, 1) to the one preceding it.

Because of this tendency to shrink a geometrically expanding series of numbers, it is often useful to convert raw data into logarithms of the original scores. It sometimes happens that the size of the increments of change of the dependent variable is not uniform but varies systematically with increases in value of the independent variable. This occurs, for example, when each successive value of the dependent variable is a constant *percentage* of the preceding value. As a practical matter, such functions grow so rapidly that it can be difficult to plot them on a graph. Furthermore, the resulting distribution of scores is skewed. When a distribution is skewed, the arithmetic mean does not represent it well, and assumptions of certain statistical tests cannot be met. Hence it is useful to convert from the scores to their logarithms.

A study done in the laboratory section of my experimental psychology class illustrates an application of logarithmic transformation. People were asked to assign numbers rating the personal value of their various bodily parts—eyes, ears, nose, and so forth. The numbers could be as large or as small as they wanted to use but should consistently reflect the relative values of the parts. (This is the psychometric method of magnitude estimation.) One participant used numbers like 100,000 for certain parts. Most subjects stayed with numbers like 100 and 60. If the arithmetic mean of these scores were used, a single subject using very large numbers could radically distort the measure of central tendency. One way to reduce the impact of the varying sizes of numbers chosen is to use a logarithmic transformation. The common logarithm of 100 is 2 and of 100,000 is 5. Thus the extreme weightiness of large numbers is made manageable by logarithmic transformation. This is, of course, essentially the same as using the geometric mean.

A second transformation of considerable usefulness is the *z* or *standard score* transformation. This transformation makes it possible to compare scores that were originally not in comparable units. For example, if a man is 6 feet tall and weighs 200 pounds, he is taller and heavier than the average man. But is he heavier to a greater extent than he is taller? This is impossible to answer with the scores in their original form but can be answered when they have been transformed into *z* scores. The formula for *z* is

$$z = \frac{\text{(Score)} - \text{(Mean of scores)}}{\text{(Standard deviation)}} = \frac{X_i - M}{\text{SD}}$$

The deviation from the mean is expressed in units equal to the standard deviation. Thus each score is expressed in terms of the relative proportion of scores in that distribution that deviate so much from the mean. It is like saying that the man is taller than 90 percent of the people but heavier than only 75 percent, thus he is taller to a greater extent than he is heavier. (These percentages are, incidentally, entirely fanciful.)

The *z* transformation as described will provide a distribution with a mean of zero and a standard deviation of 1. Since this results in both positive and negative numbers, computational ease[2] leads many investigators to go a step further and obtain a distribution with a preassigned mean and standard deviation. Since adding a constant to each score increases the mean by that same constant and multiplying each score by a constant increases both the mean and the standard deviation by that constant factor, it is easy to achieve the desired mean and standard deviation. For example,

$$Z_i = 50 + 10\frac{(X_i - M)}{\text{SD}}$$

will give a mean of 50 and a standard deviation of 10. This is because the last term in the equation is equal to the original *z* transformation, in which the mean was zero and standard deviation, 1. Adding 50 to each score increases the mean by 50. The mean was zero, so multiplying it by 10 does not change it. The standard deviation was 1, so multiplying it by 10 results in a product of 10.

Describing Degrees of Relationship

Experimenters often want a measure of *how much* relationship exists between two variables. We have a number of ways to describe the degree of a relationship. Consider what happens when two variables, H and V, are so perfectly related that $V = H$ for all values. Going back to the beginning of this discussion of describing data, remember that the geometric counterpart of this equation is a straight line.

Sometimes two variables are related very intimately, but when values of one of them rise, values of the other decline. Though the relationship is *inverse,* it is just as useful in predicting values of one variable from values of the other.

If a relationship is inverse, as when $V = 1/H$, the geometrical representation slopes downward instead of upward. The fact that some relationships can be represented by the plot of a straight line has been used to produce a measure of degree of relationship. Of course, real data will seldom come out to fit anything so simple as a straight line. There will be variability around H and there will be variability around V. Even assuming that the true measure of things would be a straight line, error of measurement would likely lead to scatter around the straight line. Consequently we are not deterred when we plot

[2]There are psychological considerations as well. How would you feel if your score on a test came out to be a negative number?

individual H and V scores against each other and get a kind of football-shaped scatter of points. Instead, we call it a *scatter diagram* and find the straight line that fits it best. There are many definitions of "best fit," but the one generally used is the straight line for which the sum of the squared deviations from the line is at a minimum. The best-fit line is called a *regression line,* and its equation is a *regression equation.* The slope of the regression line indicates the degree of relationship between the two variables.

This provides you with an intuitive notion of how the degree of a relationship can be represented geometrically and algebraically. In practice, correlation coefficients are used. The most widely used one is the *Pearson product-moment correlation coefficient,* symbolized as r. The maximum positive relationship is indicated by a value of $+1.00$, absence of relationship yields $r = 0.00$, and a maximum negative (inverse) relationship provides a value of -1.00. Intermediate degrees of relationship produce intermediate values.

Pearson's r assumes that the data can legitimately be represented as a straight line and that the standard deviations of values of the two variables are equal. A definitional formula of r is

$$r = \frac{\sum_{i=1}^{n} h_i v_i}{N(\mathrm{SD}_h)(\mathrm{SD}_v)}$$

where h and v are deviation measures from the H and V means (that is, $H_i - M_h = h_i$ and $V_i = M_v = v_i$); N = the number of individuals measured; and SD_h and SD_v are the standard deviations of the two distributions.

A computational formula is

$$r = \frac{N\Sigma HV - \Sigma H \Sigma V}{\sqrt{N\Sigma H^2 - (\Sigma H)^2}\sqrt{N\Sigma V^2 - (\Sigma V)^2}}$$

Translated into words, this says

1. $N\Sigma HV$. Multiply the V value by the H value for each of the individuals, add up the resulting products, and multiply the sum by the number of individuals.
2. $-\Sigma H\Sigma V$. Add up all the H values, then add up all the V values, and multiply the resulting sums. Subtract the result from the result of step 1.
3. $\sqrt{N\Sigma H^2 - (\Sigma H)^2}$. First, for $N\Sigma H^2$ square each H value and sum the results, then multiply by the number of individuals. For $-(\Sigma H)^2$ add up the H values, square the result, and subtract it from $N\Sigma H^2$. Take the square root of this difference.
4. $\sqrt{N\Sigma V^2 - (\Sigma V)^2}$. Do the same things to the V scores that you did to the H scores in step 3.

5. $\sqrt{N\Sigma H^2(\Sigma H)^2}$ $\sqrt{N\Sigma V^2 - (\Sigma V)^2}$. Multiply the result of step 3 by the result of step 4.

6. Divide the result of step 2 by the result of step 5.

SUMMARY

1. Data usually take the form of numbers. For many purposes, numbers, equations, and graphs are interchangeable. For a particular set of data the meaning may be clearer in one of these forms than in another. Besides numbers, graphs are commonly used to express data. Values of the independent variable go on the horizontal axis and values of the dependent variable go on the vertical axis.

2. When data are gathered, they generally vary (are "distributed") around some central value. The resulting distribution may be plotted in a bar graph (histogram) or a curve. There are many forms of distribution. Some are positively skewed (have a long tail to the right); others are negatively skewed (have a long tail to the left); and others are symmetrical. The curve of *normal* or *Gaussian distribution* is symmetrical and bell shaped. Approximations to the Gaussian distribution occur often in nature, especially when deviations from the central value are due to random influences of many small factors.

3. Data tend to vary around a central value. Several different numerical representations of that value are in common use. The most widely used, the *arithmetic mean,* is equal to the sum of scores divided by the number of scores. The *geometric mean* is the antilog of the arithmetic mean of the logarithms of the scores. It is used for highly skewed distributions because it gives less weight to extreme values than does the arithmetic mean. The *median* is the middle value of the scores in a distribution (if an even number of scores, it is the arithmetic mean of the middle two values). It, too, is relatively unresponsive to extreme values, but it only takes into account a few of the scores. The *mode* is the most frequently occurring score. It represents the distribution accurately. However, it can only be used when there are many scores repeated. This is not likely to occur with small samples, so the mode is not often used in experimental work.

4. It is important to have a number to describe the extent to which scores spread out around the central tendency of a distribution. Two distributions with markedly different degrees of spread can have the same center. The *variance* reflects dispersion. To get the variance, we subtract each score from the mean, square the resulting deviation scores, then take the mean of the squared scores. The *standard deviation* is the square root of the variance. A rough measure of dispersion is given by the *range,* which is the difference between the lowest and the highest score.

Since it only takes two of the scores into account, it is less informative than the variance and standard deviation.

5. It is not always best to work with raw data. Data may be improved by *correcting* them for constant errors. Constant errors are errors that influence data consistently in a given direction. Data may be corrected by subtracting known values, for example, scores of individuals on a pretest, from the raw scores. There are also a variety of transformations of data that aid us in handling and understanding data.

6. *Linear transformations* (adding, subtracting, multiplying, or dividing all scores by the same thing) change the zero point or the units of a set of measures. They can make computations easier, for example, by eliminating negative values.

7. *Logarithmic transformations* (converting each number to its logarithm) can make skewed distributions more symmetrical by shrinking extreme scores. This may be useful in meeting the assumptions of certain statistical tests and in making it easier to plot all the scores on one graph.

8. *Standard* (z) *scores* make it possible to compare data that were originally not in comparable units (for example, to answer the question: am I more exceptionally tall than I am exceptionally bright?). The z score indicates what proportion of the population falls above or below you on a given dimension. The Z_i transformation further permits giving the distribution any desired mean or standard deviation. The formula is

$$Z_i = \text{Desired mean} + \text{Desired SD}\,\frac{(X_i = M)}{\text{SD}}$$

9. There are many measures to describe degree of relationship. Pearson's product-moment correlation coefficient (**r**) is widely used for data on an interval scale when the standard deviations of the two variables are about equal. The formula for **r** is given in the text.

CHAPTER 8

The Reliability of Data: Some Principles of Statistical and Nonstatistical Inference

Reliability of Functional Relationships

A major goal of science is to permit us to predict natural phenomena. We can attain this goal by discovering systematic relationships between predictive (independent) variables and outcome (dependent) variables. If variations in the predictive variable correspond in an orderly way to variations in the outcome variable, we have a functional relationship and can predict outcomes not yet observed simply by knowing the values of the predictors.

Unfortunately, we have to contend with various sources of error that influence levels of the outcome variable. Sometimes a systematic relationship will occur between two variables simply by chance, when nothing but error is operating. We are always in the position of having to distinguish between results of experiments that are merely due to chance or to error and those that indicate a truly repeatable, systematic relationship between variables. This is the problem of reliability of data. The reliability of a relationship is its repeatability. If there is a truly systematic relationship between variables, the one variable will regularly predict values of the other. If a relationship between two variables is merely due to error, then that relationship will be unreliable and of no real use in predicting phenomena.

How do we tell whether or not a given observed relationship between two variables is due to error? The method scientists use for doing this is merely a well-organized version of common sense. Let me illustrate with the following story.

> Sally Howe stepped from her car and walked briskly into the house. She shivered a little as she closed the door behind her. The leaves had just begun to fall, and it had suddenly become a little chilly. Besides, she felt tense because Bill was away, and there had been a number of housebreakings in town over the past few weeks. "Why can't Bill get a job that allows him to stay home once in a while?" she thought peevishly. Then she abruptly turned on herself. "Stop it, Sally!" she thought, "You know that's the perfect job for Bill, and besides you shouldn't be so darned dependent on him!"
>
> She set her lips tight in a gesture of resolve and walked quickly upstairs to the bedroom. She closed the bedroom door and locked it behind her. Sally was tired, and hurriedly prepared herself for bed, got under the covers, and turned out the light. Her fatigue overcame her tension, and she soon drifted into that world halfway between dreams and waking.
>
> But suddenly she sat up with a start. There was a creaking sound downstairs! She felt her heart pound fast. "My God! Is there someone down

there?" she half-whispered. She listened intently for a full minute. "There it is again!" she thought.

"But no. It's just this old house creaking the way it always does when the weather gets cold," she said to herself. "You've simply *got* to quit acting like a silly child."

She lay back down, closed her eyes firmly, and tried hard to go to sleep. Then there was a sound like someone on the stairs. She bolted up and grabbed the telephone by the bed. She started to dial. But as her fingers spun the dial she began to feel that the frightening sound blended in with the other creakings of their old house. She put down the phone. Her eyes began to moisten. "I don't want to act hysterical," she thought, "it may just be the boards bending in the cold . . . but *what if someone is down there!*"

Sally's predicament is like that of an experimenter. Both of them want to know whether certain happenings are due to something important. In both cases, they have to worry whether the data might be due to uncontrolled fluctuations of uninteresting factors. They have to ask themselves: "Am I getting an important message, or is this just due to noise in the background?"

Sally doesn't want to call the police because she wishes to avoid seeming silly, hysterical, and dependent. Technically, we would say she wants to avoid a *type I error.* She makes a type I error if she sounds the alarm when no one is really there. This is like an experimenter publishing an article saying that an independent variable worked when it did not. Both are type I errors; both are "false alarms."

But there is another kind of error. What if someone is really there and Sally fails to call the police? This is like the experimenter who fails to detect it when an independent variable works. This kind of error is called a *type II error.* It is a "miss."

A major point brought out by the story of Sally is that both she and the experimenter are trying to detect a signal in the presence of a noisy background. Sally wants to know whether certain sounds in the house are different enough from creaking of the background to merit being considered a signal of danger. The experimenter likewise wants to know whether results gotten with a certain experimental treatment differ enough from what happens without the treatment to merit reporting that the variable is effective.

Basically, we assess reliability of data by deciding whether our independent variable had an effect. And we decide whether it had an effect by comparing it to some noise level, some level of fluctuating values that occurs without the independent variable. We must discriminate between a noisy background alone and a noisy background when there is a signal present.

We distinguish the combination of signal + noise from noise alone by asking ourselves how likely it is for the observed event to occur if there is just noise. Sally heard a certain level of noise. Some of the sounds were enough to make her worry that there might be a prowler. The noises seemed a bit too loud to be just part of the background noise, even in her creaky old house. We can imagine a sudden crash and the sound of a lamp falling over and Sally saying, "That's it, there *is* a prowler!" Theoretically a lamp could fall over without a prowler, but *that* is so unlikely that Sally will act on the assumption that someone is down there. Experimenters do the same thing. If the results in their treatment condition are markedly different from what occurs, or could reasonably be expected to occur, without the treatment, they take it for granted that the variable had an effect.

Technically, you can think of the judgments of Sally and the experimenter as based on a ratio. For Sally it is the following:

$$\frac{\text{Observed creaking}}{\text{Creaking without prowler}}$$

If the observed creaking is about the same as creaking without the prowler, the ratio is about 1. If the observed creaking is a lot more than the usual creaking, the ratio will be large. Implicitly, Sally has a certain cutoff point in her head. If the ratio exceeds that cutoff value, she will call the police.

For the experimenters the ratio is, roughly,

$$\frac{\text{Observation}}{\text{Error estimate}}$$

They look at the observed difference between treatment and control conditions and contrast it with differences that occur without any treatment.

A general way of saying what Sally and the experimenter are both doing is that they want to tell the ratio.

$$\frac{\text{Noise}}{\text{Noise}}$$

from the ratio

$$\frac{\text{Signal + Noise}}{\text{Noise}}$$

If what they observe is a case of

$$\frac{\text{Signal + Noise}}{\text{Noise}}$$

the ratio should be larger than if it is

$$\frac{\text{Noise}}{\text{Noise}}$$

If the ratio is large enough, they decide there is a signal.

How, in practice, do experimenters find their ratios and decide whether to say their findings are reliable? The first way is by inspection.

Judging Reliability by Inspection

Sometimes the ratio of observation to noise is so great that we can just look at the data and decide that there must be a signal. This happens if there is a *whopper variable.* A whopper variable is one that produces striking effects, clearly beyond the noise level. For example, we might find that there is no overlap at all between the results of an experimental and a control group. Say, everybody given a new teaching method did better than anybody given the old method. If no overlap occurred despite many observations, or even if a little overlap occurred, we could decide by inspection that the variable had an effect; see Figure 8.1.

We can sometimes by inspection tell that data are reliable even when we lack a whopper variable. This happens when the noise level is very low. Even a small signal may be recognizable on a background of little or no noise. Sally would have an easier time judging whether a prowler was there if she lived in a very quiet house.

Mere luck is rarely enough to give us low noise levels. We need meticulous experimental control for this. By bringing behavior under careful control prior to introducing treatment conditions, we make effects of the independent variable obvious by inspection; see Figure 8.2.

There is a whole category of psychologists who emphasize use of careful experimental control to the point where reliability can be judged by in-

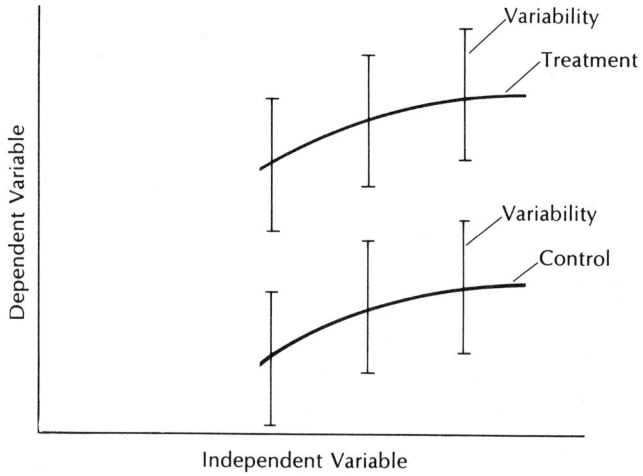

FIGURE 8.1 Idealized graph of the effects of a "whopper variable." The variable is so powerful that there is no overlap between the data with it and the data without it. The two curves are far enough apart that they do not overlap despite high variability.

spection. We call their approach the *experimental analysis of behavior.* This approach has been espoused by B. F. Skinner, and people interested in operant conditioning generally use it.

With an experimental analysis of behavior, the experimenter establishes a *baseline* of behavior to which performance is contrasted when the independent variable is put in. The baseline is usually stable and relatively free of noise. These experimenters often have to take a very long time getting the desired baseline behavior. They commonly work with small numbers of experimental subjects, and each subject receives both the experimental and control treatment. (This is called a *within-subjects design.*) They can afford to take a great deal of time and work with few subjects because the effects are made so clear. The high degree of experimental control compensates for the relatively reduced number of subjects. A more detailed account of the experimental analysis of behavior will be given in Chapter 11.

Statistical Judgments of Reliability

The eye is a relatively insensitive instrument for judging reliability. The influence of many effective independent variables would be missed if we did not compensate for this insensitivity. Reducing the noise level by exerting high degrees of experimental control helps. Another method is the use of statistics. Psychologists seem more prone to sharpen the eye with statistics than with experimental control. There is a controversy over which method is best, but we will not deal with that here.

When something gets too subtle for the eye to discriminate, scientists usually turn to instruments that enhance its power. Thus they turned in the

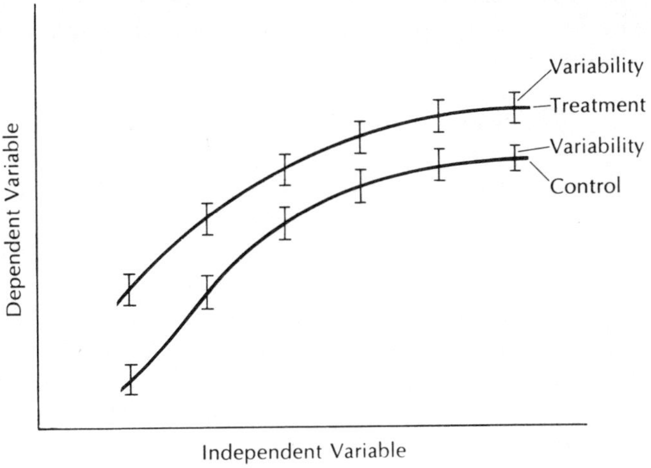

FIGURE 8.2 Idealized graph of effects produced under high experimental control. The two curves are close together, but the variability is so slight that the two sets of data do not overlap.

past to the microscope and the telescope. The idea behind statistics is to improve on the ability to discriminate the effects of experimental treatments. Many experiments have outcomes not obviously reliable by inspection, but reliable nevertheless. The reliability of such outcomes can be assessed with statistics.

Risks of Rejecting the Null Hypothesis

What is it that we use to decide that the independent variable had an influence? Think of Sally. She had to judge how likely were the sounds she heard, assuming there was no prowler. Certain sounds, like the sound of a falling lamp, would be grossly unlikely. So they would lead her to reject the notion that there was no prowler. Lesser sounds left her in doubt. Statistics help to resolve such doubts by quantifying the likelihood that the events would occur as part of background noise. They tell us what proportion of the time we could expect the observed event to occur if the independent variable were ineffective.

Suppose Sally had a complete record of a large number of household sounds that have occurred on evenings in autumn in their house. For simplicity, let's say she has recorded 1000 sounds. When a given sound occurred, she could (theoretically) compare it to the 1000. If a sound as great or greater than that had occurred 212 times, she would probably say, "See, this kind of thing happens all the time. There's no good reason to think there is a prowler." But what if that great a sound has only occurred once before in the normal course of events? She might then say, "The chances are one in a thousand that this is just background noise. I'm not taking such chances with my life. I'll assume there is a prowler."

What we are doing here is comparing the observed event to what can be expected if there is only background noise. In experiments, this would mean comparing our finding to what can be expected from random fluctuations and error. We temporarily assume that there is only error and find out how often our observation could be expected to occur if our assumption were true. This is the same as saying we assume that the independent variable had no effect. We then find out how likely our outcome is on that assumption. The assumption that the independent variable had no effect is called the *null hypothesis.*

With the experimental analysis of behavior we also find out what would happen if the independent variable did not work. We do so by running subjects for a long time without the variable. The baseline behavior is behavior without the independent variable. With statistics we try to save ourselves some work by doing at least part of this mathematically. The mathematician finds a model of the situation and finds out by computation how often the observed outcome would take place without an effective independent variable.

How can a mathematician do this? Let's take a concrete example.

Suppose you want to know whether your pet dog, Gordon, can discriminate color. You get a bunch of colored cards and, as a control for brightness, some grey cards. You order Gordon to sit, then place one card on your right and one on your left. Holding one of his favorite treats in hand, you say "Here Gordon." Gordon comes running over and jumps on you, ignoring your cards. But you "No, no!" him until he catches on that he is to nuzzle cards. You've decided to start him out on red and green. If he picks red, he is correct and you give him a treat and pet him. If not, you say "No, no!" and make him go sit. You keep changing the cards from right to left at random from trial to trial. Periodically you use the grey cards and deprive him of the treat no matter what he does. That way he should learn that you're not interested in his picking, say, the darker card.

After a few days, Gordon runs to the red card 7 out of 10 times. You ask yourself, "Is he doing better than chance?" What is the likelihood of getting 7 out of 10 correct by chance? Assuming that the red cue has no influence on Gordon, how often will he do that well? A very laborious way to find out would be to eliminate the redness of the card and to run him a thousand trials or so to find the proportion of times he performed as well as 7 out of 10 correct. But it would be easier to use a handy model. Without the red cue, there would be two equally likely choices. Anything with two equally likely outcomes could be used as a model. Why not flip a coin? Let heads indicate a correct response and tails mean an incorrect response. It would be easier to flip coins than to struggle with Gordon a thousand times. But have you ever tried flipping a coin a thousand times? It's boring.

The easiest thing is to use a mathematical model. In the eighteenth century, Blaise Pascal worked out the mathematics of such situations for some gambling friends. We call the correct model the *binomial distribution.* Appendix B shows how likely it is that Gordon would get 7 correct in 10 tries if he were not relying on the red cue. The probability is 0.172.[1] That means that you can expect to get this result about 17 percent of the time, even if Gordon has learned nothing about color. This is hardly a solid basis for deciding he has color vision.

You have to decide what probability you are willing to treat as low enough to rule out chance alone. Logically, this decision is arbitrary. But in practice, we generally accept only probabilities of 0.05 or lower. The probability we set for rejecting the null hypothesis is called the *alpha level.* The alpha level tells us the proportion of time we can expect to be wrong in rejecting the null hypothesis. At the 0.05 level we can expect to reject the null hypothesis incorrectly 5 percent of the time, or once in every 20 experiments. Rejecting the null hypothesis incorrectly, remember, is called a type I error.

[1]Actually, the situation is a bit more complex than we are pretending. Gordon is repeatedly getting 10-trial opportunities. We have calculated as though he got only one. But, for simplicity, let's leave out the mathematical details here.

To be wrong so often in thinking the independent variable had an effect seems intolerable to many people. They like to set their probability level somewhat lower. Maybe you would prefer once in a hundred experiments (0.01 level) or once in a thousand (0.001 level). But when you lower your alpha level, you increase the risk of failing to detect an independent variable that works. This is called a type II error. The probability of a type II error is called *beta.* It is, incidentally, not a single number, but a set of numbers. Its value depends on properties of the population that we normally do not know.

Demonstrating the Implausibility of Alternative Hypotheses

When an experimenter rejects the null hypothesis as implausible, this is merely one example of a more general process of making it clear that the independent variable, and not some other influential factor, was responsible for the outcome.

We can view the role of the experimenter as that of a person who wishes to make a claim that "Changes in variable A result in changes in variable B." But part of the experimenter acts as "devil's advocate" and says, "No, your results were merely due to error." This is the null hypothesis. The experimenter must show that it is an implausible hypothesis.

Experimenters do this by showing that the ratio of observation/noise is very high and that it is unlikely that such a large ratio would occur as a result of mere error. An experimenter may do this by inspection or statistically, but the underlying logic will be the same in any case. The experimenter, whether explicitly or implicitly, takes some estimate of effects attributable to the independent variable and compares it with an estimate of "noise" or *"error."* For example, the familiar t test used to compare the means of two groups, an experimental and a control, is really a ratio formed by taking the mean under experimental conditions, subtracting it from the control mean, and dividing by an estimate of "noise." Thus,

$$t = \frac{\text{Difference between means}}{\text{Standard error}}$$

where the "standard error" is an estimate of the noise level. We will not go into this in detail until Chapter 9, but other statistical tools can be shown to be the same sort of ratio.

The null hypothesis need not be the only plausible alternative. For example, recently I was involved in an experiment in which we compared depressive patients to nondepressive patients with respect to certain physiological measures. One of these was the blood flow in the hands, which reflects the degree of activation of the parts of the nervous system controlling "fight-flight" reactions.

We expected the depressive people to have less blood flow, but found instead that they had much more than the controls. The state of having more blood flow is usually thought to relate to being relaxed. Perhaps the depression was so severe that the patients had simply "given up" and relaxed. Unfortunately, depression is correlated with age, and an analysis of the ages of depressed versus control patients indicated that the depressed were significantly older. Thus we could not attribute the higher blood flow to depression, since it is equally plausible that it might be due to age. We then did a separate study looking at blood flow as a function of age and found no systematic relationship. Thus the alternative hypothesis was implausible, as we had earlier shown the null hypothesis to be.

Next we had to concern ourselves with the alternative hypothesis that the observed effects were due to drugs. Depressive people typically use different drugs than nondepressives. The alternative hypothesis that the observed effects were due to the differences in drugs is currently being evaluated. Eventually we hope to limit our plausible hypotheses to a single one.

The study just described illustrates very well the process whereby alternative hypotheses, including the null hypothesis, are dismissed as implausible. It is not a very good example of the design of experiments (though perhaps a realistic one), since the process of evaluating the alternative hypotheses should really have been incorporated in the original design of the experiment. Basically what we have been doing after the fact is ferreting out confounded variables. It would be best to anticipate such things while setting up the experiment in the first place. As you know, a major role of experimental design is to anticipate and control for confounding variables.

Power and Deciding How Many Subjects to Use in an Experiment

If we fail to detect a real effect of our independent variable, we have committed a type II error. It is important to have experimental designs and methods of evaluating their outcomes that make it likely that we will detect effects when they are there. If our method is unlikely to miss effects, we say it is of high *power*. "Power," then, is the technical term for *sensitivity to real effects of an independent variable.* Statisticians define power as 1 minus beta, where beta is the probability of missing an effect of the independent variable (type II error). The combined probabilities of detecting an existing effect and of failing to detect it must equal 1. If the probability of a type II error is, say, 0.50, the probability of detecting a real effect (the power of the method used) must be 1 minus 0.50 = 0.50.

Experimental tactics differ in their power. Several things can be varied to influence power. The most obvious of these is the alpha level, or probability of a type I error. Compare the influence of setting alpha at 0.001 and at 0.10. At 0.001 you are less likely to make a false alarm, to wrongly reject the null hypothesis. But this conservative criterion will also make it more likely for you to miss effects when they are there. Going back to Sally, if she insists on very strong evidence of a prowler, she will be unlikely to embarrass herself by calling the police when no one is downstairs. On the other hand, the risk of allowing a prowler free reign goes up when the demand for evidence is so high.

Power could be increased by choosing the alpha level of 0.10. In Sally's case this would be like her calling the police when the evidence was not very strong. She would be unlikely to fail to detect a prowler. On the other hand, she would be highly likely to make a false alarm. Thus, we can conclude that, although power can be increased by lowering the alpha level, this method of increasing power is not very desirable because it increases the rate of false alarms or type I errors.

Fortunately, there are other, more desirable ways to increase power. Anything that increases the size of the ratio of observed effect/noise increases power. For example, if the size of the signal is large, the ratio will be larger. We can deliberately choose to study highly influential, whopper variables. But this, too, has its drawbacks because it tends to limit the range of things we can study. A better approach is to concentrate on making the bottom half of the ratio, the noise level, smaller. One way to do this is to increase the number of observations we make in the experiment *(N)*. This can be done by including more subjects in the experiment or by taking more measurements on the subjects we already have. The larger the number of measurements, the more stable will be our estimate of the actual population values. Increased stability lowers noise.

One of the most desirable ways to increase power is use of technology (actively controlling the environment). As we manipulate the experimental environment, we can do so in ways that decrease noise level (error). Anything that minimizes the influence of the small extraneous variables that contribute to noise levels will improve power. Thus, exerting greater experimental control is a highly desirable way to improve power.

Reducing the noise level is exactly what experimental analysts of behavior do. Otherwise, they would have methods of very low power, since they depend on inspection to judge reliability. Statistical tests vary in power, but it would be hard to imagine one less powerful than mere inspection. High degrees of experimental control are usually needed to compensate for it. Experimental analysts of behavior also make very large numbers of observations. Both of these factors save them from low power.

Statistical Power Analysis: A Neglected Topic in Experimental Design

There would appear to be little point in doing an experiment that has small likelihood of permitting detection of effects *that are really there.* Yet, behavioral scientists commonly do so by designing experiments of low power. Cohen (1962) did a survey of research in abnormal-social psychology and found that the experiments typically had only enough power to detect effects of very large magnitude at the 0.05 alpha level. For the cases in which real effects were medium or small, Cohen (1962) estimated that the respective probabilities of failing to detect them were 0.52 and 0.82. The situation would be still worse for alpha values smaller than 0.05.

Behavioral scientists often choose sample sizes according to criteria unrelated to test power. It is common to use some arbitrary size such as the number of subjects readily available, the number of subjects used by previous experimenters who did related research, or the number of subjects the particular experimenter has used in the past. Such procedures are non-rational and dangerous. Cohen (1969) has provided tables of statistical power analysis that make it possible to arrive somewhat rationally at decisions regarding sample size, given a prior decision concerning alpha and a rough estimate of the anticipated effect size.

Often the sample sizes needed to have a reasonable degree of power are far greater than those we see in published articles. We need to be more careful about determining sample size. We should also learn a good lesson from the experimental analysis of behavior. Finding out how to control baseline behavior is very important, whether or not we prefer the experimental analysis of behavior.

It is not easy to decide rationally on a sample size. Dixon and Massey (1957) suggested the use of sequential designs. With a sequential design we determine the sample size while conducting the experiment. We start out with a small sample and, having completed a block of the experiment, decide (1) to reject the null hypothesis, (2) that the null hypothesis cannot be rejected, or (3) to increase the sample size.

Sometimes the first block of observations permits rejection of the null hypothesis. If so, it is all to the good. We have achieved our goal with great economy of effort. Keep in mind that rejection of the null hypothesis on the basis of a few observations is more impressive with respect to reliability than rejection on the basis of many.[2] This is because the test is of low power when there are few observations. Only very strong effects will be detected this way.

At other times, the overlap between experimental and control treatments may be so great at the end of the first block (or *n* blocks) that a virtual miracle would be needed to reject the null hypothesis, even in the long run. At such times it is wise to quit and rethink your experiment.

Then there are those times when the results are leaning in the direction of permitting you to reject the null hypothesis, but they have not

[2]Unfortunately, decisions made on the basis of small samples may be unsafe with respect to *generality*. Direct or systematic replication by conducting a coherent series of experiments will remedy this.

reached the stipulated alpha level. Here you can go on to make another block of observations.

Judging Reliability by Replication

In the long run we look at the results of more than one experiment to evaluate reliability of data. The technical term for repetition of an experiment is *replication.* Some published studies actually consist of many experiments. If several organisms are used and each receives identical treatment, as is often the case, the data for each organism can be considered a separate repetition of the basic experimental unit. In the Russian journals it is not uncommon to list data from each subject as a separate experiment. This makes a great deal of sense, provided the experiment is complete and not confounded within subjects. In some experimental designs, where control is across subjects, this kind of procedure would make less sense because the basic unit of information is the average of the group. For any given subject in such an experiment, important variables are confounded, and therefore repetition of the experiment requires that the same group—or, more often, a different group—be run through the experiment again. For obvious reasons the two types of repetition (or *replication*) just described are called *intersubject replication* and *intergroup replication* (Sidman, 1960). With intersubject replication the experiment done on one subject is repeated on other subjects and the results are compared. With intergroup replication the experiment done with one group of subjects is repeated with another group and the resulting averages compared.

Replication does not always consist merely in the exact repetition of an experiment. Such repetition is called *direct replication.* It is often a better strategy to start a new experiment, which yields new information and also shows whether the previous results can be replicated.

For example, I once ran an experiment that included taking measures of the ability of albino rats to perform on visual discrimination tasks with one eye when the task was learned with only the other eye open (Sheridan, 1965a). Such transfer from one eye to the other is called interocular transfer. When I moved to a new university, I wanted to replicate the experiment. One strategy would have been to move the original apparatus to the new location, obtain rats from the same colony, run the rats myself, and in general conduct the new experiment as nearly as possible in the same way as the original one. Instead, I had a new apparatus built that was similar but not identical to the original one, a different strain of albino rats was used, and a colleague ran most of the rats. If the results were like those of the original study, the experiment would not only show that the original results could be replicated, but also that the original results held despite variations in rat strain, experimenter, and other changed factors. If, on the other hand, the results were not repeated, it would be necessary to go in search of the relevant variables.

Such a search can entail much work, but it will tell a great deal about the relevant variables in the original study. The worst that can happen, then, is that variables previously thought to be irrelevant will reveal their influence. And that is not bad at all. On the other hand, obtaining results essentially similar to those of the original experiment would mean that the effort entailed in a direct replication had been spared. The results of the experiment described above were in fact virtually identical to the original ones (Sheridan & Shrout, 1965).

When we conduct a new experiment that will also show the replicability of an earlier one, the procedure is called *systematic replication* (Sidman, 1960). It is a case of systematic replication when we use the results of one experiment to create a baseline for a new experiment. For example, an early discovery that organisms rewarded only occasionally for responses are very persistent in responding when rewards are withdrawn has provided a baseline that is often used to study the effects of a wide variety of variables. Each new study is a systematic replication.

SUMMARY

1. There are essentially two methods for assessing the reliability of data (whether the independent variable really had an effect); we can do so by *inspection* or by *inferential statistics.* In both cases the magnitude of the treatment effect is judged relative to the magnitude of error variance ("random" variability) in the data.
2. There are two situations in which reliability can be judged by inspection of the data.
   - (a) *Whopper variable:* In this case the treatment effect is so great that it causes a complete or virtually complete separation of data from treated and untreated conditions. Though variability of scores may be substantial, there is little or no overlap of results from experimental and control conditions. This is illustrated in Figure 8.1.
   - (b) *High level of experimental control:* In this case the independent variable need not be a whopper variable. Stringent experimental control has led to an extremely low level of variability of the scores. Thus, despite the small magnitude of the treatment effect, there is little or no overlap. This is illustrated in Figure 8.2.
3. Mere inspection provides an insensitive test of reliability. The eye commonly fails to detect real treatment effects. Thus, for cases in which there is substantial overlap between treatment and control conditions, true effects must be detected by using statistical inference. Such inference

takes into account the apparent magnitude of treatment effects and the degree of variability of the data. It does so more quantitatively and exactly than does inspection.

4. The notion that the independent variable had no effect is called the *null hypothesis.* We determine the reliability of the independent variable's effect by contrasting it to outcomes expected if the null hypothesis were true. In the experimental analysis of behavior this is done by running subjects many, many times without the independent variable and by contrasting the results with those obtained under the influence of the independent variable. In contrast, the statistical approach is to estimate from control data the results that would occur in the long run without an effect of the independent variable. Experimental and statistical analyses both operate by contrasting null outcomes to those actually observed with the independent variable.

5. Basically, both procedures entail looking at a ratio of the effect observed *with* the independent variable to the effect *without* it. The variation found without it may be considered noise. The effect with it is either noise alone or signal plus noise. We want to decide whether there is a signal. If there is not, the ratio should be close to 1. If it is larger than that, we have evidence for a signal. How large does it have to be? We decide this arbitrarily.

6. The *alpha level* of probability is a function of the size of the ratio that we accept for rejection of the null hypothesis. It is typically set at 0.05, which means that one time in twenty we expect to reject the null hypothesis when it is true, to give a false alarm. False alarms are called *type I errors.* The alpha level is actually the probability of a type I error. Another type of error is to miss a signal when it is really there. A miss is called a *type II error.* The probability of a type II error is called *beta.*

7. The process of rejecting the null hypothesis is merely a special case of the more general process of collecting evidence against plausible alternatives to the experimental hypothesis that the treatment produced effects. Alternatives besides the null hypothesis are those that attribute observed effects to various sources of confounding.

8. The power of a test is its sensitivity to signals, to real effects of the independent variable. Since beta is the probability of missing a real effect, power is 1 - beta. Power is influenced by the size of the real effect (is it a whopper variable?), the sample size, the degree of noise in the experiment, and the arbitrary alpha level. There is evidence that many experiments done in psychology are of low power. This could be raised by increasing the degree of experimental control or increasing sample size. We have no control over the size of the real effect (except to choose whopper variables for investigation), and lowering the alpha level would increase type I errors.

9. How do we decide what sample size to use? Most investigators simply choose a size used by other investigators working in the same area. This is not necessarily safe. Cohen (1969) shows a way to estimate the sample size needed to give adequate power. Doing experiments sequentially is another alternative. This means conducting a block of the experiment, then deciding whether to reject the null hypothesis, to add another block of subjects to increase power, or to redesign the experiment more judiciously.

10. In establishing reliability of results, nothing is superior to repeating an experiment (replication). Replication may be *intersubject,* in which a controlled experiment done on one subject is repeated with others, or *intergroup,* in which a controlled experiment done on one group of subjects is repeated with another group. Replication may be *direct,* which means that the same experiment is repeated in all its details. On the other hand, it may be *systematic.* This means that a new experiment contains conditions that will tell whether the first experiment had reliable and general results. For example, a finding from the first experiment may provide a baseline for a second experiment. Systematic replications provide evidence for both reliability and generality. However, failure in systematic replication may require considerable search for the responsible variables, since several things have changed at once.

CHAPTER 9

Statistical Analysis of Data

An Overview of Statistical Inference
Statistical Testing When Mean and Variance of the Population Are Known.
From ratio to probability
Statistical Testing with Estimated Population Values
The role of degrees of freedom in estimating parameters
The *t* Test
Determining the probability of a given *t* ratio
One-tailed versus two-tailed tests
Analysis of Variance and the *F* Test
One-way analysis of variance
Multifactor Anova
Pairwise Comparisons after Analysis of Variance

In Chapter 8 it was pointed out that there is a common logic underlying statistical and nonstatistical judgments of the reliability of data. Either by inspection or statistically, we compare observed outcomes under the treatment conditions with those obtained under conditions where only error is operating. We look for a sharp *contrast* between the outcomes due to "noise" and the outcomes observed under treatment conditions. Finding such a contrast, we conclude that the treatment was effective.

The statistical approach differs from the nonstatistical one with respect to how systematically we go about identifying the contrast. With statistics we do it very systematically, and this results in very high sensitivity. Effects can be detected statistically that would likely go unnoticed by the naked eye. In this respect, statistics plays a role much like that of the microscope or telescope. It enables us to discriminate differences that might otherwise be obscured. Small differences can be discriminated by mere inspection only when the noise level has been reduced to low levels through strong technological control.

The purpose of the present chapter is to elaborate on the previous, highly general account of how we judge the reliability of a variable's effect. Here we will deal in some detail with the rationale statisticians use to reject the hypothesis that error by itself produced observed outcomes. The emphasis here will not be on procedures most convenient for calculation. These will be given in Appendixes E, F, and G for a wide array of useful statistical procedures.

An Overview of Statistical Inference

Our fundamental goal in statistical inference is to expose the implausibility of the view that a given experimental outcome was merely due to error. That view is, of course, the null hypothesis. We wish to show that the null hypothesis is not one that a reasonable person would hold.

The basic method of exposing the implausibility of the null hypothesis is to show that observed outcomes differ markedly from those expected to occur if only error were operating. But how marked must the difference be? Take the ratio

$$\frac{\text{Signal?} + \text{Noise}}{\text{Noise}}$$

If the ratio is very close to 1, it is easy to see that the top and bottom of the fraction do not differ *markedly.* Such a ratio would lead us to suspect that only noise was operating—that there was no true signal. We obviously cannot, under such circumstances, deem the null hypothesis implausible. The ratio must be larger than 1. But, again, how much larger?

What statisticians have done is to answer that question with a *probability value.* If a ratio occurs that is not likely to occur when only noise is operating, then we reject the null hypothesis. The probability will tell us how frequently, in the long run, we can expect to be wrong in rejecting the null hypothesis. The level at which we set that probability value (which is the alpha level) depends on what frequency of errors we consider acceptable. Remember, we cannot reasonably set the alpha level at extremely low levels because the result will be a statistical procedure that is insensitive to real effects of the independent variable (see Chapter 8).

Our fundamental problem, then, is one of determining the probability of some sort of ratio composed of

$$\frac{\text{Observed outcome}}{\text{Measure of error}}$$

So one of the things a statistic must achieve is the conversion of such a ratio into a probability value. But before this can be done, we have to obtain the ratio itself. In order to do *that,* we need two things: (1) a measure of the observed effect (signal? + noise) and (2) a measure of error (noise).

Since we almost never have a complete record of errors from the population of interest, we must *estimate* the true levels of error. It is usually this estimate that actually goes in the bottom of our desired ratio. The device we use for estimating error of measurement is a *variance.* But it must be a variance uninfluenced by effects of the independent variable. Since variations *within* groups cannot be due to the effects of the independent variable (that variable is either absent or held constant within the groups), variances within groups can be used as a basis for making the desired estimate.

Statistical Testing When Mean and Variance of the Population Are Known

It is relatively rare that we know the mean and variance of the target population at the time of doing a statistical test. But this is sometimes known (or it can sometimes be assumed), and tests of statistical significance under such conditions are relatively easy to understand. Thus I will begin with a test of this type, later dealing with the additional problems brought on by having to estimate variability.

Suppose you have conducted an experiment that provided a sample mean that may be different from a known population mean. Assume, for example, that you know that the mean IQ for a given population is 100, and you test a group of 50 people who were given a special program to increase IQ. You find a resulting mean IQ of 120. You want to know whether your tested group differs significantly from the known population. An appropriate statistic would be the following:

$$z = \frac{M_s - M_{pop}}{SE_{pop}}$$

where M_s = the mean of the sample, M_{pop} = the mean of the population, and SE_{pop} = the *standard error* of the population. The difference between the mean IQ of your treated group and the mean of the population may be due to error alone, or it may be due to a combination of real effectiveness of your program plus error. Thus the top part of the statistic is equivalent to our familiar "signal? + noise."

The standard error is a measure of the noise level in the population. The standard error differs from the standard deviation. It is in fact equal to the standard deviation of the population divided by the square root of the sample size.

$$SE_{pop} = \frac{s_{pop}}{\sqrt{N_s}}$$

Why introduce this new statistic, the standard error? Why not simply use the standard deviation of the population as a measure of noise? The reason is that the standard deviation will exaggerate the magnitude of the noise. If you take the means of a large number of samples of size 50, they will be less variable than the individual scores.

You may remember from our earlier discussion of measurement that a reason for calculating means is to cancel out the influence of random errors. Random errors tend, in the long run, to be equally above or below the mean of the population of scores. When we take the mean of a sample, some, though not all, of the random error will have been canceled out. Thus the variability of a large number of means will be less than the variability of the individual scores on which they were calculated. Also, the degree of that variability will be less the larger the size of the samples on which the means are calculated. Therefore, the standard deviation of the population must be corrected for the influence of sample size. For this reason the standard error, which is merely the standard deviation of a set of *means* taken from a population, includes the square root of N as a divisor. The standard error is the standard deviation of the population divided by the square root of the number of observations in the sample.

From Ratio to Probability

At this point we have established that the z statistic provides a ratio of (signal? + noise)/noise. But we want to derive a probability value from that ratio. Assuming that we are willing to risk a false alarm rate of 5 percent, how can we tell that a given z would occur less than 5 percent of the time, given that only error was operating? If the variability in our population is due to many, many small contributions of random factors, it is reasonable to assume that the distribution of the population is a Gaussian one. But we already learned in Chapter 7 that fixed proportions of the scores in a Gaussian (normal) distribution are included at given numbers of standard deviations from the mean. About 95 percent of the cases will be included within $\pm$ 1.96 standard deviations. Since the standard error *is* a standard deviation of sample means, the z statistic is in standard deviation units. Therefore if z is more than 2, we know that a z of that size will occur less than 5 percent of the time if error alone is operating. We can therefore reject the null hypothesis.

Going back to our example of IQ testing, assume that the standard deviation of the population is 15. Then

$$z = \frac{120 - 100}{15/\sqrt{50}} = 9.43$$

A value as large as that would occur much less frequently than 5 percent of the time if only error of measurement were operating (contrast 1.96 and 9.43). Thus the null hypothesis is quite implausible, and we would reject it.

Statistical Testing with Estimated Population Values

Most of the time we do not have direct access to parameters of our target population. Take the case in which we conduct an experiment with an experimental and a control group. At the end of the experiment we can calculate means and standard deviations for each group, but this only provides us with a basis for *estimating* parameters of the population. How do we construct our ratio and find its probability in such cases?

The top of the desired ratio is not hard to develop. If we calculate a mean for the experimental group and a mean for the control group, the difference between these two means is due to noise and may or may not also be due to signal. Thus we already have signal? + noise. The problem lies in estimating the noise level of the population.

There are two separate sources of information upon which to base an estimate of noise. Since the treatment condition is not present in the control group, variability *within* that group provides one estimate of the level of noise. Within the experimental group, the treatment condition is held constant. So the variability *within* that group also provides an estimate of the noise level.

Statisticians make the assumption that these two estimates of the noise level would, in the long run, yield equal values. That is to say, if we were to conduct many, many such tests, the mean values of the two estimates of variability would come closer and closer to being equal. This assumption is known as the assumption of *homogeneity of variance.*

Of course, we cannot simply use the variances or standard deviations of the experimental and control groups as estimates of error. One reason for this is that we are interested in estimating the variances of *the means of samples* of the size we used in our experiment. We are not interested in estimating the standard deviation of the population but, rather, its standard error. Thus we must correct for the size of the sample, as we did in the earlier example of the *z* statistic. Unfortunately, it is not so simple as dividing by the square root of *N*, as we did with the *z* statistic. Instead, we divide by the square root of the *degrees of freedom.* We must explain degrees of freedom before proceeding.

The Role of Degrees of Freedom in Estimating Parameters

When we do not know actual values of various parameters of our target population, we must estimate them. Obviously, we want the best possible estimate. Often, a simple descriptive statistic from a sample is the best estimate of its corresponding parameter. For example, the best estimate of the mean of a population is the mean of the sample from that population. Sometimes, though, the best estimate of the parameter is not quite the same as the corresponding descriptive statistic. Although a demonstration of it would be out of place here, it can be shown that the best estimate of the standard deviation of a population is not the sum of the squared deviations from the mean divided by *N*. Rather, it is the sum of the squared deviations from the mean divided by $N - 1$. That is, the formula for the standard deviation as a descriptive statistic is

$$\sqrt{\frac{\sum_{i=1}^{n} d_i^2}{N}}$$

whereas the formula for the standard deviation as an estimate of the standard deviation of a population is

$$\sqrt{\frac{\sum_{i=1}^{n} d_i^2}{N-1}}$$

where

d_i = the deviation of a given score from the mean
N = the number of scores
$\sum_{i=1}^{n}$ = summation of all the d_i scores,

When the standard deviation of a sample is being used as an estimate of a population value, we divide by degrees of freedom (usually abbreviated "df").

The number of degrees of freedom is the number of observations that are actually *free to vary.* It is equal to the number of scores with *independent* information. Put another way, the number of degrees of freedom equals the number of scores less the number of estimated parameters used in calculating the sum of squares. Since the mean is used in calculating the standard deviation, we must subtract 1 from N (only *one* estimated mean is used) in order to determine the degrees of freedom.

As an example to illustrate why there are fewer than N scores that are free to vary, take the simple case of a sample composed of three scores, 10, 12, and 8. The mean of these equals 10. We estimate the population mean to be 10. Now we calculate the sum of the squared deviations from the mean by subtracting each score from the estimated parameter, 10, squaring each difference, and summing the three resulting squares. Now 10 minus 10 equals zero and 12 minus 10 equals 2. Is our last score free to vary? Not if the mean equals 10 and the sample size is 3. The only number it can be is 8. If you like, try any other number for yourself. It won't work. Hence the last score does not give us independent information. The number of degrees of freedom in this case equals $3 - 1 = 2$.

The *t* Test

We are now very close to having developed the widely used statistic called the *t* test. The formula for *t* is simply:

$$t = \frac{\text{Mean}_e - \text{Mean}_c}{\text{Estimated SE}}$$

where Mean_e = the mean for the experimental group, Mean_c = the mean for the control group, and Estimated SE is the estimated standard error of the population based on the estimates of that standard error pooled for the two groups.

It is obvious how to obtain the difference between the two means. How do we obtain the desired estimate of the standard error? Remember from our discussion of the *z* statistic that the formula for the standard error as a parameter was

$$\text{SE}_{pop} = \frac{\text{SD}_{pop}}{\sqrt{N}} = \frac{(\text{SD}_{pop})^2}{N}$$

The estimated SE, based on information pooled from the experimental and the control group is

$$\text{SE}_{est} = \sqrt{\frac{(\text{SD}_{pooled}{}^2)^2}{n_1} + \frac{(\text{SD}_{pooled})^2}{n_2}} = \sqrt{(\text{SD}_{pooled})^2\left(\frac{1}{n_1} + \frac{1}{n_2}\right)}$$

where

SE_{est} = the estimated standard error of the difference between the means

$(SD_{pooled})^2$ = the pooled variance of the groups

n_1 = the number of subjects in group 1

n_2 = the number of subjects in group 2

The formula for the pooled variance of the groups, $(SD_{pooled})^2$ is

$$(SD_{pooled})^2 = \frac{(n_1 - 1)\,SD_1^2 + (n_2 - 1)\,SD_2^2}{n_1 + n_2 - 2}$$

where

SD_1^2 = the variance estimate of group 1

SD_2^2 = the variance estimate of group 2

n_1 = the number of subjects in group 1

n_2 = the number of subjects in group 2

By incorporating the formula for $(SD_{pooled})^2$ into the formula for SE_{est}, we obtain a one-step formula for SE_{est}:

$$SE_{est} = \sqrt{\frac{(n_1 - 1)SD_1^2 + (n_2 - 1)SD_2^2}{n_1 + n_2 - 2}\left(\frac{1}{n_1} + \frac{1}{n_2}\right)}$$

The formula for t then becomes:

$$t = \frac{\text{Mean}_e - \text{Mean}_c}{\sqrt{\frac{(n_1 - 1)SD_1^2 + (n_2 - 1)SD_2^2}{n_1 + n_2 - 2}\left(\frac{1}{n_1} + \frac{1}{n_2}\right)}}$$

Since the standard error was based on two estimated parameters rather than one (the mean of each group was used as an estimate), this t is based on $n_e + n_c - 2$ degrees of freedom.

Determining the Probability of a Given t Ratio

The t ratio only approximates a Gaussian distribution as the sample size becomes quite large. In particular, for sample sizes below 30, the t distribution deviates significantly from a Gaussian one. The distribution of t depends, then, on sample size—or, more exactly, on degrees of freedom. The distributions for various degrees of freedom are needed in order to determine what proportion of the time we can expect a given t value to occur if only error is operating.

The various t distributions for different degrees of freedom were long ago worked out by the mathematician, William Gossett, who used the pseudonym Student. Tables based on his mathematical functions are widely available in elementary textbooks of statistics, as well as in Appendix C of this book. Obviously, you must know the degrees of freedom in order to find the correct distribution.

The tables generally do not give the entire distribution, but only several major percentile cutoffs, including those cutoffs widely used as alpha levels. Take, for example, the case in which there are 10 subjects in each of two independent groups and the alpha level has been set at .05. There are $10 + 10 - 2 = 18$ df. Looking at the t table in Appendix C, we see that a t ratio as large as 2.101 would be expected to occur only 5 percent of the time at that number of df. Thus a t that large or larger would constitute grounds for rejecting the null hypothesis.

One-tailed versus Two-tailed Tests

If you look at Appendix C, you will see that two different percentile cutoffs (probabilities, alpha levels) are given for each size of the t ratio. One of them is for a *one-tailed test* and the other is for a *two-tailed test.* In the examples discussed so far, we have treated only the case appropriate for the two-tailed test. Usually we are interested in the hypothesis that the mean outcome under our treatment condition differs in *any way* from an outcome due to error alone. Thus, a value either significantly greater or significantly less than those reasonably expected under the null hypothesis can be used as confirmation of the statistical significance of our finding.

Sometimes, however, we may have a hypothesis that is unidirectional. In such a case we may for example be predicting that the treatment under study results in scores greater than those that would occur without the treatment. Suppose we are trying a method for increasing IQ. Our prediction focuses solely on the possibility of higher scores in the treated subjects. Under such conditions, many investigators argue that so-called one-tailed statistical tests can be used.

What is a one-tailed test? In the examples given so far to illustrate rejection of the null hypothesis, the 5 percent cutoff consisted of values *above* those expected by chance alone (2.5 percent) as well as of values *below* those expected by chance (2.5 percent). If we are only interested in one of these directions, then the alpha level is really not 5 percent. Rather, it is 2.5 percent. To keep the value at 5 percent, it would be necessary to use a one-tailed test. A substantially smaller t ratio would then permit rejection of the null hypothesis. For example, if we consider the 5 percent region of rejection mentioned in the previous section for a t with $df = 18$, the value was 2.101 for a two-tailed test. For a one-tailed test, a value of $t = 1.740$ or larger would permit us to affirm our experimental hypothesis and reject the null hypothesis.

The question of whether one should use one-tailed tests is highly controversial. Such tests are clearly legitimate in those rare cases in which a reliable outcome in the direction opposite the predicted one would be impossible or make no sense. For example, since there can be no temperatures lower than absolute zero, it would be absurd to treat this as a possible outcome in an experiment designed to test a treatment expected to produce warming above that value. Unfortunately, such cases are rare in psychology. More often, the results *might* turn out to be significantly in the direction opposite the predicted one. In such an instance, an experimenter who had opted for a one-tailed test could only legitimately conclude that the experiment provided no basis for affirming the original experimental hypothesis. It would *not* be legitimate, after the fact, to change to a two-tailed hypothesis. For this reason it is generally prudent to adhere to the use of two-tailed tests.

Analysis of Variance and the *F* Test

It is rare for contemporary experiments to be designed with only two levels of the independent variable. Much more often, experiments have several levels of the variable or variables of interest. The increasing complexity of modern experimental designs requires that we give a great deal of attention to statistical tests other than the *t* test.

Obviously we could analyze data from an experiment with three levels by doing separate *t* tests for each possible pair of levels. But this is not a desirable way to analyze the data because it increases the expected frequency of false alarms above the nominal alpha level. Suppose I take a coin from my pocket and announce to you that I am willing to bet that I can toss a "head." Assuming that you take my bet, suppose now that I at first toss a "tail," then start tossing again and again till I *do* get a head. You are likely to say that I owe you some money. But I only said I could toss a head! I did not say I could do it on the first try. Clearly, it would be a mistake to make such a bet without restricting my opportunities to make tosses. The more times I toss, the more likely it becomes that I will toss a "head."

A similar situation prevails when I set the alpha level at 5 percent, then do several *t* tests. The probability of a type I error is 5 percent only when I am limited to a single test. The more tries I get, the higher the probability becomes. Statisticians have therefore devised methods that circumvent this problem. The *analysis of variance* (anova) permits the simultaneous assessment of whether something more than error is responsible for differences observed in multilevel experiments.

The logic of the analysis of variance is almost identical to that underlying the *t* test. Once again, we need to find the familiar ratio of (signal? + noise)/noise. The bottom part of the ratio is, again, an estimate of the noise level. Since variability within groups cannot be due to the independent variable (that variable is either absent or held constant *within* groups), a measure of variability within groups is used as an estimate of the noise level. More specifically, the *variance* within groups provides the noise estimate and the bottom part of the ratio.

With the *t* test, the top of the desired ratio is provided by subtracting one mean from the other. Since there are several means (one for each of the levels of the treatment) to be compared in analysis of variance, such a simple method is not feasible. Instead, what we do is calculate another variance—the variance between groups. The result is the *F* statistic, for which a conceptual formula is:

$$F = \frac{\text{Between-groups variance}}{\text{Within-groups variance}}$$

Like the *t* statistic, the *F* statistic is not normally distributed at many of its levels. It also has various distributions, depending on the number of degrees of freedom. Furthermore, the *F* statistic has two different degrees of freedom, one for the numerator (top of the ratio, between-groups variance) and one for the denominator (bottom of the ratio, within-groups variance). Fortunately, the distributions have been worked out and are readily available, as in Appendix D.

One-way Analysis of Variance

We will now work out in some detail the rationale underlying analysis of variance for the simple case of a single-factor design.

Suppose someone has discovered a drug purporting to make people more intelligent. You have it in the form of pills—call them "smart pills." You want to test whether they work. Since they might be effective in some doses but not in others, you decide to use two widely different doses and a placebo control. Twelve people participate in the experiment. You randomly assign four subjects to each group. You find an excellent test to use as a dependent variable. Call it the "Schlepper Test of Mental Acuity." Results are as follows:

Placebo Subject Score	Low Dosage Subject Score	High Dosage Subject Score
Sam 102	Cecilia 133	Mike 140
Mary 111	April 124	Josh 141
June 107	Kelly 120	Holly 152
George 120	Bill 125	Louie 143
Means: X_P = 110.0	X_L = 125.5	X_H = 144.0
Grand Mean (T) = 126.5		

Now let's take a look at Louie. His score is 143.0. If the smart pills worked, and it looks as though they might have, his score is due to two different things. One of them is error, that is, noise. The other is an actual effect of the pills. We can view his score as a deviation from the Grand Mean ($\overline{T}$). The Grand Mean is simply the mean of all twelve scores, ignoring from which group they came. Louie's deviation from $\overline{T}$ is 143.0 – 126.5 = 17.5. If his score of 143 were a measure unalloyed by error, we could say that all of this deviation was due to an actual effect of the pills. But we know that any real observation contains an admixture of error. So this total deviation of 17.5 could be partitioned into a part that is really due to the independent variable and a part that is noise.

How can we get an estimate of what is noise? A good estimate of noise would be the amount of deviation from the mean with the influence of the pills taken out. Remember that *within* each subgroup that influence of the pills is either absent or held constant. Why not take as our estimate of noise some measure of the deviations of scores within a subgroup from the mean of that subgroup? Louie's deviation from his subgroup mean is 143.0 – 144.0 = –1. This gives us a basis for estimating how much of his 17.5-point deviation from the Grand Mean is due to noise.

Maybe now is a good time to remind you that we cannot use the simple deviations with their signs as a measure of dispersion. These deviations around the mean will always sum to zero. So we will square them and find the mean of their squares, using the *variance* as our measure of deviation. The *F* ratio is a ratio of variances.

Now that we have a basis for a noise estimate, we can put something in the bottom (denominator) of the ratio. But what shall we put in the top (numerator)? We need an estimate of the deviations (variance) due to the independent variable. We are treating $\overline{T}$ as the estimate of the true overall mean. The obvious thing is to use the mean of each subgroup as the estimate of the population mean for a given drug condition. There are three subgroup means, and they can be treated as scores deviating around $\overline{T}$.

We took out the influence of the independent variable and calculated variance within groups to get an estimate of noise. Conversely, to get an estimate of the effect of the independent variable we must take out the noise, the variance within groups. Taking the mean for each group does just that. The deviations *within* groups are of individual scores around the group means. Now we calculate a variance *between* groups. For each group, we take the group mean, subtract $\overline{T}$ from it, and square the result. This gives us a squared group deviation from $\overline{T}$. That squared deviation is due to differences between groups, with differences within groups taken out. The resulting number can be applied to each subject in the group, to represent this subject's contribution to the variance between groups. Thus, the squared "between-groups" deviation for a given group must be multiplied by the number of subjects in that group.

To get the total sum of squares between groups you must add the between-groups sums of squares for each group. So, for your experiment on smart pills, you would figure a between-groups sum of squares for the Placebo Group, for the Low Dosage Group, and for the High Dosage Group. You would then add them all up. Thus

$$n_{\text{Placebo}} (\text{Mean}_{\text{Placebo}} - \overline{T})^2 + n_{\text{Low Dosage}} (\text{Mean}_{\text{Low Dosage}} - \overline{T})^2 + n_{\text{High Dosage}} (\text{Mean}_{\text{High Dosage}} - \overline{T})^2 = \text{Sum of squares between groups}$$

Now, keep in mind that the variance is an *average* or *mean* of squared deviations. The number obtained at this point is a sum of squared deviations. To get a mean, you sum, then divide by something. To get the variances for the F ratio, you divide by *degrees of freedom.*

The variance between groups is based on one estimated population mean, $\overline{T}$ (the Grand Mean), and the means of each of the groups, treated as scores. In our "smart pill" example, there are three groups. The number of degrees of freedom for the variance between groups is therefore again 3 – 1 = 2. In general, the number of degrees of freedom for the variance *between* groups is equal to the number of groups minus one. Calculation of variance *within* groups is based on deviations around the means of each individual group. In the "smart pill" experiment, there were three groups of four subjects each. Three means were used as estimates. Thus, instead of taking the total number of subjects (12) as the divisor for the sum of squares of deviations from the respective group means, we must subtract one for each estimated mean. So we subtract one per group. Hence the number of degrees of freedom within groups is equal to the total number of subjects minus the number of groups. In our example this is 12 – 3 = 9.

We started out by saying that Louie's deviation of 17.5 from $\overline{T}$ could be broken down into two parts. These were the deviation between groups (signal) and the deviation within groups (noise). This says that the total deviation is equal to the sum of deviations from these two component sources. The total variance is equal to the sum of the variance between groups plus the variance within groups. How many degrees of freedom are there for the total sum of squares? The deviation values on which it is based are obtained by subtracting each individual's score from $\overline{T}$. Hence the number of degrees of freedom equals the total number of scores minus one for the estimated parameter $(\overline{T})$.

The F ratio is the mean square (MS) between groups over the mean square within groups; that is,

$$F = \frac{\text{MS}_{\text{between}}}{\text{MS}_{\text{within}}}$$

Each mean square is simply the sum of squares divided by its appropriate number of degrees of freedom.

Some Basic Formulas for One-Way Anova

Detailed computational procedures for one-way anova are given in Appendix F. In the present section I will give an overview of formulas for such an anova.

Total Sum of Squares. A sum of squared deviation from the mean is called a *sum of squares.* The total sum of squares is defined as

$$SS_T = \Sigma(X - \overline{X})^2$$

where, $\overline{X}$ = grand mean for all scores in the experiment and Σ = summation across all scores. This is merely the top of the formula for variance. A more generally useful formula may be obtained by carrying out the squaring operation indicated in the definitional formula and then simplifying.

$$\begin{aligned} \Sigma(X - \overline{X})^2 &= \Sigma X^2 - 2\Sigma X\overline{X} + N\overline{X}^2 \\ &= \Sigma X^2 - \frac{2\Sigma X \Sigma X}{N} + N\left(\frac{\Sigma X}{N}\right)^2 \\ &= \Sigma X^2 - \frac{2(\Sigma X)^2}{N} + \frac{(\Sigma X)^2}{N} \\ &= \Sigma X^2 - \frac{(\Sigma X)^2}{N} \end{aligned}$$

where N = the total number of scores in the experiment. Since the final part of this formula $(\Sigma X^2)/N$ is inevitably subtracted in the process of deriving a sum of squares, it is commonly called a *correction factor,* symbolized C.

Sum of Squares between Groups. The definitional formula for the sum of squares between groups is

$$SS_b = \Sigma N_G (\overline{X}_G - \overline{X})^2$$

where

N_G = number of scores in group G
$\overline{X}_G$ = mean for group G
$\overline{X}$ = grand mean
Σ = summation across all *groups*

A simpler computing formula is

$$SS_b = \frac{(\Sigma X_1)^2}{N_1} + \frac{(\Sigma X_2)^2}{N_2} + \cdots \frac{(\Sigma X_k)^2}{N_k} - C$$

where

ΣX_1 = sum of scores in group 1
ΣX_2 = sum of scores in group 2
ΣX_k = sum of scores in group k
k = the number of groups
N_1 = the number of scores in group 1
N_2 = the number of scores in group 2
N_k = the number of scores in group k
C = the correction factor

Sum of Squares within Groups. The definitional formula for the sum of squares within groups is

$$SS_w = \Sigma(X_1 - \bar{X}_1)^2 + \Sigma(X_2 - \bar{X}_2)^2 + \cdots + \Sigma(X_k - \bar{X}_k)^2$$

where

X_1 = score in group 1, X_2 = score in group 2,...
k = last group
$\bar{X}_1$ = mean of group 1, $\bar{X}_2$ = mean of group 2,...
Σ = summation across the number of cases within the given group.

A more commonly used formula is based on the fact that the total sum of squares equals the sum of squares between groups plus the sum of squares within groups. Thus

$$SS_w = SS_T - SS_b$$

Mean Squares and *F* ratio. In general, estimated variances can be derived only by taking sums of squares and dividing by their appropriate degrees of freedom. The resulting estimates of population variances are called mean squares. The sum of squares between groups must be divided by df = $k - 1$, where k = the number of groups. The sum of squares within groups must be divided by df = $N - k$, where N = the total number of scores in the experiment and k = the total number of groups.

The F ratio is simply the mean square between groups divided by the mean square within groups:

$$F = \frac{MS_b}{MS_w}$$

Obtaining the Significance of an F Ratio

As I pointed out earlier, there are different distributions of F for different degrees of freedom. There are also degrees of freedom for the numerator and for the denominator. In order to determine the cutoff for a given alpha level, it is necessary to enter the F table (Appendix D) with specification of df for the numerator and for the denominator. The columns from top to bottom of the table correspond to the numerator (degrees of freedom between groups) and the rows across the table correspond to the denominator (degrees of freedom within groups).

Multifactor Anova

The basic principles of analysis of variance are represented by the simple one-way anova just described. The total variance is partitioned into two parts, variance between groups and variance within groups. This partitioning permits formation of an F ratio, which, in turn, makes it possible to determine whether the outcome is reasonably explained by the null hypothesis.

With more complex experimental designs, the same basic process of partitioning into different sources of variance is also used. However, there are more possible sources. Take, for example, a 2 × 2 completely randomized factorial design (see Chapter 6). This design can be represented in the following matrix:

		Factor A Level 1	Factor A Level 2
Factor B Level	1		
	2		

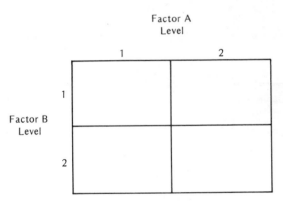

When we partition the variance into the various possible sources, there are all of the following possibilities:

1. Within-groups variance
2. Variance due to factor A (between groups for factor A)
3. Variance due to factor B (between groups for factor B)
4. Variance due to the *interaction* of factor A and factor B.

It is therefore necessary to determine the sums of squares and mean squares for each of these potential sources of variance.

Detailed methods of computation for various complex multifactor designs are given in Appendix G. But let us overview the method of partitioning variance in a multifactor design like the present example. In order to identify the variance due to the single factor of interest in one-way analysis of variance, we obtained means *within levels* of the factor. We then regarded the mean for each level as representing each subject's contribution to the influence of the between-groups factor. Thus the formula for the between-groups variance was

$$SS_b = \Sigma N_G (\bar{X}_G - \bar{X})^2$$

where

N_G = number of scores in group C
$\bar{X}_G$ = the mean of group G
$\bar{X}$ = the grand mean
Σ = summation across all groups

The mean for each group is being treated as though it were each subject's individual score. Indeed, it *is* each subject's score after influences of all other factors have been canceled out by averaging across those factors.

Remember that a sum of squares can be calculated by the formula

$$\Sigma X_i^2 - \frac{(\Sigma X_i)^2}{N} = \Sigma X_i^2 - C$$

Thus the process of obtaining a mean within factors and treating that as if it represented each subject can be done as well by the computationally simpler formula. This formula is especially advantageous because the correction factor, *C*, proves to be the same regardless of which factor or interaction is being partitioned.

Obtaining the Sum of Squares for Factor A

The process of obtaining the sum of squares for factor A is fundamentally identical to the process used for obtaining a sum of squares between groups in a single-factor design. The only difference lies in the fact that summation within levels of factor A requires that you ignore levels of factor B, that you sum across the latter levels. Since each level of factor B is equally represented within a given level of factor A, the influence of factor B is controlled within those levels. We therefore sum within levels of factor A, square each resulting sum, then add the resulting squares together. This means, in the present example, summing down each column of the matrix, squaring the sums, dividing each sum by the number of scores on which it was based, and then adding the results together. The sum of squares for factor A will result merely by subtracting the correction factor from the previously obtained value.

Obtaining the Sum of Squares for Factor B

The process of obtaining the sum of squares for factor B is identical for that used for factor A, except that we sum within levels of factor B and ignore levels of factor A. For the present example this means that we sum each row of the matrix, square it, divide by the underlying *n*, add up the resulting squares, and subtract *C*.

Obtaining the Sum of Squares for the Interaction of A × B

The same basic process is used to get the sum of squares for the interaction of A × B. In this case, however, summation is within each *combination of levels* of factors A and B. The possible combinations are factor A, level 1 with factor B, level 1; factor A, level 1 with factor B, level 2; factor A, level 2 with factor B, level 1; factor A, level 2 with factor B, level 2. Thus we sum within each of the *cells* of the matrix, square the resulting sums, divide by the number of scores underlying the sum, and add the results. Finally, we subtract *C*.

Obtaining the Total Sum of Squares

In order to get the total sum of squares, we simply ignore all levels of all factors and square all the scores and then add them up into one grand total. We then subtract *C* from that total.

Obtaining the Sum of Squares Due to Error

The total sum of squares is simply the sum of all the different partitions. Thus

$$SS_T = SS_{\text{factor A}} + SS_{\text{factor B}} + SS_{A \times B} + SS_{\text{error}}$$

Therefore we can obtain SS_{error} by the following formula:

$$SS_{\text{error}} = SS_T - SS_{\text{factor A}} - SS_{\text{factor B}} - SS_{A \times B}$$

Obtaining the Mean Squares

In order to obtain the mean squares, we must divide each of the sums of squares by their appropriate degrees of freedom. The degrees of freedom for various analyses are given in Appendices E-G, along with computational methods and worked examples. For the present example, the following degrees of freedom would be appropriate:

$df_{SST} = N - 1$
df_A = number of levels of factor A - 1
df_B = number of levels of factor B - 1
$df_{A \times B} = df_A \times df_B$
$df_{\text{error}} = df_{SST} = df_A - df_B - df_{A \times B}$

Obtaining F Values

The *F* values for each of the partitions are given by dividing the appropriate mean square by the means square for error.

Thus

$$F_A = \frac{MS_A}{MS_{error}} \quad F_B = \frac{MS_B}{MS_{error}} \quad F_{A \times B} = \frac{MS_{A \times B}}{MS_{error}}$$

Pairwise Comparisons After Analysis of Variance

Analysis of variance tells us whether variations in the level of a given factor or interaction resulted in statistically significant variations in outcome. Suppose we have three levels of a factor and there is a significant F for that factor. This tells us that *some* difference among levels significantly exceeded that expected if only error were at work. It does *not* tell us whether any given pair of levels differ significantly from each other. Having done the anova, we want to know *which* levels differ from each other.

Statisticians have long debated about which method of making these *post hoc* pairwise comparisons is most appropriate. If we use the ordinary t test, we run against the familiar problem of having an actual probability of type I error that is higher than the nominal one. This is because several t tests must be done in order to evaluate all the possible comparisons.

A variety of techniques have been devised for making such pairwise comparisons while adjusting for the number of comparisons to be made. They vary considerably in the stringency with which they protect against false alarms (type I errors). For example, the Tukey and Scheffé methods are relatively stringent, whereas the Duncan and Newman-Keuls tests are less stringent (Keppel, 1973). Selection of the best method of testing for significant differences between pairs of means is a complex topic. For detailed discussion of it, refer either to the treatment in Keppel (1973) or in Wike (1971). I will discuss only a procedure that has, in recent times, been shown to be highly effective and adequate for most situations (see, for example, Carmer & Swanson, 1973; Welkowitz, Ewen & Cohen, 1976). This is the use of the protected t test.

Keep in mind that the goal of the protected t is to identify significant differences between *pairs* of means *after* a significant F has been obtained by analysis of variance. If no significant F was obtained, this means that only error is operating, and (except under special circumstances to be discussed in Chapter 10), it would not make sense to do pairwise comparisons. The protected t must identify significantly different pairs of means while holding the frequency of type I errors approximately at levels specified by the chosen alpha level.

With the protected t we calculate t in the usual way, except that our estimate of error is based on the *mean square within groups* of the anova instead of on the usual calculation of the standard error. The MS_w is a more stable estimate of error than is the standard error because it is based on the pooling of data from all subjects. Since the MS_w is used, the degrees of freedom must be those for that error term, namely, the overall number of scores minus the number of levels of the independent variable ($N - k$). The formula for the protected t is

$$t = \frac{M_1 - M_2}{\sqrt{MS_w\left(\frac{1}{N_i} + \frac{1}{N_j}\right)}} \qquad \text{with df} = N - k$$

A simpler computational method is to calculate the smallest significant difference between any two means. The least significant difference is given by the formula:

$$\text{LSD} = t\sqrt{MS_w\left(\frac{2}{N_j}\right)}$$

where

t = the t value for the chosen alpha level and df = $N - k$.
MS_w = the mean square within groups from the anova
N_j = the sample size of each of the k groups

This formula can be used only when the different groups have equal sample sizes.

Assuming that we have a sample size of 10 per group with three groups, and that we set alpha at .05 (two-tailed), $t = 2.052$. For the sake of an example, assume that $MS_w = 0.7$ (as it does in the worked example of one-way anova given in Appendix F).

$$\text{LSD} = 2.052\sqrt{0.7\left(\frac{2}{10}\right)} = 0.77$$

Thus any pair of means differing by 0.77 or more differ significantly at the .05 level.

SUMMARY

1. Statistics permit us to stipulate the probability that an observed effect occurred by chance. There are two main steps to this: (a) finding a ratio of observation/noise and (b) determining the probability of the obtained ratio on the assumption that it is merely a ratio of noise/noise.
2. If the variability of the population is known, we can use a variance as the measure of error. However, the variance in question is not simply

the population variance. Since a set of samples of a size more than 1 will inevitably have a smaller variance than does the population itself, we must use the variance of samples of size *n* (of the sampling distribution) as our measure of noise. This measure, which is merely the population variance divided by the square root of the sample size, is called the *standard error* of the population.

3. With the *z statistic,* the population mean and variance must be known or assumed. The needed ratio (see item 1 above) is obtained by subtracting a mean observed in a sample from the known population mean. The bottom half of the ratio is merely the standard error of the population.

4. The *z statistic* is normally distributed and expresses the difference between population mean and sample mean in what are basically standard deviation units (but keep in mind that this is the standard deviation of the sampling distribution, not of the population). Since we can tell the proportion of cases under a normal curve from the number of standard deviations included, the *z statistic* provides an index of how infrequently a ratio of that size would occur if there were in fact no difference between the sampled mean and that of the population. It tells us how often the observed deviation of sample mean from population mean would occur if it were merely due to chance variations around the mean of a normal curve.

5. Usually we do not know the parameters of the population, so we have to *estimate* them. We generally do this by obtaining measures of variability with the treatment held constant. Since there is no variation in the level of the independent variable as long as we are within groups, measures of variability within groups are used as estimates. It is assumed that variability within treated and untreated groups is the same (*homogeneity of variance*).

6. In order to obtain the *best estimate* of variances, standard deviations, or standard errors of a population, we have to divide by *degrees of freedom* instead of by *n*. Degrees of freedom are equal to the number of scores minus the number of estimated parameters required to calculate the measure of variability.

7. The *t statistic* is merely a ratio of the difference between means of two samples divided by the estimated standard error. It is not normally distributed, and the shape of its distribution depends on the number of degrees of freedom. The distributions of *t* for various degrees of freedom are given in Appendix C. These permit us to say how often a given-size *t* ratio would occur if chance alone were operating.

8. *One-tailed tests* can be used if predicted differences are only in one direction. A given *t* ratio is only half as likely to occur if we stipulate that it must deviate in a given direction from (above or below) the con-

trol mean. The use of one-tailed tests for *t* and other statistics should probably be limited to those cases in which deviations in the opposite direction would be impossible or meaningless.

9. The analysis of variance is based on the *F statistic.* The *F* is also a ratio of observation over estimate of error. It is a ratio of the variance between levels of the independent variable to the variance within levels of the independent variable. It is generally used when there are more than two levels of the independent variable. There are different *F* ratios for different numbers of degrees of freedom related to the numerator *and* the denominator. The probability of a given *F* can only be obtained by specifying both sets of df.

10. The *F* ratio only tells us whether there is a statistically significant difference somewhere among all the possible comparisons between groups. To tell which comparison is significant, we must do *pairwise comparisons.* There is much controversy over which method of pairwise comparisons is best for giving an optimal balance of type I and type II errors. The text recommends and shows how to obtain the *protected t.*

CHAPTER 10

Some Special Topics in Designing, Implementing, and Analyzing Experiments

When experimenters decide to carry out a research project, there are many highly complex matters to be taken into account. The intricacy of the processes of measuring psychological phenomena, assuring adequacy of generality, selecting and implementing research design, providing clear descriptions of the resulting data, and determining the reliability of those data will be apparent to anyone who has studied the previous chapters. In order to reduce that intricacy, I have saved certain topics for this chapter. In this way, I hope that the reader will be able to see the forest before having to focus closely on the trees.

Unprotected Comparisons, Planned Comparisons, and the Analysis of Variance

In the preceding chapter, I briefly discussed the issue of how to make pairwise comparisons following the analysis of variance. The problem of pairwise comparisons stems from the fact that the anova only tells us whether there is some statistically significant comparison somewhere among all the possible pairwise comparisons of the study. Although the likelihood of a type I error is specified by the alpha level for any single comparison, it is underestimated if many comparisons are made. One useful way to put this is to say that the rate of type I errors is held at the alpha level per comparison but not per experiment.

It has long been known that the nominal alpha level is not the actual one if multiple pairwise comparisons are made. In spite of this, some investigators use *unprotected t tests.* This means that, without doing an overall anova, they make each of the possible pairwise comparisons with the familiar t test. Sometimes a large table of comparisons showing some significant ones will be published in an article using unprotected t tests. It is important to keep in mind that the probability of a type I error is greater than alpha under such circumstances. For alpha = .05, we expect one statistically significant finding to occur in every twenty comparisons, even if only chance effects are operating. Thus, it is wrong to make a large number of pairwise comparisons with unprotected t tests and then pick out the significant ones as though the nominal alpha levels truly reflected the probability of a false alarm—a type I error.

Normally we do an analysis of variance before going on to pairwise comparisons. The analysis of variance simultaneously tests whether there are significant differences among the various pairwise comparisons. Since the analysis of variance fails to tell us which contrasts between pairs are significant, we must subsequently make pairwise comparisons to localize the effect. The method of doing pairwise comparisons should be one that strikes a proper balance between risks of type I and type II errors ("misses").

The relative costs of each of these types of error varies from situation to situation. If one wishes to protect very strenuously against false alarms, the best choice might be a very stringent, relatively insensitive test like the Sheffé. If, on the other hand, one's orientation is toward detecting effects and avoiding type II errors, the Scheffé would be a poor choice. Perhaps the Duncan Multiple Range test or even the ordinary *t* test might be appropriate. An example of the sort of circumstance I have in mind here is one in which the experimenter intends to do further work on the topic and wants to prescreen for levels of the variable that are likely to be of interest.

Most of the time we have no particular preference for type I or type II errors. In such cases I have recommended the protected *t* test, which was in Chapter 9.

Although we ordinarily do an analysis of variance before conducting pairwise comparisons, this is not always necessary or appropriate. The exception is the case in which we use *planned comparisons.* The legitimacy of planned comparisons may be seen by returning to the coin-tossing analogy I used in Chapter 9 while discussing pairwise comparisons. If I say that I am willing to bet that I can toss a "head," you will lose money (assuming an even-money bet) unless you limit me to a single toss. But suppose I say that I will toss several times, but that the fourth toss will be a head. I have now limited myself to a single opportunity to get a head. It is really not different from betting on a single toss. Similarly, an experimenter can specify ahead of time that a certain comparison is of prime interest. For example, a given theory may indicate that one select comparison is crucial, or the experiment may primarily consist of a single meaningful pairwise comparison with various other controls thrown in for the sake of thoroughness. In such cases, an unprotected *t* test can legitimately be done prior to or instead of the anova. However, before any further pairwise comparisons were done, the anova would be required.

Useful sources of further information on pairwise comparisons include Keppel (1973), Welkowitz, Ewen, and Cohen (1976), and Wike (1971). Computational methods for the major methods of doing pairwise comparisons after the anova may be found in Bruning and Kintz (1977).

Measures of the Proportion of Variance Accounted For

Tests such as the *t* and *F* tests can give us evidence supporting rejection of the null hypothesis. This simply says that there is something more than error operating. It does not tell us the magnitude of the influence of the independent variable on outcomes. Sometimes there may be a statistically reliable effect of a variable, but the magnitude of the effect may be so small as to be trivial. It is therefore of considerable value to obtain some statistic that indicates the magnitude of effect—the "proportion of variance accounted for" by the independent variable.

It is well known that the variance common to a predictor and an outcome variable can be derived from a correlation coefficient merely by squaring that coefficient. If we have a correlation of, say, .50, then $.50^2$, which we generally convert into a percentage, indicates the proportion of variance accounted for. We would therefore say that 25 percent of the variance is accounted for by the predictor (independent) variable.

In order to determine the proportion of variance accounted for from a given t value, the following formula may be used:

$$r_{pb}{}^2 = \frac{t^2}{t^2 + \text{df}}$$

where

r_{pb} = the point-biserial correlation coefficient
t = the t ratio
df = degrees of freedom

For the F statistic, a measure of the strength of the tested relationship may be obtained from the statistic *epsilon* (Welkowitz, Ewen & Cohen, 1976). The formula for epsilon is:

$$\varepsilon = \sqrt{\frac{\text{df}_b\,(F-1)}{\text{df}_b F + \text{df}_w}}$$

where

df_b = degrees of freedom between groups
df_w = degrees of freedom within groups
F = the F ratio

The matter of just how much variance was accounted for by a given relationship is extremely important, but it has received far too little attention from psychologists. If investigators have shown that there is a statistically significant relationship between variables, they commonly tend thereafter to act as if the relationship indicated that one variable is an important determinant of another. It may or may not be, and the degree of relationship is an important consideration in deciding whether it is.

A good example of "much ado about very little" recently came to my attention. There is quite a literature indicating that measures of the amount of "life change" (for example, changing jobs, getting married or divorced, moving) is related to the likelihood of getting physically ill (see, for example, Dohrewend & Dohrewend, 1974). Many people would be inclined on the basis of such findings to limit their life changes out of fearful anticipation of future illness. Yet a recent paper indicates that the proportion of variance accounted for by such relationships is only .01 percent (Rahe & Arthur, 1978)!

Pilot Studies and Sequencing of Experiments

Earlier in this chapter, I mentioned the possibility of conducting experiments in order to prescreen variables for more extensive later work. A relatively small, preliminary study designed to put us in a better position to conduct a fuller investigation is called a *pilot study.* Pilot studies are useful for working through practical details that are difficult to anticipate. They also familiarize the experimenter with logical and theoretical facets of the experiment that might not be apparent from merely thinking about the study. One often recognizes needed controls, flaws in logic, and so on while conducting a pilot study. A further advantage of pilot studies is that they can, if done correctly, prove highly economical. A small study can be done prior to making the major investment of time, effort, and money that is often required by the fuller investigation.

Some thinkers (for example, Sidman, 1960) have argued against the use of pilot studies. There are circumstances in which it is unwise to do such studies. If, for example, a question cannot be answered even tentatively without considerable effort, the investigator might be wiser to plunge into the full study. Thus the relative ease of an adequate pilot study and the relative difficulty of the fuller study weigh heavily in the decision whether to do pilot work. The optimal case for the pilot study is one in which the pilot study is very easy to do and the complete study is very hard to do.

A pilot study may be of virtually no value if it is done carelessly. It is true that a pilot study need not meet the standards of sampling and full control of a fuller investigation, but one must not go too far with the lack of control. For example, a correlational study is often used to indicate whether it would likely be worthwhile to carry out a tightly controlled investigation. The correlational study might even be done on less than a fully representative sample (e.g., all women). But the pilot study should nevertheless be done with care, lest the preliminary information prove more misleading than enlightening.

If a pilot study is sufficiently well done, it may become all or part of the main study itself. For example, pilot studies are sometimes fully controlled, but simply involve fewer subjects than the experimenter anticipates as necessary to establish the effects of interest. In such cases the effects may reveal themselves clearly enough with the smaller number of subjects. In such cases it may not be necessary to go further. In effect, pilot studies can become the first tier in a sequential design, as discussed in Chapter 8.

Violations of Statistical Assumptions and Unequal *n*

In several places I have alluded to certain assumptions underlying statistical tests. For example, the *t* test assumes that there is an equal-interval scale of measurement, that the variances of experimental and control groups are equal, and that the population of scores is normally distributed. In what sense do these assumptions *underlie* the test? It is only in the sense that the derivation of the tests entails making the assumptions.

In recent years, statisticians have found that, even though such assumptions were made while deriving our familiar statistical tests, it is not necessary to meet those assumptions for the tests to accomplish their purpose. That is, despite sizable violations of such assumptions, the frequencies of type I and type II errors are usually roughly as we would expect them to be if the assumptions were met. This has been shown by doing computer simulations of many, many statistical tests while various violations of the assumptions were in effect.

Consequently, most experimenters now worry very little about violations of assumptions of statistical tests unless those violations are very extreme. Nevertheless, one circumstance in which the violations may lead to trouble is when there are unequal numbers of subjects at the different levels of the variable(s). For this reason, and sometimes in the name of computational simplicity, it is usually best to see to it that there are equal *n*'s in the various groups.

Unfortunately, it is sometimes not at all easy to provide equal *n*'s without creating unwanted problems of sampling bias. If certain subjects drop out of the study (people fail to show up, animals get sick or die), replacement of them by random sampling from a pool may lead to biased sampling. For example, suppose that the animals susceptible to a given disease also differ behaviorally from other animals? One can imagine various circumstances in which animals filled in after the appearance of the disease might create a biased sample of subjects. If some subjects fail to show up, they may have characteristics that set them aside from the average subject. Suppose they are nonconformists. By replacing them, the experimenter may end up with a sample of subjects biased in the direction of conformity. The most difficult aspect of this, though, is that one never knows in what respects the dropouts differ from the remaining subjects.

There is no simple solution to these problems. Experimenters must simply do their best. Ultimately they may have to rely on various replications that take in a wider and wider swath of subjects before becoming secure in the belief that their findings are solid.

Special Problem of Experiments Designed to Affirm Null Statements

A further potentially avoidable problem of design centers on setting up experiments to verify null statements. Experimenters sometimes design their experiments so that the main conclusion, if the experiment is successful, will be that an independent variable does *not* have an effect rather than that it *has* an effect. It is generally wise to avoid experimental designs of this type. This is not to say that it is entirely impossible to conclude with reasonable certainty that a variable does not have an effect. It is simply difficult. And sometimes it is easy to modify an experiment of this sort so that the conclusion can be that an independent variable *has* an effect. So why not avoid troubles and change the experimental design?

Specific Objections

There are many objections against designing experiments to affirm null statements. Some of them are too complicated to deal with here, but I will list the major ones.

Probably the most striking case against them is that experimenters sometimes make very slight changes in an experimental procedure and find that an effect is produced where none appeared before. For example, the great physicist Hans Christian Oersted regularly gave demonstrations showing that there was no observable interaction between electric currents and magnetism. He would place a compass next to a wire, run current through the wire, and show that the compass needle did not deflect. He made the reasonable assumption that any magnetic effects would be in the same direction as the flow of electric current. One day, after one of the demonstrations, someone thoughtlessly changed the orientation of the compass and threw the switch. The needle deflected! We know now that the magnetic field is not parallel but at right angles to the flow of electric current. A seemingly slight procedural variation changed the null finding to a positive one that launched the new field of electromagnetism.

In psychology, a classic dispute between Paul Fields and Norman Munn, which took place during the 1920s, was centered on affirmation of a null statement. It was widely accepted at that time that rats could not discriminate visual patterns. To say that they could not discriminate such patterns is to maintain that the independent variable (pattern) does not, under any circumstances, exert control over the organism's behavior. Fields (1931) devised a technique that enabled him to obtain pattern discrimination, but only after hundreds of trials. Many experimenters had been unable to get rats to discriminate pattern and were so convinced that their null findings represented the real state of affairs, that they could not bring themselves to believe Fields.

Later, Karl Lashley (1930) invented a discrimination apparatus called the *Lashley jumping stand,* in which rats discriminated all sorts of complex patterns in very short order, commonly fewer than 100 trials. Lashley actually showed the rats could discriminate patterns in his apparatus when only a few hundred of their visual brain cells had been spared following brain surgery. Today, psychologists seem to have forgotten that there was ever any difficulty in getting rats to discriminate pattern; contemporary psychologists accomplish this every day, using various types of apparatus.

Statistical Objections

Experimental psychologists know that they are sometimes wrong. Indeed, they go to great lengths to quantify the probability of their being wrong. The major tool they use to determine that probability is statistics. Thus, it is at the very heart of the statistically oriented experimental psychologists' procedure that they be able to assign a number to the probability of their committing an error. Unfortunately, this is not practical if they affirm a null statement. The probability of being wrong in deciding that an independent variable had no effect is called *beta,* and it is not a single number. It is a function, a whole curve. The information necessary to know which of the many points on that curve represents our particular probability of error is generally not available to experimenters. Hence a major goal of statistics is lost by accepting null statements.

Experimenter Effects

Any contemporary account of the problems involved in doing research must include some discussion of the problem of *experimenter effects.* As the old saying goes, the last thing a fish will discover is water. It seems that experimenters were almost as tardy in discovering that one very important factor limiting the generality of experimental findings is the experimenter's own psychology. People have long been aware of the possibility of *experimenter bias.* This term refers to the tendency of experimenters—usually inadvertently—to influence or select their results in such a way as to invalidate them. Many familiar aspects of experimental procedure were originally introduced to cope with the problem of experimenter bias. For example, we suspect, as Darwin did (Wilson, 1952), that experimenters tend to be especially forgetful about facts that do not fit well with their theory or hypothesis. Thus scientists are trained to keep careful records of all their data.

Some experimenters get so wrapped up in their results that they want to throw out data that fail to fit their expectations. Recently some students who were conducting research with me had findings that, by and large, supported our expectations until the last few days of the experiment. They wanted to ignore the late data, arguing that, since the subjects were college students, and since the disagreeable data came near the end of the week, and since (they conjectured) more exams come at the end of the week, only the earlier data were valid. This would be a very dangerous thing to do. It is a mistake so common that it has been given a name all its own: "the early returns effect." It means that experimenters tend to build up expectations on the basis of the early data, then to bias the later data in such a way as to make them fit in with the expectations.

The procedures of experimental design have been devised to avoid such obvious mistakes. However, experimenters may still influence their results without meaning to. One way that I have seen many times lies in the calculation of statistical significance. Few experimenters enjoy doing the long, drawn-out calculations involved in testing the statistical significance of data. And few people like checking calculations by doing them more than once. I have noticed that an experimenter who has done a statistical analysis, if it comes out significant, smiles and quits; but if it falls short of significance, the experimenter frowns and starts mumbling about a possible *error* of calculation. Experimenters are more likely to check the calculations on data that they dislike, and can thereby bias the outcomes of experiments. This is easily corrected by making it a policy to check all calculations, painful though it may be to look for errors in calculations that have yielded pleasing results.

These problems of experimenter bias are relatively easy to handle, but there are other experimenter effects that sneak up on you even when you are very careful. One is hardly surprised to learn that an experimenter can read a desired result into data if measures are vague. Nor is it surprising to learn that scientists, being human, tend to forget items of information that do not support their pet theories. But it *is* surprising to find that the attitudes of experimenters can influence experimental outcomes when measurement and recording are done by machine. For example, in one experiment involving the training of rats in completely automated operant chambers, the experimenters were led to believe that they had a "stupid" or a "bright" rat. The performances of the rats were in accord with the artificially induced expectations of the experimenters (Rosenthal & Lawson, 1964). Apparently the manner in which experimenters dealt with the rats outside the experimental chamber was able to cause major variations in the animals' performances.

The term *experimenter effect* is broader than the term "experimenter bias." Bias is something in the behavior of the experimenter. But even nonbehavioral cues and expectations can have an effect on subjects. The experimenter's appearance, personality, sex, social status, and the like may be important.

There have been many, many demonstrations that various characteristics of experimenters influence their data (Kintz et al., 1965; Rosenthal,

1966), and, though certain limitations in these studies have been pointed out (Barber & Silver, 1968), they have been convincing enough for us to conclude that the experimenter's personage should be treated as an important variable in an experiment. Oddly enough, it is the experimenters in the "hard-nosed" branches of psychology who seem most likely to neglect considering the experimenter effect. "Tenderminded" psychologists, such as researchers in clinical psychology, are more likely to be aware of the importance of such influences, probably because it is very obvious that human judgments play an important role in their research.

There are several ways of minimizing, or at least of detecting, experimenter effects. For example, it is possible to have several experimenters in the same laboratory conduct a given research project so that the influence of a given experimenter's individual characteristics can be assessed at the end of the experiment. Indeed, it is common for several investigators to participate in the execution of a given research project, but it is relatively rare for the personal influence of the investigators to be assessed with the same rigor as are the influences of more obvious variables. A second technique is to conduct experiments *blind.* This means that the experimenter administering the treatment does not know whether the experimental factors (variables) of interest are present or absent, and the person keeping records of the variables reveals them only after the experiment is completed and its outcome judged. An experiment with human subjects is called *double blind* if neither the experimenter nor the subjects know which treatment they are receiving at the time of the experiment. For example, an experiment on the behavioral effects of a drug might be done by coding the vials of drugs and placebos so that no one knows which is which during the experiment. This can only be determined after decoding.

None of these procedures is foolproof, but at least they can be helpful. In any case it is important to realize that characteristics of the experimenter must be taken into account very carefully and regarded just as seriously as any other potentially influential factor. There is little point in meticulously taking into account the subject's background, environmental surrounds, and all other factors that plague psychological experiments, only to allow the experimenter factor to control the situation.

Anticipating the Operation of Levinson's Law[1]

Levinson's law states, "If anything can possibly go wrong, it will." (Levinson, 1967.) The experimenter who fails to operate with an eye to Le-

[1]Sometimes called "Murphy's law." I term it Levinson's law because it was so named in the only printed statement of it I have found *(Levinson's Unafraid Dictionary,* 1967), and in honor of my colleague, Dr. Daniel M. Levinson, whose appreciation of this law is unexcelled.

vinson's law faces dire consequences. To illustrate, a colleague of mine was directing research on animal learning for almost a year before he learned that two of the three people running the animals were defining an "error" incorrectly. The research director was a highly seasoned experimenter, and well aware of Levinson's law, but he permitted himself to relax and fall into a fatal optimism.

People *will* fail to understand instructions or *will* perceive what are thought to be agreed-upon procedures incorrectly. Apparatus *will* break down or, worse, malfunction to give spurious data. Human subjects *will* fail to show up and *will* do unexpected things not anticipated in the procedure. Animal subjects *will* fall ill at critical moments in the experiment or find ways to confound the experimenter's intended procedure.

I once worked for days behaviorally shaping a cat to press a bar for milk reward, only to have it discover a technique for dipping its paw in the milk reservoir and licking ample quantities of milk from it. I have had monkeys escape from a complex automated apparatus and play at tearing the wires up for half an hour before their unauthorized leave from the apparatus was noticed.

Levinson's law is the dark side of research—an aspect that is seldom revealed in the fine, glossy reports in the journals, and the still finer and glossier reports in the textbooks. But the willingness of experimenters to go through this sort of thing indicates how gratifying the rewards are when they come.

A researcher is bound to suffer from the inexorable operation of Levinson's law from time to time. But you can devise means of coping with it. You should work on projects that you envision as important enough to make the sacrifices worthwhile. You should keep in mind that many of your research efforts will end in failure. You must simply do more work in anticipation of such failures. You should also *check* and *check* and *double check* your experiments in all their facets.

A research director who never participates in or observes the project's experiments in operation is asking to be smitten by the mighty hand of Levinson. Be a subject in your own experiments when possible. Even if you cannot use the data, you will learn a great deal. You will probably come away with many new ideas about how the experiment should be run and will have a good chance at detecting procedural flaws. Whether it is possible to participate as a subject in an experiment or not, it is a good idea for members of research teams to watch each other in operation from time to time. Procedural discrepancies are relatively easy to detect in this way.

The data themselves will often tip off an experimenter that a procedural flow has intruded. The fiasco mentioned earlier, in which animals were run incorrectly in a learning experiment for almost a year, was detected by looking at the data and noticing that implausibly long runs of errors were produced by many of the subjects. If the experimenters had been sharing their data, presenting them to each other on a regular basis, and summarizing them frequently in lucid ways, the discrepancy would have been detected much earlier.

There are sundry ways to minimize the dangers of procedural and logistical error in experiments. Each new experimental situation presents unique possibilities for error and for taking care to avoid error. The most important thing is to leave to chance as few things as possible, never to get overly optimistic about how smoothly things are running, and always to *remember Levinson's law.*

Special Problems in Dealing with Human Subjects

Several years ago it came to the public's attention that certain subjects in medical research had been grossly mistreated. For example, one news item indicated that people with syphilis had been randomly assigned to treatment and *control* conditions. No treatment at all was given under the control conditions. Since syphilis is a long-term progressive disease leading ultimately to destruction of major organs, especially the brain, there was a just public outcry against such work. The result was that investigators who would never have considered doing such things became embroiled in various regulations limiting the ways in which they can deal with human subjects in research.

Currently it is almost impossible to work with human subjects without being under the supervision of a "human experimentation committee." Such committees review proposals for research and determine whether there are risks, whether subjects have been fully informed of those risks, and whether the potential benefits of the study outweigh the potential human costs.

Many experimenters initially regarded such committees as a pointless obstacle to research. After all, virtually all psychological research is thoroughly harmless, so why the need to go through all that red tape? However, there may be times when research is not so harmless, and occasionally the investigators get so wrapped up in their scientific (and personal) goals that they overlook potential risks. Thus, the supervision by committees protects people in these relatively unusual cases.

The realization that one's research protocol will be scrutinized no doubt also leads to some fairly careful assessment of potential risks on the part of investigators. In general, all of us seem to have become more alert to the full range of human rights in the research setting. This has important benefits, but such benefits also have their costs. For example, it is doubtful whether certain classic studies could be done today.

Most students of psychology learn about the case of "Little Albert," John B. Watson's subject in an experiment on induction of a phobia in a child. Watson associated a white rat with a fear-inducing stimulus in order to show that an irrational fear could be induced through a process like Pavlovian conditioning. I feel confident (and, to be honest about it, gratified) that such a study could not be done today.

Another example is the classic study by Ax (1953) in which he showed that fear and anger could be differentiated physiologically. This had been a problem of interest for many years, ever since William James had put forth the view that emotions are nothing but the conscious awareness of bodily states (James, 1884).

Ax was able to show that fear and anger have different physiological patterns, but this required that he actually frighten and anger people. It is most unlikely that he could do such an experiment today.

Whatever your attitudes may be toward the relative value of research outcomes versus minimization of human risks, you should recognize that some balance must be struck between the two. Any intervention with human beings entails risks. Someone once asked me if there were any risk that a person could "go crazy" from answering routine questions on a mental test. I could not say that there was *no* risk of that. I think the risks entailed in going to certain movies are far greater, though.

The investigator is often not the one to make a balanced decision about these issues. There is a conflict of interests in such cases. We are fortunate, then, in having well-balanced committees, composed of scientific peers as well as persons from outside the research environment, to make such judgments.

It is important that you be aware of the ethical standards that apply to psychological research. These have been summarized by the American Psychological Association (1974) and are reproduced below.

Ethical Principles of the American Psychological Association in Relation to Research with Human Subjects

The decision to undertake research should rest upon a considered judgment by the individual psychologist about how best to contribute to psychological science and to human welfare. The responsible psychologist weighs alternative directions in which personal energies and resources might be invested. Having made the decision to conduct research, psychologists must carry out their investigations with respect for the people who participate and with concern for their dignity and welfare. The Principles that follow make explicit the investigator's ethical responsibilities toward participants over the course of research, from the initial decision to pursue a study to the steps necessary to protect the confidentiality of research data. These Principles should be interpreted in terms of the context provided in the complete document offered as a supplement to these Principles.

1. In planning a study the investigator has the personal responsibility to make a careful evaluation of its ethical acceptability, taking into account these Principles for research with human beings. To the extent that this appraisal, weighing scientific and humane values, suggests a

deviation from any Principle, the investigator incurs an increasingly serious obligation to seek ethical advice and to observe more stringent safeguards to protect the rights of the human research participant.

2. Responsibility for the establishment and maintenance of acceptable ethical practice in research always remains with the individual investigator. The investigator is also responsible for the ethical treatment of research participants by collaborators, assistants, students, and employees, all of whom, however, incur parallel obligations.
3. Ethical practice requires the investigator to inform the participant of all features of the research that reasonably might be expected to influence willingness to participate and to explain all other aspects of the research about which the participant inquires. Failure to make full disclosure gives added emphasis to the investigator's responsibility to protect the welfare and dignity of the research participant.
4. Openness and honesty are essential characteristics of the relationship between investigator and research participant. When the methodological requirements of a study necessitate concealment or deception, the investigator is required to ensure the participant's understanding of the reasons for this action and to restore the quality of the relationship with the investigator.
5. Ethical research practice requires the investigator to respect the individual's freedom to decline to participate in research or to discontinue participation at any time. The obligation to protect this freedom requires special vigilance when the investigator is in a position of power over the participant. The decision to limit this freedom increases the investigator's responsibility to protect the participant's dignity and welfare.
6. Ethically acceptable research begins with the establishment of a clear and fair agreement between the investigator and the research participant that clarifies the responsibilities of each. The investigator has the obligation to honor all promises and commitments included in that agreement.
7. The ethical investigator protects participants from physical and mental discomfort, harm, and danger. If the risk of such consequences exists, the investigator is required to inform the participant of that fact, secure consent before proceeding, and take all possible measures to minimize distress. A research procedure may not be used if it is likely to cause serious and lasting harm to participants.
8. After the data are collected, ethical practice requires the investigator to provide the participant with a full clarification of the nature of the study and to remove any misconceptions that may have arisen. Where scientific or human values justify delaying or withholding information, the investigator acquires a special responsibility to assure that there are no damaging consequences for the participant.
9. Where research procedures may result in undesirable consequences for

the participant, the investigator has the responsibility to detect and remove or correct these consequences, including, where relevant, long-term aftereffects.

10. Information obtained about the research participants during the course of an investigation is confidential. When the possibility exists that others may obtain access to such information, ethical research practice requires that this possibility, together with the plans for protecting confidentiality, be explained to the participants as a part of the procedure for obtaining informed consent.

SUMMARY

1. When data require several possible pairwise comparisons, overall analysis of variance should normally be done prior to tests of individual pairs. Only if the *F* for the anova is significant should we go on to do pairwise comparisons. If *t* tests are done without doing prior anova or if they are done when the *F* for the anova is not significant, we have an *unprotected t.* The actual probability of a type I error is greater than the nominal alpha level in such cases.
2. It is legitimate to do *t* tests unprotected by anova when they are *planned comparisons.* This means that the particular pair to be compared is stipulated prior to gathering the data.
3. There are many methods of doing protected pairwise comparisons after getting a significant *F.* Since different tests vary in their sensitivity to effects, the proper test must be selected according to the requirements of the experiment.
4. To show that there is a statistically significant relationship between variables is important, but it is also important to indicate the degree of the relationship between the variables. Formulas for determining the proportion of variance accounted for in a functional relationship are given in text for Pearson's *r* and for the *t* and *F* ratios.
5. A relatively small preliminary study done to put us in a better position to conduct a fuller investigation is called a *pilot study.* Pilot studies permit prescreening of variables for their importance, familiarization with practical problems and with logical and theoretical facets of the experiment that are not immediately apparent. Pilot studies can contribute to the economy of experimentation, provided they are done with reasonable care and are substantially more easy to do than the full study. Sometimes a really well-done pilot study will make it unnecessary to go further.
6. Statistical investigations done by computer simulation have indicated that familiar statistical tests tend to be quite accurate despite sizable violations of their assumptions. However, this rule may not

hold up if different groups or levels have different numbers of subjects. It is therefore best to have equal *n*'s at the different levels of the independent variable(s). This may also make computations easier. However, if unequal **n**'s are due to selective dropping out of subjects, their replacement may result in biasing of samples as well as in confounding.

7. The *experimenter effect* is a name given to the many ways in which an experimenter may personally influence the experimental results. With *experimenter bias,* the experimenter behaves in ways that influence the results. Other experimenter effects might come from the experimenter's appearance, sex, or other factors. The use of *blind* procedures, especially *double blind* ones may be useful in preventing experimenter effects. A procedure is said to be blind when the experimenter or subject do not know whether the subject is receiving active treatment. A double-blind procedure is one in which neither subject nor experimenter knows whether the subject is a control.
8. It is best not to design experiments to show that a variable does *not* have an effect (experiments to affirm null statements). Failure to show a relationship between variables may merely indicate that the experiment was insensitive or that the circumstances were not appropriate. It is also difficult to stipulate the probability of being wrong when a null statement is accepted. Furthermore, an experimenter who categorically states that there is no relationship between two variables is implying that there are no limiting conditions to that statement.
9. Levinson's law states, "If anything can possibly go wrong, it will." Check and double check everything. Look over data for tipoffs that an error has occurred.
10. The rights of human subjects must be protected while doing research, and the experimenter has personal responsibility for the ethical acceptability of the study. Subjects must be fully informed of relevant issues before giving their consent to participate and must be free to decline to participate. The investigator is responsible for protecting the well-being of participants and must inform them of the full nature of the study when it is finished. The investigator must correct any undesirable consequences of participation in the study and must keep information confidential.

CHAPTER 11

Single-Subject Experimental Designs

Characteristics of the Experimental Analysis of Behavior
- Emphasis on the individual organism
- Emphasis on the experimental control of variability
- Nonstatistical evaluation of reliability
- The use of direct behavioral measurement
- Rate of responding as a dependent measure
- The use of rapidly changing designs
- The atheoretical approach
- Other emphases

Techniques of Design in the Experimental Analysis of Behavior
- Baselines
- Some common experimental designs

Characteristics of the Experimental Analysis of Behavior

The approach to experimental design that I have emphasized so far has been one that is most widely used in contemporary psychology. It places emphasis on the use of formalized designs with subsequent statistical analysis of data. But statistics were not available at all during the early development of science, nor were the formalized designs. In fact, elegant statistics and codification of the designs are twentieth-century phenomena. Thus most of the great achievements of science took place in another context. Many contemporary psychologists hold to a view that the application of formal designs and statistical methods of analysis to psychology was undesirable. I have referred to these psychologists in several previous contexts as devotees of a point of view known as the "experimental analysis of behavior."

Do not make the mistake of believing that all, or even *any,* of the attitudes characteristic of the experimental analysis of behavior originated with experimental analysts ("Skinnerians," to use a more popular parlance). Single-subject designs were used by some of the earliest psychologists in the nineteenth century. Furthermore, students of so-called "higher nervous activity" in the Soviet Union approach problems with many of the same attitudes as experimental analysts. The reason for presenting these views in the context of the experimental analysis of behavior is that it is a very energetic movement in contemporary psychology. Single-subject designs seem to be having a strong impact on many psychologists, and an objective view of contemporary methodology cannot ignore that approach. Books describing this type of methodology include that of Sidman (1960) and Hersen and Barlow (1976).

Here, I will attempt to outline the most striking attitudes characterizing this approach to psychological research. To some degree I have dealt with aspects of the experimental analysis of behavior in other contexts, (see, for example, Chapter 6 on effects of order). This is not to favor one approach or the other but, rather, to recognize the continuity of the major approaches to methodology. In the past, methodological differences have often been emphasized at the expense of the similarities.

Emphasis on the Individual Organism

Since the title of the chapter includes "single-subject experimental designs" you might guess that the experimental analysis of behavior places great emphasis on the study of individual organisms. Several methodologists have pointed out that grouped data (that is, data averaged across individuals) are not necessarily representative of the underlying individual data. Figure 11.1 makes this point very well. The top part of the figure shows ten graphs representing individual organisms. The curve at the bottom and center of the figure shows the result of averaging the ten individual graphs. The graph based on averages of groups is of quite a different form from any of the individual curves. Yet psychologists—unlike sociologists, political scientists, and other students of group or mass behavior—typically want to understand individuals. Only in special cases will averaged data yield a good account of individual behavior, so it would seem wise to deal with individual data, if at all possible. Experimental analysts of behavior insist that it is generally, if not always, possible to deal with individuals.

With this method, the individual organism is studied by the use of repeated measures on the same subject. It is not enough simply to use repeated measures. Special adaptations must be developed in order to deal with such things as order effects, irreversible effects, and the like. Some of these have already been discussed in the section on experimental designs with repeated measures (Chapter 6). Others will be discussed in this chapter.

With this approach to experimental psychology, each subject provides complete experimental data. If more subjects are run (intersubject replication), this is to provide empirical confirmation of the generality of findings. All necessary controls must be provided *within* subjects.

Emphasis on the Experimental Control of Variability

Instead of treating variability of outcomes as error ("noise"), the experimental analyst will treat it as a challenge to identify the sources of variability. If there are sources of variation powerful enough to obscure the influence of the independent variable, perhaps the experimenter is studying the wrong variable. The appropriate tack might be to change the nature of the experimental goal until any substantial sources of "error" variance have been identified. Then the influence of the original variable of interest can be demonstrated in a relatively "noise-free" context.

A difficulty inherent in this approach is that it might take a rather long time to identify the sources of variability. Experimenters inclined toward the group-statistical approach are likely to feel that they want to get on with the experiment of main interest. It sometimes takes months or even years to track down major sources of variability. A friend of mine once conducted experiments on several pigeons over a period of about three years, after which time the pigeons were accidentally killed as a result of a malfunctioning thermostat!

The price paid for tracking down sources of variability is not usually so high, although it is often substantial. An experimental analyst is likely to argue that such difficulties are unfortunate, but they must be tolerated if accurate prediction and control of individual behavior are to be achieved.

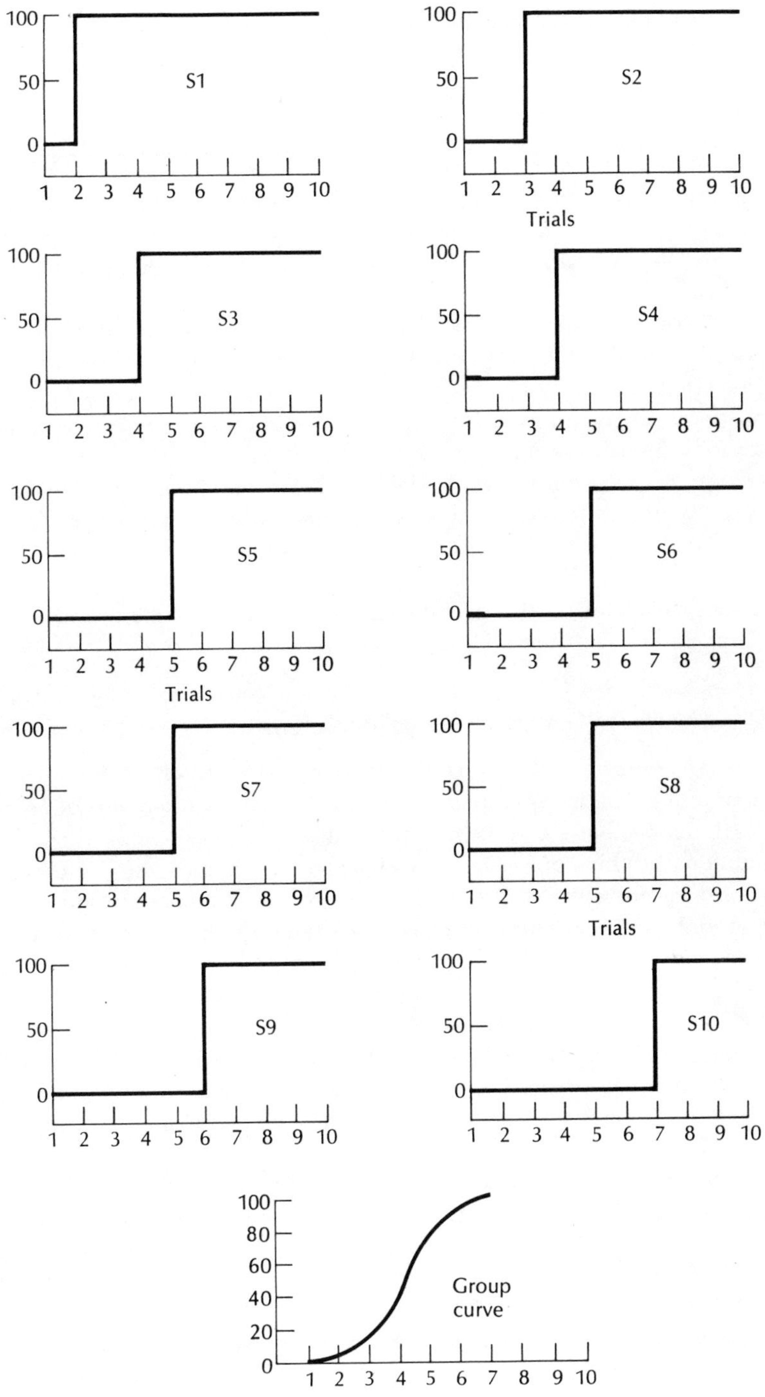

FIGURE 11.1 All-or-none learning curves that rise at different times, when grouped, yield a gradual, S-shaped curve, which is not representative of any individual's learning.

Nonstatistical Evaluation of Reliability

In the section on reliability, I explained both statistical and nonstatistical approaches to evaluating reliability. Experimental analysts of behavior prefer the nonstatistical approach. This emphasis is consistent with the attitude that "noise" must be eliminated through manipulation of controlling variables. When such control has been attained, findings will tend to manifest themselves clearly enough so that statistics will be unnecessary.

In recent years there has been some compromise of the principles that major sources of variability must be controlled and that statistics must not be used. This is largely because experimental analysts of behavior have become increasingly interested in applied psychology ("applied behavioral analysis"). Sometimes one lacks the social power to do the manipulations needed to get full control over variability. In other instances, ethical limitations may prevent ferreting out sources of variability. The result is that statistical analyses are sometimes used to evaluate reliability of studies done within the framework of the experimental analysis of behavior. A discussion of appropriate statistical procedures may be found in Hersen and Barlow (1976).

The Use of Direct Behavioral Measurement

The experimental analysis of behavior was born of a behaviorist tradition, and it continues to place emphasis on the measurement of *behavior*. Indeed, the emphasis is on behavioral measurement of the most direct kind. Traditionally, this approach to psychology has opposed the use of verbal measures except when verbal behavior *as such* was of interest. Originally, the use of direct behavioral measurement took the form of recording bar presses or key pecks in an operant chamber (see Figure 11.2). But as the method was applied to a wider and wider variety of settings, the experimenters developed behavioral measures of many psychological phenomena that had previously been measured only through rating scales and questionnaires (for example, marital happiness, depression). There have been some striking demonstrations that one need not rely on indirect, verbal measures, despite long tradition to the contrary.

Here again, there has been some compromise in the use of direct behavioral measurement, presumably because of the practicalities of studying applied behavioral problems and also as a result of an interest in studying inner mental events, which are deemed covert behaviors. Thus, a recent book on "behavioral assessment" (Cone & Hawkins, 1977) contains sections on the use of self-report measures and behavioral checklists. Many investigators report on such mental events as "urges," treating them (with some success!) as though they were observable behaviors.

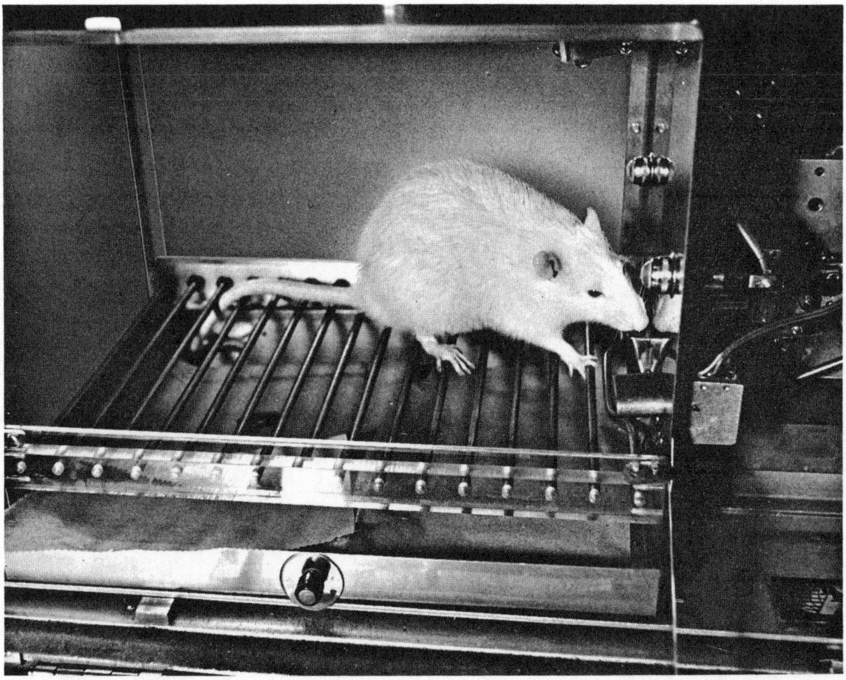

FIGURE 11.2 A free-operant test chamber (Skinner box). The rat is pressing a bar with its left paw while drinking liquid reinforcement from the reinforcement magazine. Another bar is visible to the rat's right. Stimulus lights, which can be used to bring the rat's behavior under stimulus control, are visible on the front wall of the chamber. The rat is standing on grids that can be used to deliver shock.

Rate of Responding as a Dependent Measure

Customarily there has been a great emphasis on the use of rate of responding as a dependent measure in the experimental analysis of behavior. The advantages of such a measure were discussed in Chapter 3. In research done on animals, and sometimes also in human research, the direct measures of rate of responding were obtained via a *cumulative recorder* (See Figure 11.3). A cumulative recorder is a device that bypasses the usual methods of describing data. Responses are recorded directly by having them cause a pen to move across paper that is unrolling at a constant speed. If no responses are made, the pen stands still and a line is drawn parallel to the edge of the paper. The faster the rate of responding, the closer the line comes to being perpendicular to the edge of the paper.

Cumulative records are customarily presented unaltered, with a *legend* to help the eye judge the rate of responding associated with a given angle of

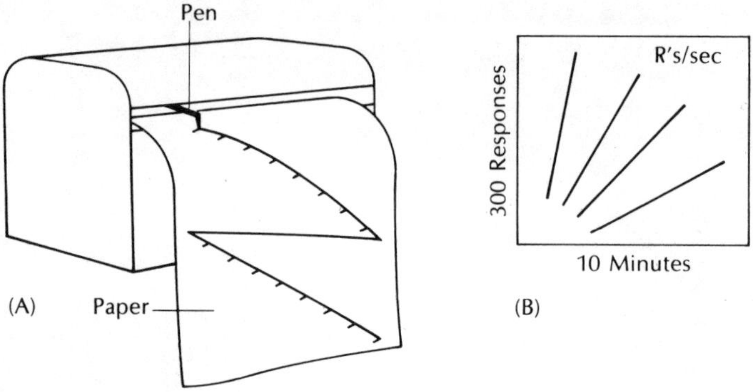

FIGURE 11.3 A cumulative recorder (A). The pen moves a step sideways each time a response occurs. The paper unrolls at a constant speed. The result is that the rate of the behavior is proportional to the angle of the line made by the pen. Reinforcements are indicated by slash marks created by a jiggle of the pen. The legend (B) helps the eye judge the relationship between angle and rate. The paper must be rotated 90 degrees to correspond with the legend.

line. No descriptive numbers are given to summarize the results. The record is a rather direct reflection of the behavior. However, cumulative plotting has a tendency to conceal variability. It is not uncommon today to supplement the cumulative record with histograms representing the distribution of *interresponse times* (time from one response to another). These provide a more fine-grained analysis.

When responses are of a type that does not permit direct mechanized recording, they can, nevertheless, be recorded cumulatively on a graph. Cumulative records have a tendency to reduce the appearance of variability. Records of interresponse times usually seem far more variable than do cumulative records. The more variable method of recording is of great value for fine-grained analyses. Contemporary students of applied behavioral analysis commonly use various forms of noncumulative recording.

The Use of Rapidly Changing Designs

Instead of attempting to anticipate all the needed controls in an experiment, experimental analysts have a tendency to improvise as they go along. At one point, Skinner (1959) denied that he was using experimental design at all. By this he seems to have meant that his experiments were not predesigned, but were flexible responses to challenges presented by the data themselves. Only after the fact could one recognize them as a particular design. The discussion of serendipity in Chapter 2 suggests that such improvisation may be one of the most fruitful ways to conduct research.

The Atheoretical Approach.

Experimental analysis of behavior has generally adopted the view that theory testing is not a particularly useful way to go about developing a science of psychology. The fundamental attitude has been that if one tracks down the sources of variability and identifies reliable and general functional relationships, wider generalizations will emerge "of themselves," and these will, in the long run, develop into theories. Though there was a time when a great deal of support for this point of view could be gained from philosophers of science, that support has been greatly undermined. A widely accepted contemporary view is that theory making is a separate creative function in its own right (see, for example, Hanson, 1968; Polanyi, 1966; Toulmin, 1953). However, psychology hardly seems ready for a full-fledged scientific theory, so the experimental analysts may, for all practical purposes, be right.

The atheoretical approach is consistent with the emphasis on experimental technological elimination of "noise" and with the use of rapidly changing improvised designs. If we are to take the attitude that important experiments are those that test a certain implication of a theory, it will be difficult then to regard the best study to be done as one that ferrets out sources of variability due to error. We are much more likely to shift to a design with more noise that answers the theoretical question. This will also incline us toward the use of statistics.

Other Emphases

There are various other emphases prevalent among experimental analysts of behavior. Since experimental analysis of behavior is a *method* developed in the context of operant conditioning (the type of conditioning in which responses are controlled by their consequences or reinforcements), many prevalent attitudes are simply residua from the traditions of operant conditioning. However, the method as such is quite independent of operant conditioning. In fact, one can argue, as I did in the beginning of this chapter, that it is much like the method used by physical and other scientists prior to the rather recent development of statistically oriented methodology.

Since these attitudes seem less than essential to the methods of experimental analysis, I will discuss them only briefly here. This is in spite of the fact that they will be almost universally encountered among experimental analysts. One of them is the emphasis on manipulation of behavior through the manipulation of its *consequences* (for example, rewards). This is the essence of operant conditioning, but there is no real reason that the methods of experimental analysis cannot be used in other contexts. A second attitude is that the *function* rather than the *structure* of behavior is of greatest interest.

TABLE 11.1 Some Major Schedules of Reinforcement

Name of Schedule	Abbreviation	Has or Does Not Have S^d
Continuous Reinforcement	CRF	Either way
Extinction	EXT	Either way
Fixed Ratio	FR	Either way
Variable Ratio	VR	Either way
Fixed Interval	FI	Either way
Variable Interval	VI	Either way
Differential Reinforcement of Low Rates of Responding	DRL	Either way
Differential Reinforcement of High Rates of Responding	DRH	Either way
Chained	Chain	Has S^ds
Tandem	Tand.	No
Multiple	Mult.	Has S^ds
Mixed	Mix	No
Concurrent	Conc.	Either way

Response Contingency	Patterns of Responding
Reinforcement after each response	Moderate rates, not very stable, low resistance to extinction
No responses reinforced	Depends on preceding schedule at first, then rate drops to criterion of extinction
Reinforcement for a fixed number of responses greater than one	Very high rates; pauses occur after reinforcement if ratio is high; resistance to extinction high and in runs of responses about equal to the ratio
Reinforcement after varying numbers of responses with a specified mean number	High stable rates, very great resistance to extinction
Reinforcement for each response provided a fixed interval has passed since the last reinforcement	"Scalloping," that is, low rate after reinforcement with positive acceleration up to next reinforcement
Reinforcement after varying intervals with a mean interval specified	High stable rates, very great resistance to extinction
At least a minimum interval between responses to be reinforced. Responding prior to the interval resets the clock timing the interval to zero	Stable low rates
Rate of response must be at a specified high value for reinforcement to be given	Stable high rate
Two or more consecutive simple schedules; S^d indicates each; primary reinforcement after all component schedule requirements have been completed	Varies with variations in component requirements. Components influence each other. The last component is especially influential, presumably because the frequency of reinforcement in that component controls the reinforcing properties of its S^ds, which in turn, controls behavior in preceding components
Two or more consecutive simple schedules; no S^ds; primary reinforcement after all component schedule requirements have been completed	Depends on component schedules, size of ratio or interval of components, and sometimes on the order of components
Two or more simple schedules; each indicated by S^d; primary reinforcement after completion of each component (called *ply*)	Behavior in component plys resembles that of simple schedule alone. Sometimes interactions occur, such as contrast effects (in which rate of responding in one ply is inversely related to frequency of reinforcement in a neighboring ply. Interactions are controlled by briefly withdrawing the opportunity to respond before shifting to a new ply (called "Time out")
Two or more simple schedules sequentially presented; not distinguished by S^ds; primary reinforcement after each component	Behavior not strongly under control of individual schedules, more under combined control of simple schedules, as when two FRs are combined for a VR. Rates higher than on multiple schedule
Two or more simple schedules simultaneously	Rates tend to match frequency of reinforcement in a given option.

This distinction might best be made by pointing out the difference between transactional analysis (TA), which is heavily structural, and applied behavioral analysis, which is heavily functional. In TA there is a great deal of emphasis on the particular patterned behavioral stratagems we use to get what we want ("strokes"). Such things as "games" and "scripts" are examples. In applied behavioral analysis such emphases are not nearly so common. The emphasis is much more likely to be on what one gets out of certain behaviors ("reinforcing consequences") than on the description of just *how* one gets it.

Techniques of Design in the Experimental Analysis of Behavior

Since, with this approach to research, each subject is to provide a fully controlled experiment, we are faced with special problems of providing controls. Behaviors under treatment conditions are generally compared to behaviors under control conditions. The behaviors under control conditions are termed *baselines,* and comparisons between baseline and treated conditions are the very lifeblood of this methodological approach.

Baselines

There are various types of baseline, and they may be introduced at various times in an experiment. Selection of a baseline and determination of the particular pattern of introducing it are central considerations in these types of designs. Intuitively it might seem that the most sensible baseline would be one taken prior to the introduction of any manipulations, in the naive organism. But the behavior obtained prior to manipulation does not constitute a "zero baseline," as some experimenters have supposed. Instead, it depends on levels of various unmeasured factors that influenced the subect prior to the experiment. It is therefore an unknown (instead of a "zero") baseline. Since it is under the control of a variety of unknown variables, it is likely to be highly noisy. Therefore, it is preferable to establish a known baseline prior to introduction of active treatments.

Baselines may be *stable* or *dynamic.* Most investigations are done with stable baselines. However, it is good to keep in mind that baselines that vary *systematically* can be used as well. For example, if a behavior is systematically increasing without active treatment, simply getting it to stay steady can provide a demonstration of the impact of the independent variable.

Schedules of Reinforcement as Baselines

Baselines are commonly established by manipulating the consequences of behavior. The rules according to which various consequences are delivered have a great impact on the rate of the behavior. When a given set of rules is in effect, we have what is called a *schedule of reinforcement.* Major schedules of reinforcement are summarized in Table 11.1.

Some Common Experimental Designs

There are two basic classes of experimental designs used by experimental analysts of behavior. The first type requires that we assume reversibility of the behavior under investigation. The second is intended to circumvent problems of "irreversibility." An "irreversible" process is one that has persistent effects once it has been introduced. Thus we might teach an organism something during a treatment phase, then lack any method of erasing the memory of what has been taught. Obviously, certain variables have temporary effects—for example, short-term effects of drugs such as alcohol. Reversal of others may be entirely beyond our capacity at the time of the experiment.

It is important to keep in mind that various things can be done to minimize the effects of irreversibility. Many of these procedures were discussed in Chapter 6 as procedures for minimizing the effects of "order of presentation." The designs that require reversibility can, to a great extent, be used with irreversible processes by such techniques of minimization.

Designs Requiring Reversibility

The A-B-A Design. The A-B-A design is one in which a baseline is taken, the treatment then introduced, and then the baseline is reinstated. Each of these phases should be *long.* Brief time samples can give very misleading impressions of the behavior that will eventually stabilize under a given condition. Highly variable data may appear briefly to be stable. If a treatment is then introduced, "noisy" variations will seem to be due to that treatment.

The A-B-A design is a clear improvement over the A-B design described in Chapter 5 under the name "Pretest-Posttest Design." However, it is not entirely free from some of the same objections, especially if phases are of short duration, if literally only one subject is run, or if several subjects are run *simultaneously.* The problem is that behavior might change as a function of some external factor that influences responding during the treatment phase. It is, in particular, helpful to run subjects at different times in order to discount the alternative hypothesis of variation due to external factors. Even then, there remains the possibility that there is some long-term cyclical process triggered by introduction to the experimental setting that causes differences between the two baseline conditions on the one hand and the treatment condition on the other. The probability of this is, presumably, not high. But we have no way to say just how low it is and are therefore plagued by the null hypothesis. It is probably better simply to go to the more complex single-subject designs, where the alternative hypothesis I am proposing becomes absurd.

The A-B-A-B Design and Its Extensions. The fundamental principle with single-subject designs for studying reversible processes is to introduce and remove the treatment variable of interest until we have shown that certain changes of outcome occur reliably if and only if the treatment is present. The more often we introduce, remove, and reintroduce the treatment condition, the more firmly we may reject certain alternative hypotheses that might account for changes of outcome. The A-B-A-B design is simply an extension of the A-B-A design. In the A-B-A-B design, the treatment is reintroduced one more time. It can provide a more convincing demonstration of effects. It can also be extended until even the most cautious experimenter is convinced that the treatment is responsible for effects.

Interaction Designs. Sometimes we want to know the way in which two or more variables interact to produce effects. Variables in combination may produce very different effects than when taken separately. Interactions may be observed in multifactor group designs (See Chapter 6), but they may also be observed in single-subject designs. This is done simply by sometimes introducing the variables alone and at other times by introducing them in combination. A large number of observations will often be needed to get clear evidence of the interaction. A design of this type described by Barlow, Blanchard, Hayes, and Epstein (1977) is the A-B-A-B-BC-A-BC. This is basically an A-B-A-B design followed by introduction of the combined variables ("BC"), a baseline phase, and reintroduction of the combined variables. Keep in mind, however, that it is incompatible with the spirit of the experimental analysis of behavior to adhere to such fixed designs in any rigid fashion. It may well be necessary to extend or modify them in order to get solid evidence for apparent effects of variables or their combinations.

Designs to Circumvent Irreversible Effects

In other contexts I have already discussed various ways to minimize or isolate carry-over effects due to influences of treatments that fail to go away upon withdrawal of the variable that produced them (See Chapter 6). At this point I will describe the use of *multiple-baseline designs.* The multiple-baseline design is one in which a treatment is introduced repeatedly to a subject, but at different times and with different dependent variables or in different settings. Sometimes such designs are used across subjects. In the latter case the baseline is given to several subjects, then the treatment is introduced at different times for each of the subjects. If the effects are seen to correspond to the introduction of the treatment, we have powerful evidence that the independent variable produced the effect. When the multiple baseline is used within subjects, we get baselines for several behaviors or in several settings for a given individual. Then we introduce the treatment sequentially in the context of the various baselines.

Multiple Baselines Across Dependent Variables One form of multiple baseline involves having several different dependent variables for a given subject. The treatment condition is introduced on each of the dependent-variable baselines, but at different times for each of the variables. For example, suppose you were interested in studying the effects of "time out" on undesirable classroom behaviors. Time out means that opportunities to make certain responses are withdrawn. The old-fashioned method of making children sit in the corner is an example of time out.

To study the effect of time out with a multiple baseline across dependent variables, you would first have to identify and select a measurement procedure for several of the undesirable behaviors. Assume this has been done for, say, talking in class, hitting other children, and getting out of one's seat during class. Baseline rates of each of these three behaviors would be taken for enough time to have a solid notion of what the rates were really like. Usually the rates would be taken until they stabilized at some predetermined level or "criterion." Next, time out would be made contingent on one of the behaviors. This simply means that, say, talking in class would be swiftly followed by removing the child from opportunities to make desired responses. This contingency would be kept in effect until the impact of it could be clearly discerned. Later, the same contingency would be introduced with a second dependent variable, say, getting out of one's seat. Having assessed the impact of the contingency on the second behavior, it would be superimposed on the baseline of the final behavior.

The result of all of this would be that, even if the treatment happened to have irreversible effects, three different assessments of its effectiveness would have been provided within a single subject. No comparisons across subjects or group averages would be required.

A major problem that might occur would be "crosstalk" between baselines. It would not be surprising if suppression of one or two of the behaviors had an influence on the remaining ones. For example, the child might suddenly come in touch with the benefits of being "good" and change all the measured behaviors in the desired direction. Another possibility might be that the child would compensate for missed opportunities to "act out" with misbehavior by increasing rates of the remaining behaviors. Such effects might well tend to make it difficult to see pure effects of the contingency separately on each of the baselines.

Multiple Baselines Across Situations A process very similar to the use of multiple baselines with several dependent measures can be applied to multiple situations. This means that the baselines are taken in several different settings and the treatments introduced sequentially in each of the settings.

Suppose an investigator was working with highly anxious subjects and found that they were anxious while interacting with older family members, while interacting with members of the opposite sex, and while speaking up in public situations. If a treatment for anxiety were being assessed, baselines would be taken in each of the different settings. Next, the treatment would be given sequentially in each of the situations.

Here, again, you can see that a problem might arise if there happened to be crosstalk between the different baseline situations. It would not be surprising if, in the process of learning to relax in one situation, some change might generalize to other situations. Perhaps it should be mentioned that generalization often does *not* occur from one situation to another.

For both of the preceding types of multiple-baseline design, data are gathered within single subjects. This does not mean that the experimenters necessarily content themselves with only one subject. However, the main purpose in running more subjects is to assess the *generality* of the original findings. The idea is to achieve adequate control for the identification of controlling variables and adequate establishment of reliability *within* a single subject.

Because of the difficulties inherent in crosstalk between the multiple baselines, a third type of multiple baseline design may be used. In this type, comparisons are made *across* subjects.

Multiple Baselines Across Subjects When we use multiple baselines across subjects, several different subjects are employed. Baselines are taken for each of the subjects, and, for one subject after another, the treatment is introduced. No two subjects receive the treatment simultaneously, so each subject has a different length of time under baseline conditions.

You may note that this is basically a pretest-posttest design of the type discussed in Chapter 5. The purpose of staggering the subjects with respect to introduction of the treatment and of varying the duration of their baseline measures is to render implausible the alternative hypothesis that changes occurred as a result of extraneous events or of spontaneous changes.

An unfortunate feature of the multiple baseline across subjects is that it makes a transition into a type of design that requires comparisons between subjects. Unlike the previous two types of multiple-baseline design, this one does not provide for a complete experiment within each subject. For any given subject, it is merely a preexperimental design of the uncontrolled pretest-posttest variety. Consequently, the present type of multiple-baseline design does not quite meet the standards of a pure single-subject design. Nevertheless, it has come to be widely accepted by experimental analysts.

You may note that the methodology of the experimental analysis of behavior runs up against serious difficulties when irreversible processes are studied. Sidman (1960) has argued essentially that there may be no irreversible processes. Irreversibility may depend on present limitations that will eventually be overcome. To maintain that a process is irreversible is to accept a null statement, and we know that that is a risky thing to do. Unfortunately, one must face the fact, in spite of Sidman's argument, that there are many processes we have no way of reversing today or in the foreseeable future (for example, effects of removing parts of the brain, or perhaps even the effects of learning). My own view would be that we should face the fact that we have no fully adequate solution to the problem of irreversibility when working within the framework of single-subject designs. Not even the multiple-baseline designs will provide a complete solution. But the growth of science has often taken place despite such limitations. As pointed out previously, physicists get by without a perfect vacuum.

SUMMARY

1. Single-subject designs were used early in the history of psychology. In recent years they have been developed largely by those identified with the *experimental analysis of behavior,* the methodology identified with B. F. Skinner.
2. The experimental analysis of behavior emphasizes the study of *individual organisms* on the grounds that group averages may not be representative of individuals in the group. The focus is on designs with repeated measures taken within subjects. The treatment of each subject should include a completely controlled experiment.
3. *Variability* is largely controlled by identifying its sources and manipulating them until noise levels are quite low. Judgments of reliability are then made by *inspection* instead of statistically.
4. Emphasis is on *direct measurement of behavior* with *rate of responding* as the dependent measure. However, there are many exceptions to this approach, especially recently and in applied behavioral analysis.
5. There is a de-emphasis on fixed designs in favor of flexible, *rapidly changing designs.*
6. Experimental analysis of behavior regards theory as something that will emerge spontaneously after enough functional relationships have been established. For now, there is *little interest in theorizing.*
7. There are other emphases, especially an emphasis on the importance of the *consequences* of behavior in its control.
8. Treatment conditions are compared to *baselines.* Baselines may be rates of behavior prior to treatment, but can also be rates determined by manipulations other than the treatment condition under study. Baselines may be *stable* or may vary consistently in a given way *(dynamic).*
9. Certain designs that are commonly used in the experimental analysis of behavior require that the effects of the treatments be *reversible.* The *A-B-A design* involves taking a baseline, introducing the treatment, then withdrawing the treatment again. Treatment effects might be due to an

extraneous factor, especially if the different segments are short, if only one subject is run, or if several subjects are run simultaneously. With the *A-B-A-B design,* the method is like that of the A-B-A design, but treatment is reinstated at the end. Alternation of baseline and treatment can be repeated until the effectiveness of the treatment is clearly established. Interactions can be studied with designs of this type merely by introducing combinations of treatments some of the time. This would be called an *interaction design.*

10. Sometimes effects of a treatment cannot, at least for the present, be reversed. *Multiple-baseline designs* have been devised to cope with irreversible effects. Multiple baselines may be *across dependent measures, across situations,* or *across subjects.* This means that measures are taken using several baselines, then treatment is introduced sequentially on each baseline. Since the treatment is not introduced simultaneously on all the baselines, several different assessments of treatment effects can be obtained even within a single organism. If assessments are obtained within subjects by using different dependent measures or different situations, there may be *crosstalk* between the different baselines. If separate subjects are used, as when multiple baselines are across subjects, a transition has been made to a between-subjects comparison, which does not really meet the standards of the experimental analysis of behavior. Thus *no fully adequate solution* to the problem of dealing with irreversible effects seems to be available at present.

CHAPTER 12

Communicating the Results of Research

The final stage in experimental psychology is communication. Science is inherently social. Remember the emphasis on agreement among observers early in this book. We can only be scientific by being objective, and to be objective is to have agreement among observers. So the very definition of a *fact* is, at bottom, a social one. Science begins with a social act, and it also ends in a social act—the act of communicating findings.

Many investigators balk at the stage of communication. They feel hesitant to communicate their findings to others in any systematic way. But this amounts to leaving the task unfinished. The results of our work should be communicated to others. The skills necessary to do this are well within reach.

Even the work done while one is a student can be publishable. My impression is that students, especially undergraduates, commonly carry out projects that, with a little extra effort, could be published. Why not put in the extra effort? It is personally rewarding, and it makes the contribution of experimental subjects worthwhile.

Even if work is not to be published, it generally has to be described in writing as part of a course requirement. So you will likely have to learn to write in a style appropriate to psychological journals. The main purpose of this chapter is to guide you in such writing, whether it stops with your teacher or goes on to a journal. I will also discuss some special problems involved in oral presentation of research.

Writing in APA Style

There is a fairly strict set of requirements for writing in the style of the American Psychological Association. These requirements have been summarized in the *Publication Manual of the American Psychological Association*, 2nd ed. (1974). You should refer to that manual for details. Here, I will summarize highlights and also provide specific recommendations based on errors commonly made by students.

The general style used by APA has been developed under certain inevitable restraints. This accounts for some of its rigidity and for the differences between "journal style" and the more breezy styles used in newspapers and magazines. Publication is costly, and therefore space is short for professional journals. The need for accuracy is, at the same time, very great. So a rather curt, concise style has been developed. And there is little toleration for deviations from that style.

Title

The title should summarize the main idea of the paper. One rule is to mention the independent variable, dependent variable, and a relationship between them. For example, "On extrinsic reward" is not good. It would be better to say "Effects of extrinsic reward on intrinsically motivated behaviors."

Author's Name and Institutional Affiliation

Beneath the title list the name of the author or authors, without titles or degrees. Beneath that, list the institutional affiliation. Spell out the title of the institution. A common error is to use an abbreviation or nickname that is only locally understood. For example, "OSU" means "Ohio State Univeristy" if you are in the Midwest, but it means "Oklahoma State University" if you are in the Southwest. In foreign countries, it may mean nothing. You may feel that it is unlikely that your paper will reach Vladivostok, but the idea is to establish the right habits in case future papers of yours do get that far.

Abstract

A brief summary (100-175 words) of the problem, method, results, and conclusions is next. The most important thing is to tell what you did and what results you got. The abstract must be capable of being understood by itself. Since it is so short, you cannot ramble. Be succinct. The abstract is very important because it is all many people will ever read.

Introduction

State the problem, its relationships to past literature or theory, and show why you selected your research tactic to solve that problem. Your awareness of the pertinent literature should be obvious here, but you should avoid getting lengthy. You can refer to previous summary reviews. For classroom papers, if you had limited sources of literature, you should explain those limitations. If you have a novel problem, you can usually at least mention literature relevant to its components. For example, a study of the influence of alcohol on chess playing might have few, if any, predecessors. But there is literature on the influence of alcohol on behavior. Incidentally, if you make claims in the introduction, or anywhere else in the paper, support them with references to literature sources. We cannot rely on common lore here. In science we are trying to improve on that.

Method

In the method section you should describe how the study was conducted. It should enable investigators to repeat your study. It customarily has the following subheadings: "Subjects," "Apparatus," and "Procedure."

Under *Subjects* explain how many and what kind of subjects you employed. Also tell how they were sampled from the population of interest. Mention any variables that might influence your results, especially their generality. Answers to such things as "What strain of rat did you use?" "How old were the subjects?" "What were their socioeconomic backgrounds?" should be included if potentially relevant to your findings. Loss of subjects (by dropping out or otherwise) should also be explained here.

Under *Apparatus,* describe your apparatus systematically. If it is a standard apparatus describe it so that another person could obtain it. If you are going to publish in a real journal, or rehearse for such publication, keep in mind that the article may find its way to foreign readers. So do not be provincial in your identification of the apparatus. A novel apparatus will have to be described in some detail. Keep a constant perspective while describing it (imagine yourself standing in front of it, or on top of it). A drawing or photograph may be very helpful.

The *Procedure* subsection is a description of what you did to the subjects. It includes a description of the experimental design with its methods of achieving control of important variables. Be sure to include descriptions of how each thing was measured and enough detail for another person to replicate your study. On the other hand, be as economical as possible with words.

Results

The next major section after "Method" is the section reporting results. A common error here is to begin with a report of outcomes of statistical analyses before presenting the data. First describe the main thrust of your results. Always describe the data (usually in figures and tables) before going on to demonstrate their reliability by such devices as statistical analyses. Since results are usually described in tables and figures, I will discuss their construction in some detail.

Constructing Tables and Figures

Tables and figures are useful both at the end of an experiment, when experimenters want to communicate their findings to others, and during an experiment, to make the findings intelligible to the experimenters themselves. There is, to be sure, a distinction between the quality of tables and figures constructed for private use and those constructed for public use; there can be some reduction in the clarity of labeling and in the attractiveness of the work when it is only for local use. However, avoid being too lax. Errors can easily creep in or important aspects of the data be missed if experimenters are careless about how they present the data to themselves or to other members of the research team.

Tables and figures are the very heart of a report. People often look at them before they look at accompanying text. Hence, the tables and figures should convey their message completely and, as far as possible, independently of the text. Labels should be clear; avoid mystifying the reader with unintelligible abbreviations. Both for yourself and for the reader, the data will be easier to understand if the labels and headings are immediately and directly intelligible. The use of arbitrary codes such as "Group A" and "Condition 1" requires the memorization of that code before the data can be interpreted. The interpretation of data is too important for us to permit any unnecessary obstacles. If abbreviations must be used, try developing them so that they readily suggest the thing they represent.

Tables and figures should be uncluttered. It is tempting to try putting all or most of the information from an experiment in one table or figure, because this has the potential of laying out the various results side by side for comparison. But the eye does not easily discern curves and numbers when they are in a crowd.

When do we choose tables rather than figures? There are no hard and fast rules. In many cases data can be communicated in either way. Tables are to be preferred when exact numbers need to be put down. For this reason, and because of the greater expense of figures, the APA manual advocates giving preference to tables. However, in psychology, the error of measurement is commonly so great that it is relatively unimportant, even sometimes misleading, to put down highly exact numbers (say, out to several decimal places). In these cases figures will do nicely. On the other hand, larger quantities of information can sometimes be put in a table better than in a figure.

Figures have the advantage of presenting trends and relationships in visible form. Deviation of a given datum is more likely to be seen in a figure than in a number. For personal use it is often best to construct both tables and figures for the same numbers. Afterwards, you can select the most successful method for presentation to others. Figures must, of course, be used to present pictorial information such as photos and drawings of apparatus or sections of brain tissue.

It is easy to overlook one of the major advantages to be gained from constructing tables and, especially, figures. The act of constructing them *forces the experimenter to get close to the data.* A datum unnoticed might just as well never have been gathered; much of the process of discovery takes place when the experimenter is tabulating and graphing the data.

Specific guidelines for the construction of tables have been laid down by Woodford (1968).

Table Title. Titles should be concise, with the key concepts emphasized by placing them at or near the beginning of the title. Detailed information goes in footnotes. The first table can bear the brunt of communicating to the reader; you can drop out some details in the titles of later tables. Avoid vague titles like "Results of experiment one," or long-winded ones like "The effects of hair length on the attractiveness of 40 male humans as measured in a natural setting in 312 female humans by the method of pupillary dilation." Instead, try "Amount of pupillary dilation as a function of hair length." You should avoid unnecessary changes of pattern, such as changes from one table to the next in the order of the words in the title and headings.

Column Headings. Items should be grouped logically. Give control values first, in the far left column or in the top row. Data from other treatment conditions should be placed in their natural order, if one exists. For example, if you were reporting the results of an experiment comparing the effects on learning of three different levels of shock, then you could put your unshocked control results to the far left, place the results from the lowest shock level next to the controls, the intermediate level to the right of that, and the highest level to the far right. Woodford (1968) recommends modifying this in the event that there is a particular pattern laid down in earlier tables that can be maintained in later ones. Readers might be better off with the familiar pattern instead of having to adjust to a change.

Footnotes. More detailed information should go in footnotes. This particularly includes mention of statistical values. For example: "Long hair condition differed significantly from controls ($p < 0.02$)." Abbreviations are explained in footnotes. Here also, special conditions and qualifications are mentioned. For example "A 300-trial cutoff was employed," in an experiment using trials to a learning criterion as a dependent measure.

Journal Format. A final point about constructing tables is that they should be in the correct format for the place in which they are to be used. If this is a psychology journal, the format will probably be that of the American Psychological Association. The APA style is also commonly required by teachers in psychology classes.

In APA style, tables are typed, double-spaced, each on a separate page. The top heading is the word "Table" and its Arabic numeral (for example, "Table 1"). This is centered at the head of the table; then comes the title, centered, with principal words capitalized. Column headings and subheadings are centered with the initial letter of the first word capitalized. Footnotes are typed, paragraph indented, double-spaced, at the foot of the table.

Figures. I will restrict this discussion to the construction of datagrams. The word "figures" includes such things as photomicrographs of brain sections, which do not require discussion here.

As with tables, the figure should be a complete unit of communication. It consists of the figure itself with *labeled* axes: some sort of legend for indicating the meaning of the included bars, lines, and so on; a title; and a caption giving explanatory details. Titles and captions are typewritten, double-spaced, on a separate sheet, not placed on the figure itself. (This rule may be modified for classroom purposes.)

If the figure is to be used for publication, you should consider how it will look in the format of the journal. It makes a difference whether the journal is physically large or not, for example. People often make the lettering on their figures so small that it becomes unreadable once the figure has been reduced to journal size. Color printing is generally not available, so differentiations cannot be made by using different colors.

Many different dimensions can be used to indicate differences in a datagram. We usually indicate differences in the variables of interest by differences in the height or length of bars or points on a graph. By paging through this book you can see many different examples of reasonably well made figures.

Datagrams should not be cluttered. Usually no more than four curves should appear on a given graph. Labeling should be very clear. Avoid using abbreviations if possible, and if they are necessary, try to make them easily related to the full words. It is often helpful to use meaningful coding symbols instead of dots on a line graph. For example, a datagram showing the effects of some treatment on male and female subjects might use ♂ and ♀ instead of dots for the two groups. Letters of the alphabet can also be used in this way. For example, I often use little H's and V's instead of dots to indicate treatments where an animal was learning to choose a horizontal or vertical cue. Another aid to understanding can be provided if labels identifying the various lines and bars are placed near them, with arrows specifying which label goes with which bar or graph.

Accuracy of Data in Tables and Datagrams

Before finishing this discussion, it is important to point out that errors often crop up in transcribing data from raw form to tables and datagrams. You should always check the data against your end product very carefully. Recalculating totals of columns of numbers from the typescript is often worthwhile. Also, check for discrepancies when tabulated or graphed numbers are cited in the text.

Reliable and Unreliable Results

Experimenters sometimes report mean differences between conditions that are unreliable by their stipulated test (such as the 0.05 level), but then go on to treat the differences as though they were confirmed. This is not legitimate. Keep in mind that the test for reliability of the data tells us whether or not we have reason to suppose that there is anything but error underlying them. If we fail to reject the null hypothesis, we have no reason to suppose that there is anything more underlying observed differences in central tendency than underlies a good poker hand. It is unscientific to infer trends from results that "almost meet the 0.05 level."

Discussion

Here you discuss the implications of your data. A common error is to forget about the statement of the original problem when it is time for the discussion. You should start by saying how your results relate to the original problem posed. Another common error is to turn this section into a kind of confession of errors. It is not necessary to obsessively point out every conceivable flaw in your methods. A third common error is to ignore your findings. This may take the form of adhering to a previous theoretical predilection despite your data's having indicated the contrary. Another form it takes is to disparage your results because they do not seem to agree with other published findings. It is not out of the question that the other investigators had flaws in their experiments.

You should accept your findings, relate them to your introductory statements, and draw out their theoretical and practical implications, as well as their implications for future research.

References

Throughout the paper, statements should be supported by references. The usual style in the text is to refer to such things as "...the pioneering study of Jones (1975)..." or "There have been many studies on chess playing in chimpanzees (Jones, 1975; Smith, 1976)." At the end of the paper a reference list is provided. It includes only papers cited in the text. There is a standard APA format for citations. Begin with a list of all authors of the work, last name first, followed by initials. Next put the title of the article, chapter, or book. For journals, next put the name of the journal in full, the date of publication, the volume number, and the first and last page numbers. For books, next put the city of publication, the publisher's name, and the date of publication. Articles and books referenced should be listed in alphabetical order of the first author's last name.

Appendixes

Appendixes are sometimes permitted by journal editors. These contain material that would be distracting in the main body of the text but would be useful in understanding, evaluating, or replicating your study. Appendixes are quite commonly used in papers presented as requirements for class and in theses. In these cases they often include raw data presented in an orderly and intelligible way. You should find out whether your teacher wants you to include such appendixes.

Oral Presentations

Second only to published articles in communicating the results of research is the oral presentation. People often follow the same format as the journals require. This is usually a source of suffering for the listeners, who generally find such presentations boring and incomprehensible.

There are a number of major differences between the oral and the written mode. When a written article is available, the reader can reread points not remembered or perhaps not even comprehended. No such opportunity exists with the oral mode. Generally oral presentations are done at conventions where time is severely limited (often 10-20 minutes), and little time is available for questioning. So it is best to depart from journal format and present things in a more breezy style with a great deal of redundancy.

One of the best techniques I have ever seen was one used by neuroscientist Ronald Myers. He presented not only the customary slides summarizing his data, but also a series of slides that summarized the main ideas made in his presentation up to that point. This way, if something was missed, the main ideas were repeated at regular intervals and could be recaptured. Perhaps you will not go that far (then again, why not?), but at least you can repeat your main points in one form or another at various stages of your presentation. Incidentally, be sure the details on your slides are large enough to be seen at the back of a lecture hall. Remarkably often, slides presented at conventions are well below readable size!

Another major difference between oral and written presentation is the tendency for fear to impair oral performance. Close to 90 percent of us fear speaking in front of groups. The symptoms of that fear can be virtually incapacitating. The best way to deal with it is to realize that nearly everyone has to go through the same thing, and therefore virtually everyone will understand if you display the symptoms. Do not feel that you lose face by showing nervousness in front of a group. In fact, it is far better simply to accept that nervousness and try to present the *facts* in spite of it.

Notice my emphasis on presenting the facts. You are there for that purpose, and your audience is there to hear those facts, not to evaluate you. If you get the facts across, you have done better than many people who use journal format and illegible slides and leave their listeners in the dark. You can arrange to make sure the facts get across by putting them on eminently clear slides. In fact, if you are nervous it is sometimes best to begin with a slide. That will get you started, and it is relatively easy to describe a familiar slide (being in the dark may help, too!).

You may spend a lot of time before the presentation anticipating all kinds of incisive criticisms. This is good up to a point. But only up to a point. Make yourself aware of potential criticisms, but do not get repetitious about it. Remember, you know your experiment better than anyone else. Chances are that the audience will be preoccupied with understanding what you did and what you got for results. They will hardly have time to think through the study better than you did, if you are at all careful. Unfortunately (or fortunately, depending on your point of view), there is usually little time for discussion and questioning anyway.

The only way you get over fear of oral presentations is through practicing them. Avoidance behaviors can last a very long time, even when the aversive stimulus is not there. So take every opportunity to sharpen your ability to present data in this way. Sometimes teachers will let you rehearse in class. Be the first volunteer.

If your problems in front of an audience overwhelm you, try special relaxation procedures such as autogenic training (Lindemann, 1973), progressive relaxation (Jacobson, 1957), or self-hypnosis (Anderson & Savary, 1972). If necessary, find someone to give you training in desensitization. Above all, don't give up on extinguishing the responses.

SUMMARY

1. Communication of data is an essential aspect of the scientific enterprise. It is most often done in *journal format.* Journal articles are composed of:

(a) *Title:* usually including statement of functional relationship between independent and dependent variables.

(b) *Author's name and affiliation.*

(c) *Abstract:* a 100-175 word summary of what you did and what you got.

(d) *Introduction:* it is not labeled, but includes a statement of the problem, the relevant literature, and the relationship of your study to that problem.

(e) *Method:* includes *Subjects* (how sampled and any other relevant information), *Apparatus* (described systematically, so it could be reproduced or obtained); *Procedure,* which tells what you did to the subjects, including experimental design and methods of measurement.

(f) *Results,* in which you describe your data, usually in tables or figures, and tell how you assessed their reliability.

(g) *Discussion,* in which you tell how the results relate to the originally stated problem and give other implications for theory and future research.

(h) *References,* in which you list, in alphabetical order by last name of first author, all articles referred to in the paper (and no other articles).

(i) *Appendix:* it is only occasionally used, but contains detailed material that would be distracting in the main body of the article.

first author, all articles referred to in the paper (and no other articles).

(i) *Appendix:* it is only occasionally used, but contains detailed material that would be distracting in the main body of the article.

2. *Oral presentations* should not be in journal format, though they should provide most of the relevant details. They differ from written presentations in that they require repetitiousness and overcoming of fear. The text describes methods of achieving redundancy and of reducing fear.

Appendixes

A. **Table of Random Numbers**
B. **Table of Binomial Probabilities**
C. **Table of Percentile Points for** t
D. **Table of Percentile Points for** F
E. **Computational Methods for Single-Factor Designs with Two Levels**
   - E1. Computing t for independent means
   - E2. Computing t for correlated means

F. **Computational Methods for Single-Factor Designs with More Than Two Levels (Anova)**
   - F1. Analysis of variance for single-factor, completely randomized design
   - F2. Analysis of variance for randomized blocks design
   - F3. Analysis of variance for single-factor design with repeated measures on the same subjects

G. **Computational Methods for Factorial Designs (Anova)**
   - G1. Computation of analysis for completely randomized factorial design for two factors and any number of levels
   - G2. Computation of analysis for completely repeated factorial design for two factors and any number of levels
   - G3. Computation of analysis for mixed factorial designs for two factors and any number of levels

APPENDIX A Table of Random Numbers

Row	00000 01234	00000 56789	11111 01234	11111 56789	22222 01234	22222 56789	33333 01234	33333 56789
				1st Thousand				
00	23157	54859	01837	25993	76249	70886	95230	36744
01	05545	55043	10537	43508	90611	83744	10962	21343
02	14871	60350	32404	36223	50051	00322	11543	80834
03	38976	74951	94051	75853	78805	90194	32428	71695
04	97312	61718	99755	30870	94251	25841	54882	10513
05	11742	69381	44339	30872	32797	33118	22647	06850
06	43361	28859	11016	45623	93009	00499	43640	74036
07	93806	20478	38268	04491	55751	18932	58475	52571
08	49540	13181	08429	84187	69538	29661	77738	09527
09	36768	72633	37948	21569	41959	68670	45274	83880
10	07092	52392	24627	12067	06558	45344	67338	45320
11	43310	01081	44863	80307	52555	16148	89742	94647
12	61570	06360	06173	63775	63148	95123	35017	46993
13	31352	83799	10779	18941	31579	76448	62584	86919
14	57048	86526	27795	93692	90529	56546	35065	32254
15	09243	44200	68721	07137	30729	75756	09298	27650
16	97957	35018	40894	88329	52230	82521	22532	61587
17	93732	59570	43781	98885	56671	66826	95996	44569
18	72621	11225	00922	68264	35666	59434	71687	58167
19	61020	74418	45371	20794	95917	37866	99536	19378
20	97839	85474	33055	91718	45473	54144	22034	23000
21	89160	97192	22232	90637	35055	45489	88438	16361
22	25966	88220	62871	79265	02823	52862	84919	54883
23	81443	31719	05049	54806	74690	07567	65017	16543
24	11322	54931	42362	34386	08624	97687	46245	23245

Reprinted with permission from M. G. Kendall and B. B. Smith, Randomness and random sampling numbers. *Journal of the Royal Statistical Society*, 1938, *101*.

APPENDIX B Table of Binomial Probabilities

NX	*0*	*1*	*2*	*3*	*4*	*5*	*6*	*7*	*8*	*9*	*10*	*11*	*12*	*13*	*14*	*15*
5	031	188	500	812	969	*										
6	016	109	344	656	891	984	*									
7	008	062	227	500	773	938	992	*								
8	004	035	145	363	637	855	965	996	*							
9	002	020	090	254	500	746	910	980	998	*						
10	001	011	055	172	377	623	828	945	989	999	*					
11		006	033	113	274	500	726	887	967	994	*	*				
12		003	019	073	194	387	613	806	927	981	997	*	*			
13		002	011	046	133	291	500	709	867	954	989	998	*	*		
14		001	006	029	090	212	395	605	788	910	971	994	999	*	*	
15			004	018	059	151	304	500	696	849	941	982	996	*	*	*
16			002	011	038	105	227	402	598	773	895	962	989	998	*	*
17			001	006	025	072	166	315	500	685	834	928	975	994	999	*
18			001	004	015	048	119	240	407	593	760	881	952	985	996	999
19				002	010	032	084	180	324	500	676	820	916	968	990	998
20				001	006	021	058	132	252	412	588	748	868	942	979	994
21				001	004	013	039	095	192	332	500	668	808	905	961	987
22					002	008	026	067	143	262	416	584	738	857	933	974
23					001	005	017	047	105	202	339	500	661	798	895	953
24					001	003	011	032	076	154	271	419	581	729	846	924
25						002	007	022	054	115	212	345	500	655	788	885

APPENDIX C Table of Percentile Points for *t*

df	*one-tailed* *p* = 0.4	0.25	0.1	0.05	0.025	0.01	0.005	0.001
	two-tailed *p* = 0.8	0.5	0.2	0.1	0.05	0.02	0.01	0.002
1	0.325	1.000	3.078	6.314	12.706	31.821	63.657	318.31
2	.289	0.816	1.886	2.920	4.303	6.965	9.925	22.326
3	.277	.765	1.638	2.353	3.182	4.541	5.841	10.213
4	.271	.741	1.533	2.132	2.776	3.747	4.604	7.173
5	0.267	0.727	1.476	2.015	2.571	3.365	4.032	5.893
6	.265	.718	1.440	1.943	2.447	3.143	3.707	5.208
7	.263	.711	1.415	1.895	2.365	2.998	3.499	4.785
8	.262	.706	1.397	1.860	2.306	2.896	3.355	4.501
9	.261	.703	1.383	1.833	2.262	2.821	3.250	4.297
10	0.260	0.700	1.372	1.812	2.228	2.764	3.169	4.144
11	.260	.697	1.363	1.796	2.201	2.718	3.106	4.025
12	.259	.695	1.356	1.782	2.179	2.681	3.055	3.930
13	.259	.694	1.350	1.771	2.160	2.650	3.012	3.852
14	.258	.692	1.345	1.761	2.145	2.624	2.977	3.787
15	0.258	0.691	1.341	1.753	2.131	2.602	2.947	3.733
16	.258	.690	1.337	1.746	2.120	2.583	2.921	3.686
17	.257	.689	1.333	1.740	2.110	2.567	2.898	3.646
18	.257	.688	1.330	1.734	2.101	2.552	2.878	3.610
19	.257	.688	1.328	1.729	2.093	2.539	2.861	3.579
20	0.257	0.687	1.325	1.725	2.086	2.528	2.845	3.552
21	.257	.686	1.323	1.721	2.080	2.518	2.831	3.527
22	.256	.686	1.321	1.717	2.074	2.508	2.819	3.505
23	.256	.685	1.319	1.714	2.069	2.500	2.807	3.485
24	.256	.685	1.318	1.711	2.064	2.492	2.797	3.467
25	0.256	0.684	1.316	1.708	2.060	2.485	2.787	3.450
26	.256	.684	1.315	1.706	2.056	2.479	2.779	3.435
27	.256	.684	1.314	1.703	2.052	2.473	2.771	3.421
28	.256	.683	1.313	1.701	2.048	2.467	2.763	3.408
29	.256	.683	1.311	1.699	2.045	2.462	2.756	3.396
30	0.256	0.683	1.310	1.697	2.042	2.457	2.750	3.385
40	.255	.681	1.303	1.684	2.021	2.423	2.704	3.307
60	.254	.679	1.296	1.671	2.000	2.390	2.660	3.232
120	.254	.677	1.289	1.658	1.980	2.358	2.617	3.160
∞	.253	.674	1.282	1.645	1.960	2.326	2.576	3.909

Reprinted with permission from Table 12 of the *Biometrika Tables for Statisticians*, Vol. I (ed. 3), 1966, edited by E. S. Pearson and H. O. Hartley.

APPENDIX D Table of Percentile Points for F

$\alpha = 0.05$

ν_2 \ ν_1	1	2	3	4	5	6	7	8	9	10	12	15	20	24	30	40	60	120	∞
1	161.4	199.5	215.7	224.6	230.2	234.0	236.8	238.9	240.5	241.9	243.9	245.9	248.0	249.1	250.1	251.1	252.2	253.3	254.3
2	18.51	19.00	19.16	19.25	19.30	19.33	19.35	19.37	19.38	19.40	19.41	19.43	19.45	19.45	19.46	19.47	19.48	19.49	19.50
3	10.13	9.55	9.28	9.12	9.01	8.94	8.89	8.85	8.81	8.79	8.74	8.70	8.66	8.64	8.62	8.59	8.57	8.55	8.53
4	7.71	6.94	6.59	6.39	6.26	6.16	6.09	6.04	6.00	5.96	5.91	5.86	5.80	5.77	5.75	5.72	5.69	5.66	5.63
5	6.61	5.79	5.41	5.19	5.05	4.95	4.88	4.82	4.77	4.74	4.68	4.62	4.56	4.53	4.50	4.46	4.43	4.40	4.36
6	5.99	5.14	4.76	4.53	4.39	4.28	4.21	4.15	4.10	4.06	4.00	3.94	3.87	3.84	3.81	3.77	3.74	3.70	3.67
7	5.59	4.74	4.35	4.12	3.97	3.87	3.79	3.73	3.68	3.64	3.57	3.51	3.44	3.41	3.38	3.34	3.30	3.27	3.23
8	5.32	4.46	4.07	3.84	3.69	3.58	3.50	3.44	3.39	3.35	3.28	3.22	3.15	3.12	3.08	3.04	3.01	2.97	2.93
9	5.12	4.26	3.86	3.63	3.48	3.37	3.29	3.23	3.18	3.14	3.07	3.01	2.94	2.90	2.86	2.83	2.79	2.75	2.71
10	4.96	4.10	3.71	3.48	3.33	3.22	3.14	3.07	3.02	2.98	2.91	2.85	2.77	2.74	2.70	2.66	2.62	2.58	2.54
11	4.84	3.98	3.59	3.36	3.20	3.09	3.01	2.95	2.90	2.85	2.79	2.72	2.65	2.61	2.57	2.53	2.49	2.45	2.40
12	4.75	3.89	3.49	3.26	3.11	3.00	2.91	2.85	2.80	2.75	2.69	2.62	2.54	2.51	2.47	2.43	2.38	2.34	2.30
13	4.67	3.81	3.41	3.18	3.03	2.92	2.83	2.77	2.71	2.67	2.60	2.53	2.46	2.42	2.38	2.34	2.30	2.25	2.21
14	4.60	3.74	3.34	3.11	2.96	2.85	2.76	2.70	2.65	2.60	2.53	2.46	2.39	2.35	2.31	2.27	2.22	2.18	2.13
15	4.54	3.68	3.29	3.06	2.90	2.79	2.71	2.64	2.59	2.54	2.48	2.40	2.33	2.29	2.25	2.20	2.16	2.11	2.07
16	4.49	3.63	3.24	3.01	2.85	2.74	2.66	2.59	2.54	2.49	2.42	2.35	2.28	2.24	2.19	2.15	2.11	2.06	2.01
17	4.45	3.59	3.20	2.96	2.81	2.70	2.61	2.55	2.49	2.45	2.38	2.31	2.23	2.19	2.15	2.10	2.06	2.01	1.96
18	4.41	3.55	3.16	2.93	2.77	2.66	2.58	2.51	2.46	2.41	2.34	2.27	2.19	2.15	2.11	2.06	2.02	1.97	1.92
19	4.38	3.52	3.13	2.90	2.74	2.63	2.54	2.48	2.42	2.38	2.31	2.23	2.16	2.11	2.07	2.03	1.98	1.93	1.88
20	4.35	3.49	3.10	2.87	2.71	2.60	2.51	2.45	2.39	2.35	2.28	2.20	2.12	2.08	2.04	1.99	1.95	1.90	1.84
21	4.32	3.47	3.07	2.84	2.68	2.57	2.49	2.42	2.37	2.32	2.25	2.18	2.10	2.05	2.01	1.96	1.92	1.87	1.81
22	4.30	3.44	3.05	2.82	2.66	2.55	2.46	2.40	2.34	2.30	2.23	2.15	2.07	2.03	1.98	1.94	1.89	1.84	1.78
23	4.28	3.42	3.03	2.80	2.64	2.53	2.44	2.37	2.32	2.27	2.20	2.13	2.05	2.01	1.96	1.91	1.86	1.81	1.76
24	4.26	3.40	3.01	2.78	2.62	2.51	2.42	2.36	2.30	2.25	2.18	2.11	2.03	1.98	1.94	1.89	1.84	1.79	1.73
25	4.24	3.39	2.99	2.76	2.60	2.49	2.40	2.34	2.28	2.24	2.16	2.09	2.01	1.96	1.92	1.87	1.82	1.77	1.71
26	4.23	3.37	2.98	2.74	2.59	2.47	2.39	2.32	2.27	2.22	2.15	2.07	1.99	1.95	1.90	1.85	1.80	1.75	1.69
27	4.21	3.35	2.96	2.73	2.57	2.46	2.37	2.31	2.25	2.20	2.13	2.06	1.97	1.93	1.88	1.84	1.79	1.73	1.67
28	4.20	3.34	2.95	2.71	2.56	2.45	2.36	2.29	2.24	2.19	2.12	2.04	1.96	1.91	1.87	1.82	1.77	1.71	1.65
29	4.18	3.33	2.93	2.70	2.55	2.43	2.35	2.28	2.22	2.18	2.10	2.03	1.94	1.90	1.85	1.81	1.75	1.70	1.64
30	4.17	3.32	2.92	2.69	2.53	2.42	2.33	2.27	2.21	2.16	2.09	2.01	1.93	1.89	1.84	1.79	1.74	1.68	1.62
40	4.08	3.23	2.84	2.61	2.45	2.34	2.25	2.18	2.12	2.08	2.00	1.92	1.84	1.79	1.74	1.69	1.64	1.58	1.51
60	4.00	3.15	2.76	2.53	2.37	2.25	2.17	2.10	2.04	1.99	1.92	1.84	1.75	1.70	1.65	1.59	1.53	1.47	1.39
120	3.92	3.07	2.68	2.45	2.29	2.17	2.09	2.02	1.96	1.91	1.83	1.75	1.66	1.61	1.55	1.50	1.43	1.35	1.25
∞	3.84	3.00	2.60	2.37	2.21	2.10	2.01	1.94	1.88	1.83	1.75	1.67	1.57	1.52	1.46	1.39	1.32	1.22	1.00

Abridged from Table 18 of the *Biometrika Tables for Statisticians*, Vol. I (ed. 3), 1966, edited by E. S. Pearson and H. O. Hartley.

$\alpha = 0.025$

ν_2 \ ν_1	1	2	3	4	5	6	7	8	9	10	12	15	20	24	30	40	60	120	∞
1	647.8	799.5	864.2	899.6	921.8	937.1	948.2	956.7	963.3	968.6	976.7	984.9	993.1	997.2	1001	1006	1010	1014	1018
2	38.51	39.00	39.17	39.25	39.30	39.33	39.36	39.37	39.39	39.40	39.41	39.43	39.45	39.46	39.46	39.47	39.48	39.49	39.50
3	17.44	16.04	15.44	15.10	14.88	14.73	14.62	14.54	14.47	14.42	14.34	14.25	14.17	14.12	14.08	14.04	13.99	13.95	13.90
4	12.22	10.65	9.98	9.60	9.36	9.20	9.07	8.98	8.90	8.84	8.75	8.66	8.56	8.51	8.46	8.41	8.36	8.31	8.26
5	10.01	8.43	7.76	7.39	7.15	6.98	6.85	6.76	6.68	6.62	6.52	6.43	6.33	6.28	6.23	6.18	6.12	6.07	6.02
6	8.81	7.26	6.60	6.23	5.99	5.82	5.70	5.60	5.52	5.46	5.37	5.27	5.17	5.12	5.07	5.01	4.96	4.90	4.85
7	8.07	6.54	5.89	5.52	5.29	5.12	4.99	4.90	4.82	4.76	4.67	4.57	4.47	4.42	4.36	4.31	4.25	4.20	4.14
8	7.57	6.06	5.42	5.05	4.82	4.65	4.53	4.43	4.36	4.30	4.20	4.10	4.00	3.95	3.89	3.84	3.78	3.73	3.67
9	7.21	5.71	5.08	4.72	4.48	4.32	4.20	4.10	4.03	3.96	3.87	3.77	3.67	3.61	3.56	3.51	3.45	3.39	3.33
10	6.94	5.46	4.83	4.47	4.24	4.07	3.95	3.85	3.78	3.72	3.62	3.52	3.42	3.37	3.31	3.26	3.20	3.14	3.08
11	6.72	5.26	4.63	4.28	4.04	3.88	3.76	3.66	3.59	3.53	3.43	3.33	3.23	3.17	3.12	3.06	3.00	2.94	2.88
12	6.55	5.10	4.47	4.12	3.89	3.73	3.61	3.51	3.44	3.37	3.28	3.18	3.07	3.02	2.96	2.91	2.85	2.79	2.72
13	6.41	4.97	4.35	4.00	3.77	3.60	3.48	3.39	3.31	3.25	3.15	3.05	2.95	2.89	2.84	2.78	2.72	2.66	2.60
14	6.30	4.86	4.24	3.89	3.66	3.50	3.38	3.29	3.21	3.15	3.05	2.95	2.84	2.79	2.73	2.67	2.61	2.55	2.49
15	6.20	4.77	4.15	3.80	3.58	3.41	3.29	3.20	3.12	3.06	2.96	2.86	2.76	2.70	2.64	2.59	2.52	2.46	2.40
16	6.12	4.69	4.08	3.73	3.50	3.34	3.22	3.12	3.05	2.99	2.89	2.79	2.68	2.63	2.57	2.51	2.45	2.38	2.32
17	6.04	4.62	4.01	3.66	3.44	3.28	3.16	3.06	2.98	2.92	2.82	2.72	2.62	2.56	2.50	2.44	2.38	2.32	2.25
18	5.98	4.56	3.95	3.61	3.38	3.22	3.10	3.01	2.93	2.87	2.77	2.67	2.56	2.50	2.44	2.38	2.32	2.26	2.19
19	5.92	4.51	3.90	3.56	3.33	3.17	3.05	2.96	2.88	2.82	2.72	2.62	2.51	2.45	2.39	2.33	2.27	2.20	2.13
20	5.87	4.46	3.86	3.51	3.29	3.13	3.01	2.91	2.84	2.77	2.68	2.57	2.46	2.41	2.35	2.29	2.22	2.16	2.09
21	5.83	4.42	3.82	3.48	3.25	3.09	2.97	2.87	2.80	2.73	2.64	2.53	2.42	2.37	2.31	2.25	2.18	2.11	2.04
22	5.79	4.38	3.78	3.44	3.22	3.05	2.93	2.84	2.76	2.70	2.60	2.50	2.39	2.33	2.27	2.21	2.14	2.08	2.00
23	5.75	4.35	3.75	3.41	3.18	3.02	2.90	2.81	2.73	2.67	2.57	2.47	2.36	2.30	2.24	2.18	2.11	2.04	1.97
24	5.72	4.32	3.72	3.38	3.15	2.99	2.87	2.78	2.70	2.64	2.54	2.44	2.33	2.27	2.21	2.15	2.08	2.01	1.94
25	5.69	4.29	3.69	3.35	3.13	2.97	2.85	2.75	2.68	2.61	2.51	2.41	2.30	2.24	2.18	2.12	2.05	1.98	1.91
26	5.66	4.27	3.67	3.33	3.10	2.94	2.82	2.73	2.65	2.59	2.49	2.39	2.28	2.22	2.16	2.09	2.03	1.95	1.88
27	5.63	4.24	3.65	3.31	3.08	2.92	2.80	2.71	2.63	2.57	2.47	2.36	2.25	2.19	2.13	2.07	2.00	1.93	1.85
28	5.61	4.22	3.63	3.29	3.06	2.90	2.78	2.69	2.61	2.55	2.45	2.34	2.23	2.17	2.11	2.05	1.98	1.91	1.83
29	5.59	4.20	3.61	3.27	3.04	2.88	2.76	2.67	2.59	2.53	2.43	2.32	2.21	2.15	2.09	2.03	1.96	1.89	1.81
30	5.57	4.18	3.59	3.25	3.03	2.87	2.75	2.65	2.57	2.51	2.41	2.31	2.20	2.14	2.07	2.01	1.94	1.87	1.79
40	5.42	4.05	3.46	3.13	2.90	2.74	2.62	2.53	2.45	2.39	2.29	2.18	2.07	2.01	1.94	1.88	1.80	1.72	1.64
60	5.29	3.93	3.34	3.01	2.79	2.63	2.51	2.41	2.33	2.27	2.17	2.06	1.94	1.88	1.82	1.74	1.67	1.58	1.48
120	5.15	3.80	3.23	2.89	2.67	2.52	2.39	2.30	2.22	2.16	2.05	1.94	1.82	1.76	1.69	1.61	1.53	1.43	1.31
∞	5.02	3.69	3.12	2.79	2.57	2.41	2.29	2.19	2.11	2.05	1.94	1.83	1.71	1.64	1.57	1.48	1.39	1.27	1.00

$\alpha = 0.01$

ν_2 \ ν_1	1	2	3	4	5	6	7	8	9	10	12	15	20	24	30	40	60	120	∞
1	4052	4999.5	5403	5625	5764	5859	5928	5982	6022	6056	6106	6157	6209	6235	6261	6287	6313	6339	6366
2	98.50	99.00	99.17	99.25	99.30	99.33	99.36	99.37	99.39	99.40	99.42	99.43	99.45	99.46	99.47	99.47	99.48	99.49	99.50
3	34.12	30.82	29.46	28.71	28.24	27.91	27.67	27.49	27.35	27.23	27.05	26.87	26.69	26.60	26.50	26.41	26.32	26.22	26.13
4	21.20	18.00	16.69	15.98	15.52	15.21	14.98	14.80	14.66	14.55	14.37	14.20	14.02	13.93	13.84	13.75	13.65	13.56	13.46
5	16.26	13.27	12.06	11.39	10.97	10.67	10.46	10.29	10.16	10.05	9.89	9.72	9.55	9.47	9.38	9.29	9.20	9.11	9.02
6	13.75	10.92	9.78	9.15	8.75	8.47	8.26	8.10	7.98	7.87	7.72	7.56	7.40	7.31	7.23	7.14	7.06	6.97	6.88
7	12.25	9.55	8.45	7.85	7.46	7.19	6.99	6.84	6.72	6.62	6.47	6.31	6.16	6.07	5.99	5.91	5.82	5.74	5.65
8	11.26	8.65	7.59	7.01	6.63	6.37	6.18	6.03	5.91	5.81	5.67	5.52	5.36	5.28	5.20	5.12	5.03	4.95	4.86
9	10.56	8.02	6.99	6.42	6.06	5.80	5.61	5.47	5.35	5.26	5.11	4.96	4.81	4.73	4.65	4.57	4.48	4.40	4.31
10	10.04	7.56	6.55	5.99	5.64	5.39	5.20	5.06	4.94	4.85	4.71	4.56	4.41	4.33	4.25	4.17	4.08	4.00	3.91
11	9.65	7.21	6.22	5.67	5.32	5.07	4.89	4.74	4.63	4.54	4.40	4.25	4.10	4.02	3.94	3.86	3.78	3.69	3.60
12	9.33	6.93	5.95	5.41	5.06	4.82	4.64	4.50	4.39	4.30	4.16	4.01	3.86	3.78	3.70	3.62	3.54	3.45	3.36
13	9.07	6.70	5.74	5.21	4.86	4.62	4.44	4.30	4.19	4.10	3.96	3.82	3.66	3.59	3.51	3.43	3.34	3.25	3.17
14	8.86	6.51	5.56	5.04	4.69	4.46	4.28	4.14	4.03	3.94	3.80	3.66	3.51	3.43	3.35	3.27	3.18	3.09	3.00
15	8.68	6.36	5.42	4.89	4.56	4.32	4.14	4.00	3.89	3.80	3.67	3.52	3.37	3.29	3.21	3.13	3.05	2.96	2.87
16	8.53	6.23	5.29	4.77	4.44	4.20	4.03	3.89	3.78	3.69	3.55	3.41	3.26	3.18	3.10	3.02	2.93	2.84	2.75
17	8.40	6.11	5.18	4.67	4.34	4.10	3.93	3.79	3.68	3.59	3.46	3.31	3.16	3.08	3.00	2.92	2.83	2.75	2.65
18	8.29	6.01	5.09	4.58	4.25	4.01	3.84	3.71	3.60	3.51	3.37	3.23	3.08	3.00	2.92	2.84	2.75	2.66	2.57
19	8.18	5.93	5.01	4.50	4.17	3.94	3.77	3.63	3.52	3.43	3.30	3.15	3.00	2.92	2.84	2.76	2.67	2.58	2.49
20	8.10	5.85	4.94	4.43	4.10	3.87	3.70	3.56	3.46	3.37	3.23	3.09	2.94	2.86	2.78	2.69	2.61	2.52	2.42
21	8.02	5.78	4.87	4.37	4.04	3.81	3.64	3.51	3.40	3.31	3.17	3.03	2.88	2.80	2.72	2.64	2.55	2.46	2.36
22	7.95	5.72	4.82	4.31	3.99	3.76	3.59	3.45	3.35	3.26	3.12	2.98	2.83	2.75	2.67	2.58	2.50	2.40	2.31
23	7.88	5.66	4.76	4.26	3.94	3.71	3.54	3.41	3.30	3.21	3.07	2.93	2.78	2.70	2.62	2.54	2.45	2.35	2.26
24	7.82	5.61	4.72	4.22	3.90	3.67	3.50	3.36	3.26	3.17	3.03	2.89	2.74	2.66	2.58	2.49	2.40	2.31	2.21
25	7.77	5.57	4.68	4.18	3.85	3.63	3.46	3.32	3.22	3.13	2.99	2.85	2.70	2.62	2.54	2.45	2.36	2.27	2.17
26	7.72	5.53	4.64	4.14	3.82	3.59	3.42	3.29	3.18	3.09	2.96	2.81	2.66	2.58	2.50	2.42	2.33	2.23	2.13
27	7.68	5.49	4.60	4.11	3.78	3.56	3.39	3.26	3.15	3.06	2.93	2.78	2.63	2.55	2.47	2.38	2.29	2.20	2.10
28	7.64	5.45	4.57	4.07	3.75	3.53	3.36	3.23	3.12	3.03	2.90	2.75	2.60	2.52	2.44	2.35	2.26	2.17	2.06
29	7.60	5.42	4.54	4.04	3.73	3.50	3.33	3.20	3.09	3.00	2.87	2.73	2.57	2.49	2.41	2.33	2.23	2.14	2.03
30	7.56	5.39	4.51	4.02	3.70	3.47	3.30	3.17	3.07	2.98	2.84	2.70	2.55	2.47	2.39	2.30	2.21	2.11	2.01
40	7.31	5.18	4.31	3.83	3.51	3.29	3.12	2.99	2.89	2.80	2.66	2.52	2.37	2.29	2.20	2.11	2.02	1.92	1.80
60	7.08	4.98	4.13	3.65	3.34	3.12	2.95	2.82	2.72	2.63	2.50	2.35	2.20	2.12	2.03	1.94	1.84	1.73	1.60
120	6.85	4.79	3.95	3.48	3.17	2.96	2.79	2.66	2.56	2.47	2.34	2.19	2.03	1.95	1.86	1.76	1.66	1.53	1.38
∞	6.63	4.61	3.78	3.32	3.02	2.80	2.64	2.51	2.41	2.32	2.18	2.04	1.88	1.79	1.70	1.59	1.47	1.32	1.00

Appendix E: Computational Methods for Single-Factor Designs with Two Levels

E1. Computing t for Independent Means

The t ratio equals the difference between the two means divided by their standard error.

$$t = \frac{\overline{X}_1 - \overline{X}_2}{SE_{\overline{X}_1 - \overline{X}_2}}$$

1. Find the difference between the means.

Experimental Scores	Control Scores
2	0
3	1
1	1
2	2
3	2
$\Sigma X_1 = 11$	$\Sigma X_2 = 6$

$$\overline{X}_1 = \frac{\Sigma X_1}{5} = 2.2 \qquad \overline{X}_2 = \frac{\Sigma X_2}{5} = 1.2 \qquad \overline{X}_1 - \overline{X}_2 = 2.2 - 1.2 = 1.0$$

2. Find the standard error.

$$SE_{\overline{X}_1 - \overline{X}_2} = \sqrt{S^2\left(\frac{1}{n_1} + \frac{1}{n_2}\right)}, \text{ where } S^2 = \frac{\left(\Sigma X_1^2 - \frac{(\Sigma X_1)^2}{n_1}\right) + \left(\Sigma X_2^2 - \frac{(\Sigma X_2)^2}{n_2}\right)}{n_1 + n_2 - 2}$$

a. Square each score and sum the squares for each group.

4	0
9	1
1	1
4	4
9	4
$\Sigma X_1^2 = 27$	$\Sigma X_2^2 = 10$

b. Square ΣX_1 and ΣX_2 and divide each by the corresponding n.

$$(\Sigma X_1)^2 = 11^2 = 121; \quad \frac{121}{n_1} = 24.2$$

$$(\Sigma X_2)^2 = 6^2 = 36; \quad \frac{36}{n_2} = 7.2$$

c. $S^2 = \dfrac{(27 - 24.2) + (10 - 7.2)}{5 + 5 - 2} = \dfrac{5.6}{8} = 0.7$

d. $SE_{x_1 - x_2} = \sqrt{0.7\left(\frac{1}{5} + \frac{1}{5}\right)} = \sqrt{\frac{1.4}{5}} = \sqrt{0.28} = 0.53$

4. $t = \dfrac{1.0}{0.53} = 1.89$

5. Degrees of freedom $= n_1 + n_2 - 2 = 8$ at $df = 8$

Appendix C shows that t at $df = 8$ must be at least as large as 2.306 to correspond to the 0.05 alpha level. Thus t is too small to permit rejection of the null hypothesis.

E.2 Computing *t* for Correlated Means

The t ratio equals $\dfrac{\bar{D}}{SE_{\bar{D}}}$

1. Find D, the mean of differences between matched subjects. List pairs of scores, subtract one from the other, and find the mean of the resulting difference.

Pairs	Experimental	Control	D_i
1.	2	0	+2
2.	3	1	+2
3.	1	1	0
4.	2	1	+1
5.	3	2	+1
			$\Sigma D_i = 6$

$$\bar{D} = \frac{\Sigma D_i}{N} = \frac{6}{5} = 1.2$$

2. Find $SE_{\bar{D}}$.

a. Square each difference and sum the squares.

4
4
0
1
1

$\Sigma D_i^2 = 10$

b. Compute standard deviation of difference.

$$S_D = \sqrt{\frac{\Sigma D_i^2}{n} - \left(\frac{\Sigma D_i}{n}\right)^2} = \sqrt{\frac{10}{5} - \left(\frac{6}{5}\right)^2}$$

$$= \sqrt{0.56} = 0.75$$

c. $SE_{\overline{D}} = \frac{S_D}{\sqrt{n-1}} = \frac{0.75}{2} = 0.38$

3. $t = \frac{1.2}{0.38} = 3.16$

4. Degrees of freedom $= n - 1 = 5 - 1 = 4$. The tabulated value for alpha $= 0.05$ at 4 df $= 2.776$, so the null hypothesis can be rejected.

Appendix F: Computational Methods for Single-Factor Designs with More than Two Levels (Anova)

F1. Analysis of Variance for Single-Factor, Completely Randomized Design.

1. Obtain the total sum of squares (SS_T).
   a. Obtain the correction factor (C) by summing all the scores, squaring the results, and dividing by the number of scores (n).

Levels of Factor

A Scores	B Scores	C Scores
1	2	3
2	3	4
1	2	3
0	1	2
2	3	4
$\Sigma X_A = 6$	$\Sigma X_B = 11$	$\Sigma X_C = 16$

$$\Sigma X_i = 6 + 11 + 16 = 33$$

$$(\Sigma X_i)^2 = 1089$$

$$C = \frac{(\Sigma X_i)^2}{n} = \frac{1089}{15} = 72.6$$

   b. Find SS_T by squaring each score, summing the squares, and subtracting C.

A Scores	B Scores	C Scores
1	4	9
4	9	16
1	4	9
0	1	4
4	9	16
$\Sigma X_A^2 = 10$	$\Sigma X_B^2 = 27$	$\Sigma X_C^2 = 54$

$$\Sigma X_i^2 = 10 + 27 + 54 = 91$$

$$SS_T = \Sigma X_i^2 - C = 91 - 72.6 = 18.4$$

2. Obtain sum of squares between groups (SS_b).

$$SS_b = \frac{(\Sigma X_A)^2}{n_A} + \frac{(\Sigma X_B)^2}{n_B} + \frac{(\Sigma X_C)^2}{n_C} - C$$

$$= \left(\frac{6^2}{5} + \frac{11^2}{5} + \frac{16^2}{5}\right) - 72.6 = 10.0$$

3. Obtain sum of squares within (SS_w).

$$SS_w = SS_t - SS_b = 18.4 - 10 = 8.4$$

4. Find MS_b by dividing SS_b by df_b.

$$df_b = \text{number of groups} - 1 = 3 - 1 = 2$$

$$\frac{SS_b}{df_b} = \frac{10}{2} = 5$$

5. Find MS_w by dividing SS_w by df_w.

$$df_w = \text{number of scores minus number of groups} = 15 - 3 = 12$$

$$MS_w = \frac{SS_w}{df_w} = \frac{8.4}{12} = 0.7$$

6. Find F by dividing MS_b by MS_w.

$$F = \frac{MS_b}{MS_w} = \frac{5}{0.7} = 7.14$$

7. Read Appendix D for F corresponding to alpha = 0.05 at 2 and 12 df. The $F = 3.89$, so the null hypothesis can be rejected.

8. It is customary to summarize results of analysis in a table like this:

Source	df	SS	MS	*F*
Total	14	18.4	—	—
Between	2	10.0	5.0	7.14
Within	12	8.4	0.7	—

F2. Analysis of Variance for Randomized Blocks Design

1. Find SS_T.
   a. Find C by summing all scores, squaring the result, and dividing by n.

	Treatments		
	A	B	C
	0	1	2
Block 1	1	2	3
	0	1	2
	1	2	3
	$\Sigma X_{A_1} = 2$	$\Sigma X_{B_1} = 6$	$\Sigma X_{C_1} = 10$
	1	2	3
	2	3	4
Block 2	1	2	3
	2	3	4
	$\Sigma X_{A_2} = 6$	$\Sigma X_{B_2} = 10$	$\Sigma X_{C_2} = 14$

$$\Sigma X_i = 2 + 6 + 10 + 6 + 10 + 14 = 48$$

$$(\Sigma X_i)^2 = 48^2 = 2304$$

$$C = \frac{(\Sigma X_i)^2}{n} = \frac{2304}{24} = 96$$

b. Square each score, sum the squares, and subtract C.

	A	B	C
	0	1	4
Block 1	1	4	9
	0	1	4
	1	4	9
	1	4	9
	4	9	16
Block 2	1	4	9
	4	9	16
	$\Sigma X_A^2 = 12$	$\Sigma X_B^2 = 36$	$\Sigma X_C^2 = 76$

$$\Sigma X_i^2 = 12 + 36 + 76 = 124$$

$$SS_T = 124 - 96 = 28$$

2. Find SS_{blocks}.

a. Add all the scores for block 1 and square the result; repeat for block 2.

Block 1: $2 + 6 + 10 = 18;\ 18^2 = 324$

Block 2: $6 + 10 + 14 = 30;\ 30^2 = 900$

b. Divide each square by the number of scores on which it is based, sum the results, and subtract C.

$$\frac{324}{12} + \frac{900}{12} = 102$$

$$SS_{blocks} = 102 - 96 = 6$$

3. Find $SS_{treatments}$.
   a. Add all the scores for each treatment and square the results.

      A: $0 + 1 + 0 + 1 + 1 + 2 + 1 + 2 = 8; 8^2 = 64$

      B: $1 + 2 + 1 + 2 + 2 + 3 + 2 + 3 = 16; 16^2 = 256$

      C: $2 + 3 + 2 + 3 + 3 + 4 + 3 + 4 = 24; 24^2 = 576$

   b. Divide each square by its corresponding *n*, sum the results, and then subtract *C*.

$$SS_{treatments} = \left(\frac{64}{8} + \frac{256}{8} + \frac{576}{8}\right) - 96 = 16$$

4. Find SS for interaction of treatments × blocks.
   a. Square the sums for each treatment group of each block $(\Sigma X_{A1})^2$, $(\Sigma X_{B1})^2$, $(\Sigma X_{C1})^2$, $(\Sigma X_{A2})^2$, $(\Sigma X_{B2})^2$, $(\Sigma X_{C2})^2$, divide each square by the *n* on which the sum was based, and sum the results.

$$\frac{2^2}{4} + \frac{6^2}{4} + \frac{10^2}{4} + \frac{6^2}{4} + \frac{10^2}{4} + \frac{14^2}{4} = \frac{472}{4} = 118$$

   b. Subtract *C*, SS_{blocks}, and $SS_{treatments}$ from the result.

$$118 - 96 - 6 - 16 = 0$$

5. Find SS_{error}.

$$\begin{aligned} SS_{error} &= SS_T - SS_{blocks} - SS_{treatments} - SS_{treatments \times blocks} \\ &= 28 - 6 - 16 - 0 \\ &= 6 \end{aligned}$$

6. Find the various degrees of freedom.

   For SS_T, $df = n - 1; 24 - 1 = 23$

   For SS_{blocks}, df = number of blocks − 1 = 1

   For $SS_{treatments}$, df = number of treatment levels − 1 = 3 − 1 = 2

   For $SS_{treatments \times blocks}$, $df = df_{treatments} \times df_{blocks} = 2 \times 1 = 2$

   For SS_{error}, df = df for $SS_T - dfSS_{blocks} - dfSS_{treatments}$
   $-dfSS_{treatments \times blocks} = 23 - 1 - 2 - 2 = 18$

7. Compute the squares.

$$MS_{blocks} = \frac{SS_{blocks}}{df_{blocks}} = \frac{6}{1} = 6$$

$$MS_{treatments} = \frac{SS_{treatments}}{df_{treatments}} = \frac{16}{2} = 8$$

$$MS_{treatment \times blocks} = \frac{SS_{treatments \times blocks}}{df_{treatments \times blocks}} = \frac{0}{2} = 0$$

$$MS_{error} = \frac{SS_{error}}{df_{error}} = \frac{6}{18} = 0.33$$

8. Divide the other mean squares by MS_{error} to get F's.

$$F_{blocks} = \frac{MS_{blocks}}{MS_{error}} = \frac{6}{0.33} = 18$$

$$F_{treatments} = \frac{MS_{treatments}}{MS_{error}} = \frac{8}{0.33} = 24$$

$$F_{treatments \times blocks} = \frac{MS_{treatments \times blocks}}{MS_{error}} = \frac{0}{0.33} = 0$$

9. Tabulate the results.

Source	SS	df	MS	F	p
Total	124	23	—	—	—
Blocks	6	1	6	18	<0.01
Treatments	16	2	8	24	<0.01
Treatments × blocks	0	2	0	0	NS
Error	6	18	0.33	—	—

F3. Analysis of Variance for Single-Factor Design with Repeated Measures on the Same Subjects

1. Find SS_T.

a. Find C by summing all the scores, squaring the result, and dividing by n.

Subjects	Treatment Conditions A	B	C
S_1	1	3	5
S_2	2	3	5
S_3	2	4	4
S_4	1	2	4
	$\Sigma X_A = 6$	$\Sigma X_B = 12$	$\Sigma X_C = 18$

$$\Sigma X_i = 6 + 12 + 18 = 36$$

$$C = \frac{(\Sigma X_i)^2}{n} = \frac{36^2}{12} = 108$$

b. Square each score and sum the squares, then subtract C.

	A	B	C
S_1	1	9	25
S_2	4	9	25
S_3	4	16	16
S_4	1	4	16
	$\Sigma X_A^2 = 10$	$\Sigma X_B^2 = 38$	$\Sigma X_C^2 = 82$

$$\Sigma X_i^2 = 130$$

$$SS_T = \Sigma X_i^2 - C = 130 - 108 = 22$$

2. Find $SS_{treatments}$.
   a. Sum scores for each treatment across subjects, square the results, sum the squares, and divide by the number of subjects.

A: $1 + 2 + 2 + 1 = 6; 6^2 = 36$

B: $3 + 3 + 4 + 2 = 12^2 = 144$

C: $5 + 5 + 4 + 4 = 18; 18^2 = 324$

$$36 + 144 + 324 = 504$$

$$\frac{504}{4} = 126$$

   b. Subtract C from the result of 2a.

$$SS_{treatments} = 126 - 108 = 18$$

3. Find $SS_{subjects}$.
   a. Sum scores across treatments for each subject, square the result for each subject, sum the results, and divide by the number of treatments.

S_1: $1 + 3 + 5 = 9, 9^2 = 81$

S_2: $2 + 3 + 5 = 10, 10^2 = 100$

S_3: $2 + 4 + 4 = 10, 10^2 = 100$

S_4: $1 + 2 + 4 = 7, 7^2 = 49$

$$81 + 100 + 100 + 49 = 330$$

$$\frac{330}{3} = 110$$

   b. Subtract C from the result of 3a.

$$SS_{subjects} = 110 - 108 = 2$$

4. Find SS_{error}.

$$SS_{error} = SS_T - SS_{treatments} - SS_{subjects}$$
$$= 22 - 18 - 2$$
$$SS_{error} = 2$$

5. Determine degrees of freedom.

df for $SS_T = N - 1 = 12 - 1 = 11$

df for $SS_{treatments}$ = number of treatments $-1 = 3 - 1 = 2$

df for $SS_{subjects}$ = number of subjects − 1 = 4 − 1 = 3

$df_{error} = dfSS_T - df_{treatments} - df_{subjects} = 11 - 2 - 3 = 6$

6. Divide $SS_{treatments}$ by $df_{treatments}$ and SS_{error} by df_{error}.

$$MS_{treatments} = \frac{SS_{treatments}}{df_{treatments}} = \frac{18}{2} = 9 \qquad MS_{error} = \frac{SS_{error}}{df_{error}} = \frac{2}{6} = 0.33$$

7. Find $F_{treatments}$ by dividing $MS_{treatments}$ by MS_{error}.

$$F_{treatments} = \frac{MS_{treatments}}{MS_{error}} = \frac{9}{0.33} = 27.27$$

8. Look up the p related to that F for $df_{treatments}$ (= 2) and df_{error} (= 6).

F for $p = 0.05 = 5.14$ at df = 2 and 6; so reject the null hypothesis.

9. Tabulate the analysis.

Source	SS	df	MS	F	p
Total	22	11	—	—	—
Subjects	2	3	—	—	—
Treatments	18	2	9	27.27	<0.001
Error	2	6	0.33	—	—

Appendix G: Computational Methods for Factorial Designs (Anova)

G1. Computation of Analysis for Completely Randomized Factorial Design for Two Factors and Any Number of Levels

1. Find SS_T.
   a. Find C by summing all the scores, squaring the result, and dividing by the total number of measures.

	Factor A Level 1		Factor A Level 2	
Factor B Level 1	S_1	0	S_9	5
	S_2	1	S_{10}	4
	S_3	2	S_{11}	5
	S_4	3	S_{12}	4
Level 2	S_5	1	S_{13}	6
	S_6	2	S_{14}	5
	S_7	2	S_{15}	6
	S_8	3	S_{16}	5

0 + 1 + 2 + 3 + 1 + 2 + 2 + 3 + 5 + 4 + 5 + 4 + 6 + 5 + 6 + 5 = 54

$$C = \frac{(\Sigma X_i)^2}{N} = \frac{54^2}{16} = 182.3$$

b. Square each score, sum the squares, then subtract C.

$$0^2 + 1^2 + 2^2 + 3^2 + 1^2 + 2^2 + 2^2 + 3^2 + 5^2 + 4^2 + 5^2 + 4^2 + 6^2 + 5^2 + 6^2 + 5^2 = 236$$

$$SS_T = 236 - 182.3 = 53.7$$

2. Find $SS_{\text{factor A}}$ (SS_A).
   a. Sum the scores within level 1 of factor A across levels of factor B, and square the result, and divide by the number of scores on which the sum is based. Repeat for level 2 of factor A; then add the resulting sums.

   Level 1: $0 + 1 + 2 + 3 + 1 + 2 + 2 + 3 = 14,\ 14^2 = 196$

   Level 2: $5 + 4 + 5 + 4 + 6 + 5 + 6 + 5 = 40,\ 40^2 = 1600$

$$\frac{196}{8} + \frac{1600}{8} = 224.5$$

   b. Subtract C from the result of 2a.

$$SS_{\text{factor A}} = 224.5 - 182.3 = 42.2$$

3. Find $SS_{\text{factor B}}$ (SS_B).
   a. Sum the scores for level 1 within factor B across levels of factor A, square the result, and divide by the number of scores on which the sum is based. Repeat for level 2 of factor B, then add the resulting sums.

   Level 1: $0 + 1 + 2 + 3 + 5 + 4 + 5 + 4 = 24,\ 24^2 = 576$

   Level 2: $1 + 2 + 2 + 3 + 6 + 5 + 6 + 5 = 30,\ 30^2 = 900$

$$\frac{576}{8} + \frac{900}{8} = 184.5$$

   b. Subtract C from 3a.

$$SS_{\text{factor B}} = 184.5 - 182.3 = 2.2$$

4. Find $SS_{\text{factor A} \times \text{factor B}}$ ($SS_{A \times B}$).
   a. Sum the scores for each of the four subgroups, square each sum, and divide each sum by the number of scores on which it is based.

   1, 1: $0 + 1 + 2 + 3 = 6,\ 6^2 = 36$

   1, 2: $5 + 4 + 5 + 4 = 18,\ 18^2 = 324$

   2, 1: $1 + 2 + 2 + 3 = 8,\ 8^2 = 64$

   2, 2: $6 + 5 + 6 + 5 = 22,\ 22^2 = 484$

$$\frac{36}{4} + \frac{324}{4} + \frac{64}{4} + \frac{484}{4} = 227$$

b. Subtract C, $SS_{factor\ A}$, and $SS_{factor\ B}$ from 4a.

$$SS_{A \times B} = 227 - 182.3 - 42.2 - 2.2$$

$$SS_{A \times B} = 0.3$$

5. Find SS_{error}.

$$SS_{error} = SS_T - SS_{factor\ A} - SS_{factor\ B} - SS_{A \times B}$$

$$= 53.7 - 42.2 - 2.2 - 0.3$$

$$SS_{error} = 9.0$$

6. Find degrees of freedom.

$df_{SS_T} = N - 1 = 16 - 1 = 15$

df_A = number of levels of factor A – 1 = 1

df_B = number of levels of factor B –1 = 1

$df_{A \times B} = df_A \times df_B = 1 \times 1 = 1$

$df_{error} = df_{SS_T} - df_A - df_B - df_{A \times B} = 15 - 1 - 1 - 1 = 12$

7. Divide each SS by its df to get the mean squares. SS_T is not needed.

$$MS_A = \frac{SS_A}{df_A} = \frac{42.2}{1} = 42.2$$

$$MS_B = \frac{SS_B}{df_B} = \frac{2.2}{1} = 2.2$$

$$MS_{A \times B} = \frac{SS_{A \times B}}{df_{A \times B}} = \frac{0.3}{1} = 0.3$$

$$MS_{error} = \frac{SS_{error}}{df_{error}} = \frac{9.0}{12.0} = 0.75$$

8. Divide MS's by MS_{error} to get the F's, look up p's for each F with df for numerator and denominator.

$$\frac{MS_A}{MS_{error}} = \frac{42.2}{0.75} = 56.26$$

$$\frac{MS_B}{MS_{error}} = \frac{2.2}{0.75} = 2.93$$

$$\frac{MS_{A \times B}}{MS_{error}} = \frac{0.3}{0.75} = 0.4$$

9. Tabulate the analysis.

Source	df	MS	F	p
Total	15	—	—	—
A	1	42.2	56.26	< 0.001
B	1	2.2	2.93	NS
A × B	1	0.3	0.4	NS
Error	12	0.75	—	—

Note: This analysis can be extended to any number of levels of the factors.

G2. Computation of Analysis for Completely Repeated Factorial Design for Two Factors and Any Number of Levels

1. Find SS_T.
   a. Find C by summing all the scores, squaring the result, and dividing by the total number of measures.

	A_1, B_1	A_1, B_2	A_2, B_1	A_2, B_2
S_1	0	5	1	6
S_2	1	4	2	5
S_3	2	5	2	6
S_4	3	4	3	5
	$\Sigma X_{A_1B_1} = 6$	$\Sigma X_{A_1B_2} = 18$	$\Sigma X_{A_2B_1} = 8$	$\Sigma X_{A_2B_2} = 22$

$$\Sigma X_i = 6 + 18 + 8 + 22 = 54$$

$$C = \frac{(\Sigma X_i)^2}{N} = \frac{54^2}{16} = 182.3$$

   b. Square each score, sum the squares, then subtract C.
   $0^2 + 1^2 + 2^2 + 3^2 + 5^2 + 4^2 + 5^2 + 4^2 + 1^2 + 2^2 + 2^2 + 3^2 + 6^2 + 5^2 + 6^2 + 5^2 = 236$

$$SS_T = 236 - 182.3 = 53.7$$

2. Find SS_{subjects}.
   a. Sum scores for each subject, square each resulting sum, and divide by the number of measures on which it was based. Add up the results.

S_1: $0 + 5 + 1 + 6 = 12,\ 12^2 = 144$
S_2: $1 + 4 + 2 + 5 = 12,\ 12^2 = 144$
S_3: $2 + 5 + 2 + 6 = 15,\ 15^2 = 225$
S_4: $3 + 4 + 3 + 5 = 15,\ 15^2 = 225$

$$\frac{144}{4} + \frac{144}{4} + \frac{225}{4} + \frac{225}{4} = 184.5$$

   b. Subtract C from the result of 2a.

$$SS_{\text{subjects}} = 184.5 - 182.3 = 2.2$$

3. Find $SS_{factor\ A}$ (SS_A).
   a. Sum scores within level 1 of factor A, ignoring levels of factor B. Square the sum and divide by the number of measures on which it was based. Repeat for level 2 of factor A. Finally, add up the resulting numbers.

$$A_1{:}\quad 0 + 1 + 2 + 3 + 5 + 4 + 5 + 4 = 24,\ 24^2 = 576$$
$$A_2{:}\quad 1 + 2 + 2 + 3 + 6 + 5 + 6 + 5 = 30,\ 30^2 = 900$$

$$\frac{576}{8} + \frac{900}{8} = 184.5$$

   b. Subtract C from 3a.

$$SS_A = 184.5 - 182.3$$
$$SS_A = 2.2$$

4. Find $SS_{factor\ B}$ (SS_B).
   a. Sum within level 1 of factor B, ignoring levels of factor A. Square the sum and divide by the number of measures on which it was based. Repeat for level 2 of factor B. Finally, add up the resulting numbers.

$$B_1{:}\quad 0 + 1 + 2 + 3 + 1 + 2 + 2 + 3 = 14,\ 14^2 = 196$$
$$B_2{:}\quad 5 + 4 + 5 + 4 + 6 + 5 + 6 + 5 = 40,\ 40^2 = 1600$$

$$\frac{196}{8} + \frac{1600}{8} = 224.5$$

   b. Subtract C from 4a.

$$SS_B = 224.5 - 182.3 = 42.2$$

5. Find $SS_{A \times B}$, the interaction of factor A and factor B.
   a. Square $\Sigma X_{A_1B_1}$, $\Sigma X_{A_1B_2}$, $\Sigma X_{A_2B_1}$, and $\Sigma X_{A_2B_2}$, divide each by the number of measures on which it was based, and sum the results.

$$\frac{6^2}{4} + \frac{18^2}{4} + \frac{8^2}{4} + \frac{22^2}{4} = 227$$

   b. Subtract C, SS_A, and SS_B from 5a.

$$SS_{A \times B} = 227 - 182.3 - 2.2 - 42.2$$
$$SS_{A \times B} = 0.3$$

6. Find $SS_{error/A}$, the sum of squares for error of factor A.
   a. For each subject, sum across levels of B within level 1 of A (A_1B_1 + A_1B_2 for S_1, A_1B_1 + A_1B_2 for S_2, and so on). Square each resulting sum

and divide by the number of measures on which it was based. Repeat within level 2 of A and sum the results.

Level A_1:	$0 + 5 = 5$	Level A_2:	$1 + 6 = 7$
	$1 + 4 = 5$		$2 + 5 = 7$
	$2 + 5 = 7$		$2 + 6 = 8$
	$3 + 4 = 7$		$3 + 5 = 8$

$$\frac{5^2 + 5^2 + 7^2 + 7^2 + 7^2 + 7^2 + 8^2 + 8^2}{2} = 187$$

b. Subtract C, $SS_{subjects}$, and SS_A.

$$SS_{error/A} = 187 - 182.3 - 2.2 - 2.2$$
$$= 0.3$$

7. Find $SS_{error/B}$, the sum of squares for error of factor B.
   a. For each subject, sum across levels of A within level 1 of B (A_1B_1 + A_2B_1 for S_1, A_1B_1 + A_2B_1 for S_2, and so on). Square each resulting sum and divide by the number of measures on which it was based. Repeat within level 2 of B.

Level B_1:	$0 + 1 = 1$	Level B_2:	$5 + 6 = 11$
	$1 + 2 = 3$		$4 + 5 = 9$
	$2 + 2 = 4$		$5 + 6 = 11$
	$3 + 3 = 6$		$4 + 5 = 9$

$$\frac{1^2 + 3^2 + 4^2 + 6^2 + 11^2 + 9^2 + 11^2 + 9^2}{2} = 233$$

   b. Subtract C, $SS_{subjects}$, and SS_B.

$$SS_{error/B} = 233 - 182.3 - 2.2 - 42.2$$
$$= 6.3$$

8. Find $SS_{error/A \times B}$, the sum of squares for error of the A × B interaction.

$$SS_{error/A \times B} = SS_T - SS_{subjects} - SS_A - SS_B - SS_{A \times B} - SS_{error/A} - SS_{error/B}$$
$$= 53.7 - 2.2 - 2.2 - 42.2 - 0.3 - 0.3 - 6.3$$
$$SS_{error/A \times B} = 0.2$$

9. Calculate df.

df_{SS_T} = number of measures − 1 = 16 − 1 = 15

$df_{SS_{subjects}}$ = number of subjects − 1 = 4 − 1 = 3

df_{SS_A} = number of levels of A − 1 = 2 − 1 = 1

df_{SS_B} = number of levels of B – 1 = 2 – 1 = 1

$df_{SS_{error/A}}$ = df for $SS_{subjects} \times df_{SS_A} = 3 \times 1 = 3$

$df_{SS_{error/B}}$ = df for $SS_{subjects} \times df_{SS_B} = 3 \times 1 = 3$

$df_{SS_{A \times B}} = df_{SS_A} \times df_{SS_B} = 1 \times 1 = 1$

$df_{error/A \times B}$ = df for $SS_{subjects} \times df_{SS_A} \times df_{SS_B} = 3 \times 1 \times 1 = 3$

10. Calculate the mean squares.

$$MS_A = \frac{SS_A}{df_A} = \frac{2.2}{1} = 2.2$$

$$MS_B = \frac{SS_B}{df_B} = \frac{42.2}{1} = 42.2$$

$$MS_{A \times B} = \frac{SS_{A \times B}}{df_{SS_{A \times B}}} = \frac{0.3}{1} = 0.3$$

$$MS_{error/A} = \frac{SS_{error/A}}{df_{error/A}} = \frac{0.3}{3} = 0.1$$

$$MS_{error/B} = \frac{SS_{error/B}}{df_{error/B}} = \frac{6.3}{3} = 2.1$$

$$MS_{error/A \times B} = \frac{SS_{error/A \times B}}{df_{error/A \times B}} = \frac{0.2}{3} = 0.07$$

11. Compute F's.

$$F_A = \frac{MS_A}{MS_{error/A}} = \frac{2.2}{0.1} = 22.00$$

$$F_B = \frac{MS_B}{MS_{error/B}} = \frac{42.2}{2.1} = 20.10$$

$$F_{A \times B} = \frac{MS_{A \times B}}{MS_{error/A \times B}} = \frac{0.3}{0.07} = 4.29$$

12. Look up p values for each F based on df for numerator and denominator in step 11.

$p(F_A) < 0.025$	$p(F_B) < 0.025$	$p(F_{A \times B})$ = NS
df = 1, 3	df = 1, 3	df = 1, 3

13. Tabulate results:

Source	SS	df	MS	F	p
Total	53.7	15	—	—	—
Between Subjects	4.7	7	—	—	—
A	2.2	1	2.2	5.23	NS
Error between	2.5	6	0.42	—	—
Within Subjects	49.0	8	6.13	—	—
B	42.2	1	42.2	39.07	< 0.001
A × B	0.3	1	0.3	0.28	NS
Error within	6.5	6	1.08	—	—

Note: This analysis may be extended to any number of levels of the factors. The repeated factor is commonly "trials," in which case the unrepeated factor is regarded as "conditions."

G3. Computation of Analysis for Mixed Factorial Designs for Two Factors and Any Number of Levels

1. Find SS_T.

   a. Add all the scores, square the result, and divide by the total number of measures.

	Factor with Independent Subjects			
	A_1		A_2	
Repeated Factor B_1	S_1	0	S_5	1
	S_2	1	S_6	2
	S_3	2	S_7	2
	S_4	3	S_8	3
B_2	S_1	5	S_5	6
	S_2	4	S_6	5
	S_3	6	S_7	6
	S_4	4	S_8	5

$$0 + 1 + 2 + 3 + 5 + 4 + 5 + 4 + 1 + 2 + 2 + 3 + 6 + 5 + 6 + 5 = 54$$

$$C = \frac{(\Sigma X_i)^2}{N} = \frac{54^2}{16} = 182.3$$

   b. Square each score, sum the squares, then subtract C.

$$0^2 + 1^2 + 2^2 + 3^2 + 5^2 + 4^2 + 5^2 + 4^2 + 1^2 + 2^2 + 2^2 + 3^2 + 6^2 + 5^2 + 6^2 + 5^2 = 236$$

$$SS_T = 236 - 182.3 = 53.7$$

2. Find the sum of squares between subjects ($SS_{between}$).

   a. Sum each subject's scores, square each sum, add them together, and divide by the number of levels of the repeated factor (B).

S_1: $0 + 5 = 5, 5^2 = 25$ S_5: $1 + 6 = 7, 7^2 = 49$
S_2: $1 + 4 = 5, 5^2 = 25$ S_6: $2 + 5 = 7, 7^2 = 49$
S_3: $2 + 5 = 7, 7^2 = 49$ S_7: $2 + 6 = 8, 8^2 = 64$
S_4: $3 + 4 = 7, 7^2 = 49$ S_8: $3 + 5 = 8, 8^2 = 64$

$$\frac{25 + 25 + 49 + 49 + 49 + 49 + 64 + 64}{2} = 187$$

b. Subtract C from 2a.

$$SS_{between} = 187 - 182.3 = 4.7$$

3. Find $SS_{factor\ A}$ (nonrepeated factor).
   a. Sum scores within levels of factor A (across levels of factor B). Square the resulting sums, divide by the number of measures on which they were based, and sum the results.

   A_1: $0 + 1 + 2 + 3 + 5 + 4 + 5 + 4 = 24, 24^2 = 576$

   A_2: $1 + 2 + 2 + 3 + 6 + 5 + 6 + 5 = 30, 30^2 = 900$

   $$\frac{576 + 900}{8} = 184.5$$

   b. Subtract C from 3a.

   $$SS_A = 184.5 - 182.3 = 2.2$$

4. Find $SS_{error/between}$.

$$SS_{error/between} = SS_{between} - SS_A = 4.7 - 2.2 = 2.5$$

5. Find SS_{within}.

$$SS_{within} = SS_T - SS_{between} = 53.7 - 4.7 = 49.0$$

6. Find SS_B (the repeated factor).
   a. Sum scores within levels of B (across levels of A). Square the resulting sums, divide by the number of measures on which they were based, and sum the results.

   B_1: $0 + 1 + 2 + 3 + 1 + 2 + 2 + 3 = 14, 14^2 = 196$

   B_2: $5 + 4 + 5 + 4 + 6 + 5 + 6 + 5 = 40, 40^2 = 1600$

   $$\frac{196 + 1600}{8} = 224.5$$

b. Subtract C from 6a.

$$SS_B\ 224.5 - 182.3$$
$$= 42.2$$

7. Find $SS_{A \times B}$.
   a. Sum scores for each subcondition (A_1B_1, A_1B_2, A_2B_1, A_2B_2), square each result, divide by the number of measures on which it is based, and sum the results.

A_1B_1: $0 + 1 + 2 + 3 = 6$
A_1B_2: $5 + 4 + 5 + 4 = 18$
A_2B_1: $1 + 2 + 2 + 3 = 8$
A_2B_2: $6 + 5 + 6 + 5 = 22$

$$\frac{6^2}{4} + \frac{18^2}{4} + \frac{8^2}{4} + \frac{22^2}{4} = 227$$

   b. Subtract C, SS_A, and SS_B from 7a.

$$SS_{(A \times B)} = 227 - 182.3 - 2.2 - 42.2$$
$$= 0.3$$

8. Find $SS_{error/within}$.

$$SS_{error/within} = SS_{within} - SS_B - SS_{A \times B}$$
$$= 49.0 - 42.2 - 0.3$$
$$SS_{error/within} = 6.5$$

9. Compute df's.

df_{SS_T} = total number of measures − 1 = 16 − 1 = 15

$df_{SS_{between}}$ = total number of subjects − 1 = 8 − 1 = 7

df_{SS_A} = number of levels of A − 1 = 2 − 1 = 1

$df_{SS_{error/between}}$ = df for $SS_{between} - df_{SS_A}$ = 7 − 1 = 6

$df_{SS_{within}}$ = df for SS_T − df for $SS_{between}$ = 15 − 7 = 8

df_{SS_B} = number of levels of B − 1 = 2 − 1 = 1

$df_{SS_{A \times B}}$ = df for $SS_B \times df_{SS_A}$ = 1 × 1 = 1

$df_{SS_{error/within}}$ = df for $SS_{within} - df_{SS_B} - df_{SS_{A \times B}}$ = 8 − 1 − 1 = 6

10. Compute mean squares.

$$MS_A = \frac{SS_A}{df_A} = \frac{2.2}{1} = 2.2$$

$$MS_{error/between} = \frac{SS_{error/between}}{df_{error/between}} = \frac{2.5}{6} = 0.42$$

$$\text{MS}_{\text{within}} = \frac{\text{SS}_{\text{within}}}{\text{df}_{\text{within}}} = \frac{49.0}{8} = 6.13$$

$$\text{MS}_{\text{B}} = \frac{\text{SS}_{\text{B}}}{\text{df}_{\text{B}}} = \frac{42.2}{1} = 42.2$$

$$\text{MS}_{\text{A}\times\text{B}} = \frac{\text{SS}_{\text{A}\times\text{B}}}{\text{df}_{\text{A}\times\text{B}}} = \frac{0.3}{1} = 0.3$$

$$\text{MS}_{\text{error/within}} = \frac{\text{SS}_{\text{error/within}}}{\text{df}_{\text{error/within}}} = \frac{6.5}{6} = 1.08$$

11. Calculate F's.

$$F_{\text{A}} = \frac{\text{MS}_{\text{A}}}{\text{MS}_{\text{error/between}}} = \frac{2.2}{0.42} = 5.23$$

$$F_{\text{B}} = \frac{\text{MS}_{\text{B}}}{\text{MS}_{\text{error/within}}} = \frac{42.2}{1.08} = 39.07$$

$$F_{\text{A}\times\text{B}} = \frac{\text{MS}_{\text{A}\times\text{B}}}{\text{MS}_{\text{error/within}}} = \frac{0.3}{1.08} = 0.28$$

12. Look up tabulated F values for appropriate df for numerator and denominator.

$F_{\text{A}} = 5.23$, df $= 1, 6$, $p =$ NS
$F_{\text{B}} = 39.07$, df $= 1, 8$, $p < 0.001$
$F_{\text{A}\times\text{B}} = 0.28$, df $= 1, 8$, $p =$ NS

13. Tabulate the results.

Source	SS	df	MS	F	p
Total	53.7	15	—	—	—
Subjects	2.2	3	—	—	—
A	2.2	1	2.2	22.00	<0.025
B	42.2	1	42.2	20.10	<0.025
A × B	0.3	1	0.3	4.29	NS
Error/A	0.3	3	0.1	—	—
Error/B	6.3	3	2.1	—	—
Error/A × B	0.2	3	0.07	—	—

References

Allport, G. W. ***Becoming.*** New Haven, Conn.: Yale University Press, 1955.

American Psychological Association. Publication Manual, 2nd ed. Washington, D.C.: American Psychological Association, 1974.

Anderson, M. S., & Savary, I. M. ***Passages: A guide for pilgrims of the mind.*** New York: Harper & Row, 1972.

Andrade, E. N. DaC. ***Sir Isaac Newton.*** Garden City, N.Y.: Doubleday, 1958.

Atkinson, J. W., & McClelland, D. C. The projective expression of needs. II. The effect of different intensities of the hunger drive on thematic apperception, ***Journal of Experimental Psychology,*** 1948, **38,** 643–658.

Ax, A. The physiological differentiation of fear and anger in humans, ***Psychosomatic Medicine,*** 1953, **15,** 433–442.

Barber, T. X. ***Hypnosis, a scientific approach.*** New York: Van Nostrand, 1969.

Barber, T. X., & Silver, M. J. Fact, fiction and the experimenter bias effect, ***Psychological Bulletin,*** 1968, **70,** (6, Pt. 2), 1–29.

Barlow, D. H., Blanchard, E. B., Hayes, S. C. & Epstein, L. H. Single case designs and clinical biofeedback experimentation, ***Biofeedback and Self-Regulation,*** 1977, **2,** 221–239.

Besley, S., & Sheridan, C. L. A sensitive method for the detection of experimental brain lesions, ***Perceptual and Motor Skills,*** 1973, **36,** 584–586.

Beveridge, W. I. B. ***The art of scientific investigation.*** New York: Random House (Vintage), 1950.

Blough, D. S. Dark adaptation in the pigeon, ***Journal of Comparative and Physiological Psychology,*** 1956, **49,** 425–430.

Bolgar, H. The case study method. In Wolman, B. B. (Ed.), ***Handbook of clinical psychology.*** New York: McGraw-Hill, 1965, pp. 28–39.

Breland, K., & Breland, M. The misbehavior of organisms, ***American Psychologist,*** 1961, **16,** 681–684.

Bruch, H. ***Eating disorders.*** New York: Basic Books, 1973.

Bruning, J., & Kintz, B. ***Computational handbook of statistics,*** 2nd. Glenview, Ill.: Scott, Foresman, 1977.

Budzynski, T., & Stoyva, J. An electromyographic feedback technique for teaching voluntary relaxation of the masseter muscle, ***Journal of Dental Research,*** 1973, **52,** 116–118.

Budzynski, T., Stoyva, J., & Adler, C. Feedback-induced muscle relaxation: Application to tension headache, ***Journal of Behavior Therapy and Experimental Psychiatry,*** 1970, **1,** 205–207.

Campbell, D. T., & Stanley, J. C. ***Experimental and quasi-experimental designs for research.*** Chicago: Rand McNally, 1963.

Carmer, S. G., & Swanson, M. R. An evaluation of ten multiple comparison procedures by Monte Carlo methods, ***Journal of the American Statistical Association,*** 1973, **68,** 66–74.

COHEN, J. The statistical power of abnormal-social psychological research: A review, ***Journal of Abnormal and Social Psychology,*** 1962, **65,** 144–153.

COHEN, J. ***Statistical power analysis for the behavioral sciences.*** New York: Academic Press, 1969.

CONE, J. D., & HAWKINS, R. P. ***Behavioral assessment.*** New York: Brunner/Mazel, 1977.

CREEL, D. J. Visual system anomaly associated with albinism in the cat, ***Nature,*** 1971, **231,** 465–466.

CREEL, D. J., & SHERIDAN, C. L. Monocular acquisition and interocular transfer in albino rats with unilateral striate ablations, ***Psychonomic Science,*** 1966, **6,** 215–216.

DILLEHAY, R. C. On the irrelevance of the classical negative evidence concerning the effect of attitudes on behavior, ***American Psychologist,*** 1973, **28,** 887–891.

DIXON, W., & MASSEY, F. ***Introduction to statistical analysis.*** 2nd ed. New York: McGraw-Hill, 1957.

DOHREWEND, B. S. & DOHREWEND, B. P. (EDS.) ***Stressful life events.*** New York: Wiley, 1974.

EDWARDS, D. D., & EDWARDS, J. Marriage: Direct and continuous measurement, ***Bulletin of the Psychonomic Society,*** 1977, **10,** 187–188.

ENGEN, T. Psychophysics II. Scaling methods. In Kling, J., & Riggs, L. (Eds.), ***Woodworth and Schlosberg's experimental psychology,*** 3rd ed. New York: Holt, Rinehart and Winston, 1971, pp. 49–86.

EYSENCK, HANS J. The effects of psychotherapy: An evaluation, ***Journal of Consulting and Clinical Psychology,*** 1952, **16,** 319–323.

FAWL, G. Electrosleep as a clinical treatment. Unpublished M. A. thesis, University of Missouri, Kansas City, 1975.

FELDT, L. S. A comparison of the precision of three experimental designs employing a concomitant variable, ***Psychometrika,*** 1958, **23,** 335–353.

FEYNMAN, R. P., LEIGHTON, R. B., & SANDS, M. ***The Feynman lectures on physics.*** Vol. 1. Reading, Mass.: Addison-Wesley, 1963, Sect. 7.

FIELDS, P. E. Contributions to visual figure discrimination in the white rat, ***Journal of Comparative Psychology,*** 1931, **11,** 327–348.

FISHER, S. ***The female orgasm.*** New York: Basic Books, 1973.

GALTON, L. ***The silent disease: Hypertension.*** New York: New American Library, 1974.

GARCIA, J., & ERVIN, F. R. Gustatory-visceral and telereceptor-cutaneous conditioning—Adaptation in internal milieus, ***Communications in Behavioral Biology,*** Part A, 1968, **1,** 389–415.

GAUQUELIN, M. ***Cosmic influences on human behavior.*** New York: Stein & Day, 1973.

GUTTMAN, N., & KALISH, H. I. Discriminability and stimulus generalization, ***Journal of Experimental Psychology,*** 1956, **51,** 79–88.

HANSON, N. R. ***Patterns of discovery.*** New York: Cambridge University Press, 1958.

HELD, R. Plasticity in sensory-motor systems, ***Scientific American,*** 1965, **213**(5), 84–94.

HELD, R., & HEIN, A. Movement-produced stimulation in the development of visually guided behavior, ***Journal of Comparative and Physiological Psychology,*** 1963, **56,** 872–876.

HERSEN, M., & BARLOW, D. H. ***Single case experimental designs.*** New York: Pergamon, 1976.

HILGARD, E. R. Pain as a puzzle for psychology and physiology, ***American Psychologist,*** 1969, **24,** 103–113.

HITE, S. ***The Hite report.*** New York: Dell, 1976.

HOFFMAN, M. ***The gay world.*** New York: Basic Books, 1968.

HOOKER, E. The adjustment of the overt male homosexual, ***Journal of Projective Techniques,*** 1957, **21,** 18–31.

JACOBSON, E. *You must relax.* New York: McGraw-Hill, 1957.

JAMES, W. What is emotion? *Mind,* 1884, **19,** 188–205.

KASAMATSU, A., & HIRAI, T. An electroencephalographic study on the Zen meditation (Zazen), *Folio Psychiatrica Neurologica Japonica,* 1966, **20,** 315–336. Also reprinted in Tart, C. (Ed.), *Altered states of consciousness.* New York: Wiley, 1969.

KEPPEL, G. *Design and analysis: A researcher's handbook.* Englewood Cliffs, N.J.: Prentice-Hall, 1973.

KIESLER, C., COLLINS, B., & MILLER, N. *Attitude change.* New York: Wiley, 1969.

KINSEY, A. C., POMEROY, W., MARLIN, C., & GEPHARD, P. *Sexual behavior in the human female.* Philadelphia: Saunders, 1953.

KINTZ, B., DELPRATO, D., METTEE, D., PERSONS, C., & SCHAFFE, R. The experimenter effect, *Psychological Bulletin,* 1965, **63,** 223–232.

KUHN, T. S. *The structure of scientific revolutions.* Chicago: University of Chicago Press, 1962.

LA PIERE, R. T. Attitudes vs actions, *Social Forces,* 1934, 230–237.

LASHLEY, K. S. The mechanism of vision: I. A method for rapid analysis of pattern-vision in the rat, *Journal of Genetic Psychology,* 1930, **37,** 453–460.

LEVINSON, L. *Webster's unafraid dictionary.* New York: Collier, 1967.

LINDEMANN, H. *Relieve tension the autogenic way.* New York: Wyden, 1973.

LOCKARD, R. B. The albino rat: A defensible choice or bad habit? *American Psychologist,* 1968, **23,** 734–742.

LORENZ, K. Z. *King Solomon's ring.* (Wilson, M. K., Trans.) New York: Crowell, 1952.

LUND, R. D. Uncrossed visual pathways of hooded and albino rats, *Science,* 1965, **149,** 1506–1507.

LURIA, A. R. (SOLOTORAOFF, L., TRANS.) *The mind of a mnemonist.* New York: Basic Books, 1968.

MASTERS, W. H., & JOHNSON, V. E. *Human sexual response.* Boston: Little, Brown, 1966.

MATHESON, D. W., BRUCE, R. L., & BEAUCHAMP, K. L. *Experimental psychology.* 3rd ed. New York: Holt, Rinehart and Winston, 1978.

MCNEMAR, Q. Opinion-attitude methodology, *Psychological Bulletin,* 1946, **43,** 289–374.

MILGRAM, S. Liberating effects of group pressure, *Journal of Personality and Social Psychology,* 1965a, **1,** 127–134.

MILGRAM, S. Some conditions of obedience and disobedience to authority, *Human Relations,* 1965b, **18,** 57–76.

MILLER, N., & DWORKIN, B. Visceral learning: Recent difficulties with curarized rats and significant problems for human research. In Obrist, P., Black, A., Brener, J., & DiCara, L. (Eds.), *Cardiovascular psychophysiology.* Chicago: Aldine, 1974, pp. 312–331.

MINKIN, N., BRAUKMANN, C. J., MINKIN, B. L., TIMBERS, G. D., TIMBERS, B. J., FIXSEN, D. L., PHILLIPS, E. L. & WOLFE, M. M. The social validation and training of conversational skills, *Journal of Applied Behavioral Analysis,* 1976, **9,** 127–139.

NEALE, J. M., & LIEBERT, R. M. *Science and behavior.* Englewood Cliffs, N.J.: Prentice-Hall, 1973.

ORNE, M. T. On the social psychology of the psychological experiment: With particular reference to demand characteristics and their implications, *American Psychologist,* 1962, **17,** 776–783.

ORNE, M., & HOLLAND, C. C. On the ecological validity of laboratory deceptions, *International Journal of Psychiatry,* 1968, **6,** 282–293.

PAGE, M. M. Social psychology of a classical conditioning of attitudes experiment,

Journal of Personality and Social Psychology, 1969, **11,** 177–186.

Page, M. M. Demand awareness, subject sophistication, and the effectiveness of a verbal "reinforcement," ***Journal of Personality,*** 1970, **38,** 287–301.

Page, M. M. Effects of evaluation apprehension on cooperation in verbal conditioning, ***Journal of Experimental Research in Personality,*** 1971, **5,** 85–91.

Page, M. M. Demand characteristics and the verbal operant conditioning experiment, ***Journal of Personality and Social Psychology,*** 1972, **23,** 372–378.

Page, M. M. Effects of demand cues and evaluation apprehension in an attitude change experiment, ***Journal of Social Psychology,*** 1973, **89,** 55–62.

Page, M. M., & Lumia, A. Cooperation with demand characteristics and the bimodal distribution of verbal conditioning data, ***Psychonomic Science,*** 1968, **12,** 243–244.

Patty, R., & Page, M. Manipulations of a verbal conditioning situation based upon demand characteristics theory, ***Journal of Experimental Research in Personality,*** 1973, **6,** 307–313.

Polanyi, M. ***The tacit dimension.*** New York: Doubleday, 1966.

Pyles, M. K., Stalz, H. R., & Macfarlane, J. W. The accuracy of mothers: Reports on birth and developmental data, ***Child Development,*** 1935, **6,** 165–176.

Rahe, R. H., & Arthur, R. J. Life change and illness studies, ***Journal of Human Stress,*** 1978, **4,** 3–15.

Robbins, L. C. The accuracy of parental recall of aspects of child rearing practices, ***Journal of Abnormal and Social Psychology,*** 1963, **66,** 261–270.

Rokeach, M. ***The open and closed mind.*** New York: Basic Books, 1960.

Rosenberg, M. J. When dissonance fails: On eliminating evaluation apprehension from attitude measurement, ***Journal of Personality and Social Psychology,*** 1965, **1,** 28–42.

Rosensweig, S. The experimental situation as a psychological problem, ***Psychological Review,*** 1933, **40,** 337–354.

Rosenthal, R. ***Experimenter effects in behavioral research.*** New York: Appleton, 1966.

Rosenthal, R., & Lawson, R. A longitudinal study of the effects of experimenter bias on the operant learning of laboratory rats, ***Journal of Psychiatric Research,*** 1964, **2** (2), 61–72.

Rosenthal, R., & Rosnow, R. L. The volunteer subject. In R. Rosenthal & R. L. Rosnow (Eds.) ***Artifact in behavioral research.*** New York: Academic Press, 1969.

Rozin, P., & Kalat, J. Specific hungers and poison avoidance as adaptive specializations of learning, ***Psychological Review,*** 1971, **78,** 459–486.

Ryle, G. ***The concept of mind.*** London: Hutchinson, 1949.

Sanderson, K. J., Kaas, J. H., & Guillery, R. W. Abnormal retinogeniculate and geniculocortical projections in the albino allelomorphic series of mammals, from ***Program and abstracts, Society for Neuroscience,*** 1972, p. 145.

Seligman, M. On the generality of the laws of learning, ***Psychological Review,*** 1970, **77,** 406–418.

Sheridan, C. L. Interocular transfer of brightness and pattern discriminations in normal and corpus callosum sectioned rats, ***Journal of Comparative and Physiological Psychology,*** 1965a, **59,** 292–294.

Sheridan, C. L. Interocular interaction of conflicting discrimination habits in the albino rat: A preliminary report, ***Psychonomic Science,*** 1965b, **3,** 303–304.

Sheridan, C. L. ***Fundamentals of experimental psychology.*** 2nd ed. New York: Holt, Rinehart and Winston, 1976.

SHERIDAN, C. L., & SHROUT, L. L. Interocular transfer in the rat: The role of the occlusion process, ***Psychonomic Science,*** 1965, **4,** 177–178.

SIDMAN, MURRAY. ***Tactics in scientific research.*** New York: Basic Books, 1960.

SIEGEL, S. ***Nonparametric statistics.*** New York: McGraw-Hill, 1956.

SILVERMAN, I., & REGULA, C. Evaluation apprehension, demand characteristics, and the effects of distraction on persuasibility, ***Journal of Social Psychology,*** 1968, **75,** 273–281.

SILVERMAN, I., & SHULMAN, A. A conceptual model of artifact in attitude change studies, ***Sociometry,*** 1970, **33,** 97–107.

SKINNER, B. F. ***Science and human behavior.*** New York: Appleton, 1953.

SKINNER, B. F. ***Verbal behavior.*** New York: Appleton, 1957.

SKINNER, B. F. ***Cumulative record.*** New York: Appleton, 1959.

SMITH, A. ***The body.*** New York: Walker, 1968, p. 179.

STAUB, E. Helping a distressed person: Social personality and stimulus determinants. In Berkowitz, L. (Ed.), ***Advances in experimental social psychology,*** Vol. 7. New York: Academic Press, 1974.

STEVENS, S. S. On the psychophysical law, ***Psychological Review,*** 1957, **64,** 153–181.

TAYLOR, D. W., GARNER, W. R., & HUNT, H. F. Education for research in psychology, ***American Psychologist,*** 1959, **14,** 167–179.

THURSTONE, L. L. A law of comparative judgment. ***Psychological Review,*** 1927, **34,** 273–286.

TOULMIN, S. ***The philosophy of science.*** New York: Harper & Row, 1953.

WELKOWITZ, J., EWEN, R. B. & COHEN, J. ***Introductory statistics for the behavioral sciences.*** New York: Academic Press, 1976.

WEST, J., & TOONDER, J. ***The case for astrology.*** Baltimore: Penguin, 1973.

WIKE, E. ***Data analysis.*** Chicago and New York: Aldine-Atherton, 1971.

WILCOXON, H., DRAGOIN, W., & KRAL, P. Illness-induced aversions in rat and quail: Relative salience of visual and gustatory cues, ***Science,*** 1971, **171,** 826–828.

WILSON, E. B. ***An introduction to scientific research.*** New York: McGraw-Hill, 1952.

WOODFORD, F. P. (ED.) ***Scientific writing for graduate students.*** New York: Rockefeller University Press, 1968.

YOUNG, J. Z. ***Doubt and certainty in science.*** Oxford: Clarendon Press, 1951.

Name Index

Subject Index